Awareness Alone

Also By This Writer

The Wandering Distanced from partner Marsha and her daughter Matty by physical and psychic wanderings into geographic places, historical scenes, other lives… the narrator Blank dances solo with his unavoidable other, claiming to alert her to opaque parts of his nature and to her own: on clinging and running, victim and perpetrator, freedom and fundamentalism, splitting and taking responsibility… and on Samsara, the trivial endless recurrence. *The Wandering* is Blank's ruminating travelogue, tainted-love diary, mythic karmic romance, meditation on being and becoming, on conscience and commitment.

The Labyrinth: Tales of Entanglement, Escape Ambiguities and escapisms of the psyche are exposed in fifteen stories - entwining motifs of conscience and repression, freedom and fixation, atonement and suicide, intimacy and responsibility - presented with forensic directness, a wide poetic vision, and a startling cast of protagonists.

The Elusive: Three Novellas Personal quests for integrity within the complications and ironies of relationships are chronicled in this trio of novellas. **The Adventures of Sally Bang** charts an unruly anti-heroine's coming of age, and a ghost writer's need to possess. At sixteen there's insight and beauty that never come again, and within every adult is a wish to get it back. What is gained and lost with growing up, and whose story is it anyway? **Commitment** ensnares a standoffish narrator in dilemmas of want, in a psychologic navel-gaze in cliffhanger style on the elusive as romance, the tango of intimacy and distance, conformism and the irrational. **In Search of Francesca Mars** exposes an artist's vision of a self-immolating media star who tilts at strange awakening, who toys with all who need to put her on a pedestal or drag her down. A close-skinned portrayal of ambition and use, the politics of giving and wanting, glamour and ugliness, the artifice of art, the problem of value.

Total Drama (Macmillan Education Australia, 2010) investigates the dynamics of interpersonal encounters and the core ingredients of drama through original scripts and exercises.

Awareness Alone

The Path of Enquiry

Nicholas Frost

Copyright © Nicholas Frost 2021

First published in 2021 in Sydney

All rights reserved. No part of this publication may be reproduced by any means without the prior written consent of the publisher.

Every effort has been made to trace (and seek permission for use of) the original source of material used within this book. Where the attempt has been unsuccessful, the publisher would be pleased to hear from the author/publisher to rectify any omission.

For purchasing information, go to:
www.mouthsofillusion.com / nfrost@odp.com.au

Cover design by Alicia Grady Struck By Violet www.struckbyviolet.com

Typeset by BookPOD

Printed and bound in Australia by BookPOD

ISBN: 978-0-6450137-0-2 (pbk) 978-0-6450137-1-9 (e-book)

 A catalogue record for this book is available from the National Library of Australia

Contents

Guide for readers   vi

Initiation   vii

PART ONE: ANALYTICS

1	The Perennial Science	3
2	Reflections on the Perennial Science	21
3	Practise Mindfulness	45
4	Real and False Knowledge	59
5	Deconstructions	73
6	Journey Without End – Journey's End	109

PART TWO: POETICS AND POLEMICS

7	Infinitude of Scintillating Pulsation	177
8	Tales of Entanglement and Escape	185
9	Polemics on Reality	197
10	Endless Dialogue of a Self	217

Guide For Readers

1. This text rewards repeated visits over a long period of time. It can be read in any order the reader chooses, dipped into at random, or pursued in chapters from beginning to end. Paragraphs tend to cluster in terms of aspects of a theme. Overall, the text iterates a single big theme, and all paragraphs illustrate it in diverse ways according to readers' tastes: some forensic and analytical, others more discursive or lyrical.

2. To deal with the pressures of using language in an exposition that intrinsically reaches beyond language, inverted commas are used to signify that the meaning of a word or statement operates in a specific context.

3. Some Sanskrit terms that appear in the science of Yoga may be useful to readers. They are included in italics in brackets. Eg: existence-awareness-bliss (*Satchitananda*).

Initiation

There is one indivisible real substance that is absolutely aware. No-one has ever been able, or will ever be able, to prove that anything exists outside it. It is literally all that you and I can ever be. Understanding that there is no Other, beyond endless becoming born of desire and fear, we should accept ourselves as eternal awareness alone.

The goals of this factual text are specific: (1) To affirm the utter transparency of ourselves as effortless existence-awareness. (2) To affirm the world's manifestations as nothing but organs and conditions of borderless existence-awareness. (3) To reconcile awareness in its modes of feeling and volition, potential and kinetic. (4) To deconstruct all limiting paradigms: of border, person, ego, name, form, time, space, cause, change, duality, context, body, independent arising, death. (5) To affirm awareness as ever-absorbed, singular, beyond polarised notions of 'subject and object'.

Those who entertain the notion that consciousness is some kind of 'evolutionary product' that 'evolves from unconscious states' without ever offering a single example of how this happens, will resist the proofs in this book: that the absolute condition of existence is consciousness itself, and that 'these words and these worlds' are its eternal affirmation. Even a cursory summary of our position reveals its absoluteness in that body, senses, feelings and thoughts function effortlessly as expressions of boundless profundity. Meanwhile, our experience at any moment is absolute, never polarised as 'seer and seen', 'self and other'.

The apparent infinite ramification of awareness as ego, sense, feeling, thought, imagination, memory and so forth, prevents us from surrendering in awe at awareness' sole and extraordinary presence. Our confusion lies in the perceived hiatus between absolute receptivity (feeling) and absolute volition (power of concentration), whereby 'awareness is obscured' as ideas and their forms: name, atom, time, space, cause... Observe this pulsing, this 'becoming' of awareness. Without utter receptivity, how could anything be discerned? How can awareness modify where the context is ever itself? And where is the border between limited and limitless? The issue turns on a single question: *To whom* does any idea, action, displacement (*etc*) occur? *Who* is the witness and dancer of all phenomena?

We must embrace the *necessity* for enquiry: our responsibility for suffering and its cause, limitation. All our phantom boundaries, mental conventions entrenched by habit, are exposed as the thieves and dictators that they are. *What* is ignorant, suffers, is born and dies, is lost? Ego (that seeker, desirer, little 'I', definer, fixator, achiever, phantom gatekeeper, material idea, superimposition) dictates experience, enforcing the lie that 'forms' independently arise, where we drown in relativities, and 'knowledge by inference and labelling' replaces that of identity, and our obsessively-built personae amount to no more than cardboard cutouts. Beyond self-distraction, beyond the clamour to build an ideational machine paradise, beyond endless fear that we will cease to be, our rock and role is *to be as we are*. Peace is the goal, a permanent security beyond the see-saw of need, dependency and dissatisfaction. Yet there's no patience, no surrender, without understanding. To deconstruct brings us detachment, which opens the way to an effortless joy. We then wear the world's jewels lightly, knowing them to be the very delight of the Supreme. While we ever appear to act, we don't cling to action's seeds and consequences. We become transparent, simple, ever now, ever here, borderless, eternal.

If this text appears persistently abstract, or solipsistic, or impractical, or absurd - chew on it, in bits, with patience. The writer has oftentimes hesitated, fearing that a plethora of words only adds to the problem. In the end he 'points a finger to the sun, plays tunes on the strings of our ever-present awareness', so that each utterance seeks to be a nugget, a homecoming.

Our liberation does not lie in the passage of time or experience or any 'future state'. It lies in surrender to an unutterable miracle: that we are one effortless absolute aware presence that, while appearing to pulse as a relentless becoming, ever affirms its own borderless freedom.

PART ONE
ANALYTICS

ONE

THE PERENNIAL SCIENCE

This chapter examines the constituent principles of the Absolute Real Substance, and the nature of their manifestation.

The Real Substance

The Absolute Real Substance is the absolute bliss of aware existence. It is everlasting, indivisible, without origin or end, one without a second, that which is forever itself, all in all in the universe. It is simple, stable, effortless, utterly present, utterly empty, inexpressible and elusive, infinitely potent and volitional yet beyond all becoming. The Absolute Real Substance is called Existence, Awareness and Bliss (*Sat-chit-ananda*). This is all we ever are, all we can ever be.

The absolute real substance is (a) utterly present without border, beginning or end, and (b) abstract, indescribable, without qualities. These two seemingly contradictory facts should deliver the most profound realisation: that existence is all we are, that we are forever present without qualification or boundary. Our ability to discern the fact of our unqualified absolute existence depends on our absolute capacity to experience. Therefore, existence and awareness are identical facts. The realised fact that we are existence-awareness, is the experience of absolute bliss, of being ever one, undivided, without a second.

The Origin of Idea of Manifestation within the Absolute Real Substance

The nature of the Aware Real Substance is Feeling and Volition. While Feeling is the absolute experiencer, Volition is its absolute power of concentration. Volition is the projecting force, the impulse, the effort, the will to form, the appearance of Idea in emptiness, the pulsation, the displacement, the polarisation, the origin of other. It is desire, seeking, the effort to define the indefinable. It is the ego, clinging, the need to personalise. It is the flood of creation, the 'external manifested world', the idea of 'independent, discrete arising'. It is the idea of the involuntary, the insentient, the limiting, the automatic. It is the notion of beginning, evolving and ending, the journey of becoming, creator of 'contextual bubbles of meaning', search for perfect enjoyment and happiness.

Existence-Awareness is identical with and inseparable from its Volition, just as burning power is inseparable from fire. The eternal real substance as volition, constitutes the absolute and primal impulse, the vibration or word (*aum*). 'In the beginning (eternal idea of creation) was the word, and the word was with god.'

The relationship between Existence-Awareness and 'impulse' or 'beginning' may be described in the following steps:

1. Existence is absolute beyond any idea.
2. Awareness is absolute beyond any idea.
3. Awareness is the absolute condition of Existence. They are identical.
4. Existence-awareness is utterly volitional, capable, pulsing, adaptable.
5. The pulsation of existence-awareness creates the idea.
6. All ideas are ideas of concentration, distinction, limitation.
7. The 'idea' of existence-awareness appears distinct from the reality of existence-awareness.
8. The idea of existence-awareness creates the idea of non-existence and non-awareness.
9. The pulsation or polarity of (8) creates the structure of separateness, of relativity, of 'mind', characterised by four cardinal ideas (below).

The Four Ideas

1. **Word** is the idea that the eternal Sound (pulsation, *Om*) becomes name in the ever-unnameable: discrete, contextual, objectified, the other.
2. **Atom** is the idea that the eternal Light (awareness) becomes limitation in the ever-illimitable: the idea of materiality, density, 'particles and waves of a universal force', discrete objects, 'things'.
3. **Time** is the idea that the eternal Presence becomes change in the ever-unchangeable: discrete event, beginning, ending, duration, linear sequence, cause and effect, past and future, birth and death.
4. **Space** is the idea that the absolute Presence becomes division in the ever-indivisible: location, region, quantity, context, relationship, independent arising, difference, arrangement, form.

Word, atom, time and space are essentially one. They are called the Force of Repulsion, and constitute the Ignorance. They generate the idea of the pulsating, the other, the ego, the polarised, the displaced, the relative, the 'bubble of context', the independently arising, the concentrated, the dense, the involved, the defined, the particular, the objective, the separate, the material, the fixed, the bound, the involuntary, the automatic, the desired, the feared, the attached, the becoming, the transient, the insubstantial, the *superimposed*.

the · World

Idea of Separate Self

The Four Ideas, and all subsequent ideas, are at once the free expression and embodiment of eternal existence-awareness, and the contextual supports, through the Projecting Power, of this universe of ignorance. The absolute real substance is kept out of our comprehension, making us identify with the volitional projecting power, embodied as ego, mind and material body, giving rise to all involuntary, automatic responses and all consequent searching, 'evolving'. The innumerable 'manifested atoms' of absolute existence-awareness are called the Veiling Power (*maya*), where each 'particle' is limitation, clinging, ignorance, transience, insubstantiality.

Genesis of 'other'

What sends unalterable existence-awareness on its 'journey of seeking'? Existence-awareness, the 'borderless I', dwells as absolute feeling, forever absorbed as eternal *this,* as 'suchness'. It is called 'impersonal, empty, abstract, absorbed'. Whence comes the idea of other? Out of *volition* a pulsation arises, the sole and original 'displacement', the 'little 'I', the limiting ego we call 'personal', which endlessly seeks, through the mind and sense organs, to 'self-maintain' by desire and aversion. Volition as *idea* (expressed as time, space, atom, *etc*) is thus the genesis of all 'externality, objectivity, context, creation, transience, insubstantiality'.

Force as Attraction and Repulsion

Absolute Feeling in its dance with Absolute Volition creates an eternal magnetic polarisation: that of Attraction and Repulsion. Universal attraction, the force of *return* to absolute existence-awareness, to absolute love, shines on the objectifying material (the Four Ideas) in order to attract every bit of it back to itself. However, the Ideas, being obscuration itself, cannot receive or comprehend the absolute awareness, but *reflect* it instead. This is termed the Repulsion. Herein, the universal magnetic 'wheel of creation' is forever maintained, expressed as the endless play of involuntary, automatic forces.

Under the force of attraction, the absolute existence-awareness manifests as the Intelligence or the Heart *(chitta)*. Its agent is Intellect *(buddhi)*, which determines what is truth. In the repulsing state, the force is called Mind *(manas)* and produces out of itself (that is, senses and imagines) all the ideal worlds for enjoyment.

The infinite magnetic field of Feeling and Volition expresses itself in terms of *egoism,* which embodies both (a) the idea of the 'discrete actor, the person', and (b) the idea of 'unlimited I' who commands the entire field of action. Existence-awareness as ego searches for its 'origin' (attraction back to boundless awareness) through the faculty of Intellect, and, by the same impulse, searches through the faculty of Mind for perfect objective enjoyment in manifestation. The secret is, that the search for perfect awareness and for perfect enjoyment are two sides of the same coin: that is, they are the eternal working out of the magnetised relationship between absolute feeling and absolute volition.

The Electricities

The idea of Atom or Particle (Repulsion, the embodiment of volitional force) gives rise to 'aura electricities'. These five electricities, being under the attracting influence of universal Feeling (awareness, love) towards the Real Substance, produce a magnetic field which is called the 'Body of the Intelligence'. These five polarised electricities exhibit three aspects: (a) positive (*Sattva*), (b) neutralising (*Rajas*) and (c) negative (*Tamas*). The **positive** attributes are the five sense organs (sight, hearing, touch, taste and smell). They are attracted under Mind, the polar opposite of the Intelligence, and thereby form its 'body'. The **neutralising** attributes of the five electricities are the organs of action: movement (feet), grasping (hands), sex, evacuation and speech. These organs constitute an 'energetic body' (*prana*). The **negative** attributes of the five electricities are the five sense objects (light, sound, touch, taste, smell). These, when united with the five sense organs through the neutralising power of the five organs of action, satisfy the desires of the heart. These fifteen electricities, plus the truth-seeking Intelligence and material-seeking Mind constitute the *fine material body*.

Seven Spheres of Creation

We now identify seven stages or spheres of 'the involution', the 'descent into manifestation'. These stages are eternally present, eternally co-existing, and they operate on any and all scales, from 'the billion-year expansion and contraction of a physical universe', to the infinite concentric cycles within that universe, right down to 'the projection and withdrawal of a single thought'. 'Scale' is a convention only. The spheres express through seven energy centres in the human body, along with five 'coverings or sheaths of the existence-awareness'.

The foremost (seventh) 'sphere' is the Real Substance. Nothing in the creation of darkness and light can designate it. It is the Nameless all-pervading Absolute. The next (sixth) sphere is called eternal patience or holy spirit, as it remains forever undisturbed by any limiting idea. The next (fifth) is the sphere of volition, of spiritual reflection ('the Sons of God'), wherein *the idea of separate existence of self originates.* Next (fourth) is the sphere of the atom or particle, the beginning of the creation of darkness, obscuration (*maya*) upon which the absolute existence-awareness is reflected. Next (third) surrounding this atom, is the sphere of magnetic auras, the electricities. Second to last, is the sphere of the electrical attributes (sense organs *etc*). Finally, the lowest (first) sphere is the objective material creation, which is always visible to everyone.

Seven Key Energy Centres

The human constitution embodies the 'spheres of creation' in terms of seven vital centres (*chakras*), through which we can perceive the manifestations of the absolute existence-awareness. These vortices or 'wheels' are polarised by attracting and repulsing channels (*nadis*) characterised as 'sun and moon'. These in turn manifest in chemical form as the double helix, and so on and so forth.

Five Sheaths

The Self, comprising the fifth sphere of creation to the first as listed above, is covered by five 'sheaths' or superimposed coverings. The first is the Heart sheath, composed of the four ideas (word, atom, time, space). It feels, enjoys and expresses, and is called the seat of Bliss. The second is the Knowledge Sheath. This is the intelligence, the intellect, the power to discriminate, judge, choose. It manifests the 'magnetic aura electricities', that is, the 'body of the Intelligence'. The third is the Mental Sheath, the power to use the five internal organs of sense to fulfill the desire for enjoyment. The fourth is the Prana Sheath, the body of energy or life force (*prana*), composed of the five organs of action. It is the power to go outward toward objects of sense. The last (fifth) is the Physical Sheath, the power of attachment to the five objects of sense. It is the gross material outer coating, which becoming 'nourishment' supports the visible world.

The Energetic Cycle

The cyclic energies that run up and down within the human spinal column embody life's energetic processes. Their polarised movements within two key energy channels are termed *Pingala* (red, masculine, hot, representing the sun, ending in the right nostril) and *Ida* (white, feminine, cold, representing the moon, ending in the left nostril). *Pingala* expresses the upsurge of desire, seeking, birth, growth, evolution, need for survival, self-definition, self-empowerment, self-articulation, self-actualisation. *Ida* expresses re-absorption into the absolute presence. The energy centres towards the base of the spine express progressively more concrete and involved aspects of the creation, while those towards the upper end express progressively more subtle, unitary, abstract aspects. Yet these polarised movements, always in magnetised motion like the breath, are sides of a single coin. Ultimately they must coalesce in a central channel (the *Sushumna*), that leads to the highest *chakra* and is their absolute synthesis: the eternal presence where no struggle or contradiction exists.

The Great Attraction

The seven spheres, seven energy centres and five sheaths described above, mark out the progressive 'manifestation' of the absolute force, that is, the action of 'involution' or *repulsion*. When this is completed, the action of *attraction* begins to manifest in the creation. We now outline the 'evolution', the 'return journey' to the Real Substance.

Under the influence of attraction, the Atoms ('particles of obscuration') come nearer and nearer, taking ethereal, gaseous, fiery, liquid and solid forms (elements). Thus comes what is called the *inanimate kingdom*, where the visible world becomes adorned with suns, planets, moons, nebulae *etc*. Next, when the action of divine love becomes more developed, the involution of Ignorance (the particles of obscuration, *maya*, the omnipotent energy manifested) begins to be withdrawn. The Atom's outer coating of gross matter is withdrawn, and the atoms are drawn more closely to their heart, so that the sheath composed of the organs of *action* (called *prana*) begins to operate, resulting in the organic state known as the *vegetable kingdom*. Next, the sheath of action becomes withdrawn, so that the sheath composed of the organs of *sense* comes to light. Hereby, the particles of darkness (atoms) *perceive* the nature of the external world, and attracting other Atoms of different nature, form bodies suitable for enjoyment, so that the *animal kingdom* appears in the creation. Next, when the sheath composed of the organs of sense becomes withdrawn, the body of *Intelligence* (called *buddhi*), composed of the Electricities, becomes perceptible. The Atom as the particle of darkness thus acquires the power of determining right from wrong (discrimination) and becomes the Human, the *rational* being in the creation. Next, when the Human cultivates all-knowing love within his heart, he is able to withdraw the rational sheath, so that the innermost sheath (the Heart, called *chitta*), composed of the four ideas (word, time, space, atom) becomes manifest. Human is therein called Angel (a being of light) in the creation. In this state, all of the 'creation' is now seen to be inert, insentient, without self-nature, substantially nothing but ideas generated within the one Real Substance (existence-awareness-bliss, *Satchitananda*). When the last sheath is withdrawn, there is nothing to keep us in the creation of obscuration, and so we become free and enter into the Light. We see the universal Light as a perfect whole, and ourself as nothing but an idea or fragment within that light. Thus we are bound to give up the vain idea of our separate existence.

The Idea as a Dream of Creation

All our conceptions are substantially nothing but superimposed ideas caused by the union of five objects of sense (the negative aspects of the five internal electricities) with the five organs of sense (the positive attributes of the electricities) through the medium of five organs of action (the neutralising attributes of the electricities). Thus we see that all our conceptions are a matter of *inference only*. We understand that the 'external world' is literally non-existent, just as the objects seen in dreams are found to be insubstantial when we awake. Even if we only suspect, or see by inference, the provisional nature of this creation, we can see that ignorance born of 'the idea of other' is the cause of all suffering. The point is to remove ourselves from obsession with the creation and maintenance of ideas.

The Idea of Ignorance

Ignorance is literally the apparent perception of the non-existent, and the non-perception of the existent. How can the awareness become 'unaware, inert, insentient, unknowing'? Ignorance is ultimately misconception: literally, the erroneous conception of the existence of the 'other'. From this we understand that this 'creation of unawareness' is literally non-existent.

Absolute existence-awareness 'occurs in two modes': feeling and volition, passive and active, static and dynamic, potential and kinetic. In reality it is never 'confined to one mode or the other'. What we call 'the ignorance in manifested nature' is apparent only: a product of volition, a concentration, a contraction, a 'contextual bubble', an intensifying of the existence-awareness caused by force in the form of heat (*tapas*), which automatically generates the idea of 'other' or counterforce or displacement. We (as unlimited awareness) then perceive the resulting differences in intensity as 'objects', which occur as the limiting awareness we term 'ego-mind'. Ignorance only appears to arise when the ego-mind grasps, clings, judges and categorises, excluding everything but the thing concentrated on. Ignorance may thus be termed 'the willed self-forgetfulness of existence-awareness for its own specific purposes'.

The Five Troubles

Our human troubles are defined as **ignorance, egoism, blind tenacity, attachment, aversion.** Ignorance is the idea of darkness (*maya*) distributed outward as a universe of particles according to two polarising properties: attachment, which means thirst for the objects of happiness, and aversion, which means desire for the removal of the objects of unhappiness. This polarisation delivers egoism and blind tenacity. Egoism engenders the idea of 'separate particles' (atoms) within the absolute volitional power of awareness. It is literally the failure to discriminate between the real self, existence-awareness, and (its) 'body'. Similarly, blind tenacity is the conditioned belief in the finality of nature's laws (known as materialism) instead of discernment of the infinitely fluid volitional delight of the aware Self.

Our Three Life Options

In this life we have three options for dealing with experience. (1) **To cling and to enjoy.** Here we view all experience as 'grist to the mill' of building and maintaining our 'identity', which we attempt to sustain by memory. Such a 'positive' view has a core drawback: we ultimately cannot hold on to anything, since everything we call ourselves, despite our best efforts to maintain and renew, is erased, both moment-by-moment and ultimately. Our failure to admit to this fact, whereby our fingers desperately plug the dyke against marching time, brings confusion, fear and suffering. (2) **To consciously erase.** This path seeks to fundamentally distrust all experience as ephemeral and therefore of no consequence. It is a conscious effort to 'detach', so that we no longer participate in 'this absurd show called life'. One drawback is that it is supremely difficult to erase the idea that we exist in and as the myriad of manifested forms. A second drawback is the fact that while all forms and events are ultimately erased, our physical and psychological structures entrench tendencies and attitudes that form an unimpeachable basis for future manifestation. (3) **To accept, without attachment.** This path seeks to integrate all experience 'in and as ourself' while forfeiting any egoic claim to ownership. We understand that we can never avoid action, but while doing it all with a good heart we never seek to hold onto any of action's results. We confront the extraordinary fact that *all* our problems stem from clinging. We realise that clinging is the automatic condition of believing that we are 'incarnated in the forms of the world' rather than understanding that we are *nothing but the eternal absorption of singular awareness*. Although this path may seem 'too subtle for mere mortals', we become courageous and resilient through continued awareness and patience in the face of our clinging, our need. Such an attitude and tendency grows, and by degrees we emerge as freedom itself.

What is our usual relationship with experience?

There are four phases to how we process information moment by moment:

1. The awareness 'perceives an external stimulus' according to one of its organs.
2. The awareness (as ego) reacts by asking: *Is this known to me, or is this unknown to me?*
3. The awareness (as ego) asks: *Do I like this, or do I not like this?*
4. The awareness makes a judgement, a choice.

We live by **ego,** the limited and limiting sense of self. We create **identity** by means of judgement, the continual binary trial-and-error process of choosing what we want (desire) and what we reject (aversion) in a process of 'know-don't know' and 'like-dislike'. This is akin to the one-zero energy pathways in computing. We usually recoil at first from a new, unknown input, unless we have 'subconsciously' been seeking it. Intellectual judgements that are taken for granted and no longer examined result in **paradigms,** that is, unconscious or semi-unconscious fixed views. **The Dance of Persona and Shadow** We always seek to **project and maintain 'personae'** (literally, masks); that is, we make judgements and choose positions that suit either our social roles or our personal vision of ourselves, in a shifting, life-long process. The material that is denied in the projection of a persona is often termed the 'shadow'. This shadow consists of unexamined, unintegrated material on the emotional level. The fixed positions (personae), maintained by force of ego, are continually threatened by the need to integrate the totality of our psychic material. There is only one context in which this can be achieved: the context of ourself as absolute awareness.

The unutterably complex mental and vital forces that dictate our 'conscious choices' are, in Jungian psychology, termed **'anima' and 'animus'.** These animating forces govern 'the marionette of the ego'. The core question is: 'who are we if we are nothing but the sum total of forces?' Logically, we would be nobody at all. To counter this, we present as the ego, the tiny 'I', floating and clinging and surviving in an ocean of infinite power. Our volition or will, expressed as this ego, is thus taken as paramount. Meanwhile, it rails against its self-imposed 'limitation by conditions', making continual adjustments in its search for power, knowledge, happiness.

How does 'I am' lead to 'I want' and 'I have'?

Absolute Feeling or Receptivity ('I am') and Absolute Volition ('I can') generate an endless and permanently unstable force and counterforce (displacement), which entrenches the need for 'little I who wants to be Unlimited I', characterised as the need to control and possess. This expresses as grasping, as 'I want', which entrenches the possessive sense 'I have'. The combination of 'I want' and 'I have' personify at once the unstable struggle for 'self-maintenance' (fixation, possession, control) and the ego's deepest impulse for 'self-actualisation as Unlimited I'.

There is no discrete person

Although our 'volitional acts' may appear like a 'continuous and connected stream', all are discrete, artificial instants in a borderless ocean of awareness. We think that 'identity' is the habituated collection of our ego-driven impulses, endlessly forged in the contexts of desire and aversion. We desperately try to 'maintain' identity through reiteration and habit, continually trying to revive or update components that are continually decaying and disappearing, while seeking to discard or forget material we cannot abide. 'Bundles of discrete experiences' can never deliver permanence: they are the epitome of fragmentation. We are never satisfied. We are like fish in water looking for a better class of water, not realising that we are never anything but water. To realise that we are *only this borderless absolute* delivers true identity: free from desire, aversion, fixation, fragmentation, automatism. This borderless absolute is forever-present bliss. Do we have the insight and the courage to identify with this alone?

Ignorance of the real material nature

Existence-awareness and its delight of volition (*satchitananda*) is the sole material, utterly pliable and free, effortlessly creating and collapsing all so-called forms and conditions in terms of time, space, atom, name, experience, evolution, cause, effect, memory, imagination, paradigm. By way of example, 'the collected experience of a lifetime' can suddenly appear to be 'as nothing' or 'an experience of long ago' can suddenly appear to be 'here and now'. The terms 'material' and 'materialist' are debased in that the 'dense' products of experience are proclaimed as causes (for example, we falsely seek 'the causes of awareness' in the brain). We subscribe to the limiting densities of a train of thought known as 'material science'. It is true that we may 'see the universe in a flower or a grain of sand', but we will find no origin in 'objects'. Nothing exists but the *unquantifiable material* of existence-awareness, and there can be no other 'cause'. Yet we invent (that is: fetishise, single out) such phenomena as 'birth, change and death'. We ask: 'at death, where do I go?' and 'after death, what will I become?' The short answers are 'you go absolutely nowhere' and 'you become absolutely nothing but what you are now'. Similarly, at 'birth' we cannot possibly 'come from' any material that we are not already.

Change the attitude: shift the perspective

Volition is 'the act of perceiving an idea, a form'. This act automatically gives rise to the idea of 'context', where name, particle, wave, time and space instantly deliver a sense of 'discreteness from other forms'. This process sums up our *egoism*, the sense of 'a discrete perceiver who filters awareness through the organs of perception'. But is 'the one who sees' located in any idea or form? Further, can 'the one who sees' claim discreteness 'other than as the object witnessed'? *Where is that perceiver?* If we were to drive from the countryside into a city, to its centre and out the other side, we would see that the city is not a separate entity at all, merely a 'densification', a 'contextual bubble', an 'idea'. Where is the border? Here is our attitude problem: we habitually build 'identity' through the discrete, while there is never anything but *the one who is looking*. Can we simply 'exist as borderless awareness'? In asking this question we reflexively wonder, 'where am I in this?' The ego again takes control as 'the perceiver and arbiter of objects'. Again we ask, to whom does anything (or nothing) 'occur'? Only to the borderless awareness, which is what we *are,* beginningless and without end. Our problem is thus nothing but 'a perspective that cements continual distinction, division, limitation, clinging, control'. It may be objected that this 'process of forming' is entirely natural, incontrovertible. Yet we should continuously and baldly ask: 'What are we, absolute awareness or invented object?' We cannot be both.

We are always the borderless absolute

1. All 'levels and expressions' of existence-awareness forever exist, and the 'human form' is an eternal blueprint, expressing in its energy centres and energetic waves the infinite play of existence-awareness. All potentiality and all conditions exist always as existence-awareness-volition. 'Infinite past' and 'infinite future' are one and the same.

2. It is quite impossible for existence-awareness to become 'particular', that is, to 'perform any single task or focus', without remaining infinitely malleable and potential. The possible ramifications of any 'particular action' are always unlimited in their scope, as any particle physicist will attest. Any 'system' or 'body' or 'microcosm' (for example, a 'person') always 'perfectly embodies that absolute'. This is illustrated by the doctrine of fractals: witness the perfect reproduction of a human embryo from a seed or fluid in conditions provided by the host bodies. That the totality exists at all junctures, gives the absolute lie to 'independent conceptions' like space, time, cause, history, particle, duality, movement. Such concepts veil what *is*. An analogy: If we look at the waves of the sea, we see that their 'states of flux' are so continuous as to make definition redundant. Do we proclaim each state as distinct, as 'being birthed and dying'? To widen our vision a little is to recognise the waves as the endlessly recurring, and thus endlessly empty, expressions of a borderless unchanging ocean. In the same way, we may understand the revolving states of waking, sleeping and dreaming as nothing but 'apparent pulsations of awareness'. Ultimately, how are manifestations to be viewed: as real or unreal?

They are real in that they embody the volitional energy of absolute awareness, and they are unreal in that they have no properties outside absolute awareness, that is, they have no independent arising.

3. We are bound to ask: 'Why do we entrench the vision of multiplicity, variety?' Let us go step by step. We are forever That Awareness which requires *nothing other* in order to be. There is nothing external to it. Yet awareness is absolute volition, which can be defined as *the absolute potentiality and power to confirm oneself.* This naturally expresses as 'the idea of self-control', which is egoism, the eternal quest for 'definition'. This generates 'idea', automatically followed by 'counter-idea', so that all ideas, being relative, represent a continuous vision of 'entity' or form. This vision's handmaid is memory, an arbitrary and elusive sketch of uncountable egoic occurrences in the service of 'personal identity'. The ego needs to self-define, to control, to judge, according to both the desire to enhance itself and the fear of losing itself. Once again, remember that awareness has no borders. Ego is therefore merely a personalised term for the innate and absolute volition of awareness.

4. Existence-awareness forever appears to exhibit two states: contraction and expansion. Our egoic need for (i) self-expression through knowledge and enjoyment, and (ii) need for freedom, are actually one and the same. Awareness can thereby seem to be both 'positional as personalised awareness', and 'non-positional as impersonal awareness'. The limited, alienating, egoic impulse ultimately seeks to 'return to the absolute', to 'rediscover' its core or essence. Such seeking leads to the revelation that there is nothing but core, nothing but essence: there is nowhere to 'return to' since the one who seeks is forever oneself.

5. Following (4), a core existential question arises for us, and its irony lies in the asking of it: 'Who or what am I, actually?' (a) We are utterly subject to the infinitude of volitional force that characterises absolute existence-awareness. A 'perfect conjunction of forces' is known as the 'human being'. You and I could not breathe, move, think, will, heal and so forth except as a total expression of the absolute. (b) Our volition (powers of creation and choice) is expressed in terms of senses, powers of action, imagination, retention and discrimination.

Yet we can only use the faculties available to us, and the ultimate test is: if these faculties did not pre-exist as 'eternal blueprint', would we be able to do or be anything at all? The answer is an obvious no. (c) We must therefore turn to 'what we are in total', as opposed to 'the sum of faculties that we are'. That you and I are *the absolute power of aware being*, both in the 'pure impersonal abstraction of it', and in 'our sense of personal presence', is incontrovertible. There is thus just one thing we have 'no choice' about: to be as we eternally are. Nothing and no-one can change what we are.

Take responsibility, practise austerity

Because existence-awareness is absolute, there can never be anything that is not eternally present. Since experience is continuous and eternal, the one to whom (in which) experience occurs must be absolute, and absolutely aware. In time, whatever there is to be felt, sensed, thought, acted, dreamed or remembered will eventually arise for each of us. Our experience is total and unavoidable. Existence-awareness is 'personal' in that 'nothing can occur except to ourself', yet 'impersonal' in that 'it is the sole fact'. Our experiences appear personal in that they 'seem to make a difference to us', yet are impersonal in that they 'ultimately make no difference to anything'. We thus oscillate between two attitudes. First, we may envision ourselves as an absolute player in and as the field of experience, whereby it would be logical to take *responsibility* for all of it. Second, we face the fact that whatever occurs in this infinite string of experiences is continually superceded or repeated, so that we endlessly oscillate between the struggle to succeed and descent into a blaming victim: against god, nature, systems, a nemesis, ourself. Yet who or what should take responsibility for the totality of experience? Is it the ego, who seeks to be 'arbiter', continually oscillating between struggle and blame? Or should we surrender to the realisation that there is never anything that is not forever present, that thereby there is nothing that is not forever ourself? *Austerity* is defined as 'the state where one is no longer affected by experience'. It is often called liberation. Since experience is continuous and endless, the austerity of 'not being affected' requires us to continually accept that our experience is simply the endless extrapolation of our own absolute existence-awareness. In summary, is there anything to be done? Absolutely yes, and absolutely no.

Deconstruct: play devil's advocate in search of real facts

At some point, we are bound, either through enquiry or through fear of death, to face the revelation that we are literally nothing at all. To look with great care at this juncture, will reveal that we are not other than existence-awareness itself. Further reflection reveals that we never were anything else. Yet we as existence-awareness appeared to relentlessly express ourselves as *quantity,* as 'the overwhelming world', when really we were nothing but a *quality*. Therefore, what power do we have in this overwhelming infinitude to influence anything? We are bound to ask: Is not our search for reality and the end of suffering a futile exercise? Surely life is the unfathomable play of opposites: both eternal and ephemeral, real and a dream, suffering and fleeting peace, where 'emptiness is form and form is emptiness', where there is no evolution, only recurrence, where mind is uncontrollable and awareness 'comes and goes', where nothing we do will change anything because we are never anything other than what we are! Answer: We cannot in all conscience continue to be mere (clever) transactional beings, sleep-walking our way through experience. The real goal of this glittering civilisation of ours is to generate a platform for liberation. This does not mean an escape into rarefaction, it means *acceptance of the totality of ourselves.* We possess the power of discrimination, and in the role of 'devil's advocate' we may burrow to the 'inevitable end' (like this writer has done). What do we find there? We find the need to accept unbreakable facts: that we exist and cannot cease to exist, that we are aware and cannot cease to be aware, that we perform extraordinary feats by the free power of volition, that we innately crave the absolute real. To deconstruct all experience does not cancel our wish to affirm and surrender to the absolute, it is our straight path to it. Integrity is all we have in our tortuous enquiry. In short, we need to *understand*. Even at the last we may exclaim: 'I have absorbed the problem, but what am I to *do* about it?' The answer is: dwell henceforward as the expanding understanding and presence that you ever are.

AWARENESS ALONE

TWO

REFLECTIONS ON THE PERENNIAL SCIENCE

The Core Contradiction

There is one indivisible real substance, and it is absolutely aware. It is all that you and I can ever be. No-one has ever been able, or will ever be able, to prove that anything exists outside awareness. Awareness has absolutely no features: it is 'empty and absolutely present'. The very idea that there are forms that differ from the absolute real substance is an absurdity, the original and only absurdity. Yet, this text exists to unmask the seeming contradiction between 'emptiness and form', between 'real and apparent'. Manifestations ('forms of awareness') always give the impression of substance. This is because they are expressions of the eternal real substance. Yet, because they 'appear to us' as expressions, as concentrations, as formations, as limitations, we are ever required to 're-establish the absolute nature of the real substance'.

All experience is self-absorption

There can never be such a thing as 'multiple experiences'. We are 'forever absorbed as one experience'. We cannot experience 'two times' or 'two places' or 'two objects'. No matter how we try to differentiate 'states' or create 'sequences', there is only ever unitary experience. In this way, no 'particular object of perception' can ever be in any way relevant. The shocking fact is: there has never been, nor ever could be, any experience but *This* - and 'this' is indefinable.

No Independent Arising

The doctrine of 'no independent arising' explains that there are no modifications of awareness, since the so-called 'current state of absorption' (current thought, sensation, feeling, act) is never anything but the absorbed experience of awareness itself. That is, a 'wave' is never anything but the ocean itself. Can there actually be a seer of the sight, a hearer of the sound, a feeler of the feeling, a doer of the deed, a thinker of the thought? There is absolutely no Other. Enquire *at any given instant* into the nature of your experience. You will find that the dualities you take for granted are non-existent, and that 'present absorption' is the only reality. We affirm that the so-called 'states' of awareness, namely 'form and emptiness' are one and the same, and therefore oneness eternally prevails.

The riddle of being and becoming

If the Real Substance eternally 'manifests expressions of itself', logically such expressions must 'appear to be relative to it'. If that is the case, these expressions must also 'appear to be relative to any and all other expressions'. Yet relativity is precisely the 'expression of illusion', which might be oxymoronically termed 'that which is there and not there'. So, can 'forms' be called 'real but impermanent (that is, ever-changing) expressions of the real substance'? Or further, can it be said that 'since they are ever-changing', and therefore 'never actually what they are' and therefore borderless, they are non-existent as forms? We at this point may be led to conclude that the problem is one of convention, of the noise of generated names, that 'form' and 'emptiness' (like 'matter' and 'energy') are words for the same thing, whereby 'word' is the original 'form'. Yet, why is it that to the seer (pure awareness, you and me) there is the continual sense of egoism, which generates the sense of modification, that is, the seeming uncontrollable pulsation or relationship between seer and object? And why is it that our ever-present source of *suffering* is precisely the feeling that 'all desired things pass away' and 'all unwanted things come again'? If you and I were truly at peace, we would have not the slightest problem with life's phenomena. In short, we would never need, or seek, or invent, or judge. This text might seem to 'self-entertain with endless conjecture', to 'chase its tail', but there is a bigger issue at stake. Genuine self-enquiry in this life is generated by (a) suffering associated with the ego's limiting need to cling and control, and (2) the sense of futility associated with inevitable loss. It is clear that the fundamental remedy is to perfect 'non-attachment through total acceptance of the real substance'.

Who is the seer?

To answer the question whether there is any *actual relationship* between 'emptiness and form' (a discipline known as *jnana yoga*) is to penetrate to life's utter reality. This yoga (meaning, to unite) urges us to continually ask: *Who* is the seer of thought, of form? *Who* is the conjuror of thought's founding paradigms: word, atom, time and space? We then repeatedly grasp that all 'forms' are apparent only. It is the *continuous* deconstruction of the so-called seer-seen relationship that will transform us, liberate us, root us in reality, dissolve the illusion of relationship.

As 'materialists', we cling to the false idea of the 'independent arising' of forms, stemming from our harnessing of energy in the form of 'ego'. We think that awareness is somehow 'validated by the appearance of form'. We fail to see that (our) awareness is only ever as it is, whatever the apparent 'condition' the awareness chooses to occupy. The concept that 'form proves the presence of the seer' may be convenient, but is ultimately absurd, since the 'form' is nothing but 'the dance of the phantom ego within undifferentiated awareness itself'.

No Object, No Context

We habitually speak of a 'relationship', that is, a difference, between 'an object and its context', with context defined as 'the conditions within which the object came into being'. But let us deconstruct this idea called context. It can only serve as 'context to the object' in the event that it creates *all* (that is, infinite) conditions whereby that object can exist. Conversely, if the object exhibited any characteristics that were not (already) contained in its context, then it could not be a representation or product of that context. The slam-dunk ironies here are: (a) any 'difference' between these so-called 'dancing ghosts' ensures the obliteration of both, and (b) any 'connection or similarity' between them also ensures the obliteration of both. We see that the terms are mere conveniences, born to uphold the fallacy of duality, of 'definition', of 'perceiver and perceived', of 'subject and object', of 'cause and effect'. If we are to speak of 'context' at all, there can be only one, and that is 'absolute awareness'.

Show me the border

All definitions, assumptions and paradigms must be challenged. Where is the border between 'thing' and 'context'? Where is the border between 'what constitutes context and what does not'? Where is the border between 'awareness and its products'? Where is the border between 'air and wind', the border between 'sleep and waking', the border between anything and anything? The concrete and practical goal here is to realise that *we are nothing but the borderless, simple, effortless absolute.*

The absurdity of mechanical chance

If we accept the statement 'No-one has ever been able, or will ever be able, to prove that anything exists outside awareness', the next logical statement will be 'The infinitude of so-called forms are but expressions of awareness'. What alternative is there? The glib materialist notion that 'things evolve out of an infinite play of forces' is never able to say what it *is* that actually evolves. Where is the border between so-called object and so-called context? And where is the conscious motivator in all this? The idea that awareness 'at some point arose or evolved' out of the infinite action of mechanical chance, that is, a combination of unconscious objects, simply beggars belief. It would be better to say: awareness eternally 'involves itself in form', thereby offering 'infinite opportunities to evolve, to reaffirm itself'.

Awareness Alone: The 'jetplane route'

1. There is awareness alone.
2. Awareness' indwelling power of volition generates displacement: the idea of egoism, of 'other' or 'object'.

3. Thereby arises the automatic notion of 'subject'.
4. For 'the subject' to ask: 'What is the object?' is to discover that the object has no boundaries, therefore cannot be discrete, therefore cannot be an object at all.
5. To similarly ask: 'Who is the subject?' is to discover that the subject has no boundaries, therefore cannot be discrete, therefore cannot be a subject at all.
6. Both subject and object are fabrications of awareness in its mode of volition.
7. Is there anything but awareness alone, that is, emptiness?
8. Alternatively, is there forever the subject-object relationship, that is, form?
9. The doctrine of Pulsation says: 'Emptiness is (forever) form, and form is (forever) emptiness.
10. Both are thereby mere names, signifying that 'all relationships are illusory', hence non-existent.

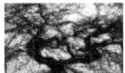 **Never Obscured**

At the risk of being absurdly precise, we should question the very basis of existence itself. Can existence arise? If yes, existence must arise from something else, since it cannot arise from nothing (non-existence). Clearly, it cannot arise at all. It is literally eternal. Can awareness arise? If so, it must arise from unawareness. How can awareness arise from unawareness? Again it cannot: it is eternal. Next, as both existence and awareness are eternal, and as there is nothing outside them, then they must be one and the same. If the notion or the fact of absolute existence cannot be posited without awareness, again they must be identical. If nothing exists but existence-awareness, then it must be bliss (oneness, self-delight). Can existence itself be obscured, in a state we call death? Never. There is no death except 'the idea of obscuration, limitation', that is, the idea of egoism. Can awareness be obscured? Never. Crucially, can awareness *appear* to be obscured, in what we call a state of ignorance? We would assume that this is so, but the question is actually equivalent to 'if awareness is obscured, to whom is it obscured?' The answer is only awareness. The question therefore means: 'can awareness be obscured to awareness?' This is clearly absurd.

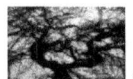

Absolute Receptivity and Absolute Volition

The absolute condition of absolute existence-awareness is (a) infinite receptivity, feeling, and (b) infinite volition, the power of concentration. Absolute volition is absolute force, the absolute vibration. It is Sound, the creative intensity of pulsating bliss. Meanwhile, there is ever and always absolute feeling. It is the absolute Light that ever thrills in (and *as*) the concentrated fissures of its own bliss-intensity, yet ever holds and tempers and cups that bliss-intensity in its ever-wide lightness. The force of volition is never so intense that it is not utterly saturated and cradled and cooled by the awareness-light, the ever-present receptivity, the feeling-lightness, the ever-sensitive, ever-aware light.

The Limiting Idea of Ignorance

(1) How does the idea of obscuration (ignorance) arise? The answer lies in the absolute pulsation of awareness as the absolute force of volition (concentration), which instantly engenders the idea called egoism. This is the effort to define and control, which instantly engenders the 'contexts' of form, name, time, space and cause. (2) No idea can arise without the substratum of awareness, and no secondary or other idea can arise without reverting to that continuous substratum. If nothing arises without an absolute substratum, does anything ever arise? The answer is no. (3) Can ignorance therefore exist? The answer is ultimately no, since we are bound to ask: who will define it? Clearly, the perceiver's volitional experience (the egoic idea of externality) is nothing but the affirmation of awareness, forever.

Does Volition innately obscure?

Why would the Absolute, that which is forever itself, appear 'not to be absolute', that is, appear obscured? Volition must be 'the absolute free play' of absolute awareness, yet it also 'appears to be the genesis of all obscuration'. Does volition innately obscure? Answer: Who has the volition to ask that question and find an answer? We must be aware that *the idea* of obscuration, limitation or concentration can only occur to one who is limitlessly aware. Therefore, there are three options only: (1) If the absolute is truly obscured it is because a superior (volitional) power has done it. This is patently absurd. (2) If the absolute is obscured, whatever reasons it has for obscuring itself can only ever be known to itself and are therefore of no relevance to anything but itself. (3) The absolute is never obscured. Only (3), shockingly, can be correct. Therefore our sole question is: What, if any, is the relationship between 'that which is absolutely itself' and 'that which appears to be other than itself'? In other words, how and why do confusion and ignorance occur to the seer, that is, to 'you and me'?

We must assert that 'volition is ever free, but its child, egoism, the limited, separate sense of self, is not'. The unbreakable signal that there is 'a problem' occurs in the fact that there is suffering. There is no suffering without limitation. In short, we entrench a sense of limitation based on the continual egoic polarisation of our awareness into 'seer and seen', which in turn arises from our continual egoic clinging to desire and aversion. In the greatest irony of all, this rampant egoism flails to actualise our ingrained need for perfect awareness, bliss and peace. Therefore, to pursue a state characterised as 'continual awareness of the unchanging reality', we may: (1) Continually recognise the absolute instability of egoic desire and aversion within the unchanging context of awareness. (2) Continually deconstruct the polarity between 'seer and seen' (the very definition of ego), recognising the 'object' to be non-different from the 'subject', so that both are therefore unreal. (3) If we realise Volition (power of concentration) to be nothing but 'the endless freedom of awareness', rather than the enchainment of need, then we recognise 'we, the perceiver' to be the eternal 'agent and affirmer' of awareness.

The true animator of systems, bodies, organs

Omniscient Feeling and Omnipotent Volition create a state whereby Intelligence (the urge toward undifferentiated self) seems polarised with Mind (the urge toward action, manifestation, the involuntary). The idea of manifestation, as atom, particle, form, the involuntary, is distributed as five electricities which express the polarity or tension of three basic states: equilibrium (*sattva*), activity (*rajas*) and inertia *(tamas)*. The electricities manifest as: 1. A state representing undifferentiated purity or equilibrium. 2. A tension between the equilibrium state and the state of activity. 3. The state of activity itself. 4. A tension between the state of activity and the state of inertia. 5. The state of inertia itself. The electricities shoot like tentacles ever outward, creating the mind's five electricities or organs of sense, which are magnetically polarised with the five objects of sense to which they attach, to create the plane of 'physical elements' (ether, air, fire, water and solid) that play out their endless ramifications through the five channels of action (movement, grasping, sex, evacuation and speech or noise). The human organism is built around seven key energy centres (*chakras*) that operate according to five internal forces or 'winds', that correspond to the five powers of action, namely: moving about, grasping, reproducing, evacuating waste, and expressing speech.

Yet, *what is it* that forever expresses itself as the cascade of organs called system or ecosystem, such as the human body, and effortlessly maintains perfect renewal and equilibrium? This system we call human is none other than the volitional power of omnipresent awareness. It is usually defined in the separative mechanical way of material science as 'a composition of elements (electricity, chemicals, air, heat, water, solids), coalescing as a partly creative, partly automatic system'. Yet *who* looks through these eyes, hears through these ears, feels through this skin, smells through this nose, tastes through this tongue, experiences through these nerves, imagines and judges through this brain? According to the mechanical view, the organ called 'brain' might be called 'mere blood and meat' if it were not for 'the polarised electricities and their resulting chemicals that animate the apparent Frankenstein's monster'. Yet, if the system is admitted to be *in any way creative or self-regulating*, the cat is truly out of the bag. Where is the border between the self-aware and the so-called inert or automatic? It does not exist. The only 'animator, producer, maintainer and arbiter' of all action, sensation, discriminating intelligence (*etc*), is the free volition of absolute awareness, effortlessly conceived by and operating at every juncture, as itself. Whether as 'organ' or 'system' or as 'animating ghost within the organs and systems', the living awareness is ever itself.

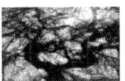 **Volition: the affirmation of awareness itself**

Why should the sole and absolute awareness appear to manifest as an infinitude of pathways and points? Awareness as the force of volition generates the idea of concentration, of manifestation, which is nothing but the idea of displacement, discreteness, egoism. Does concentration really occur in the stillness of awareness? While we may glibly assume that 'volition is the eternal action of awareness', the truth is that no action exists in its own right, since it can only be 'distinguished from its origin' where its displacement or counterforce (which ironically is immediately identified as its 'origin') is admitted. And by no stroke of genius can one ever discover a boundary between force and counterforce except as within the eternal context of awareness. We must never assume 'the thing we identify' is what it *is*. Volition (concentration) is therefore utterly indistinguishable from awareness itself, *and yet* it seems to be 'the eternal phantom, the relativity, the displacement of oneness, the obscuring play of thisness'. Its so-called dance of force and counterforce is nothing but the *apparent* repulsion (denial) of *This,* wherein we continually experience 'a birth in thisness, birth of duality in oneness, birth of time in eternal *this*, birth of entity in emptiness, birth of name out of silence'. Again we ask: Does volition innately obscure? We answer: *Who* has the volition to ask that question, and to deliver an answer? Volition is the continual and infinite *affirmation* of awareness alone. **The ego-mind** Yet doubts continually arise! Is awareness really 'forever free' in its extrapolation of point, pathway, particle, space, time, name? (1) We know that awareness is the only volitional actor, so that all points and pathways (*etc*) are mere ideas of Itself. (2) We know that because volition's action is nothing but 'the false idea of limitation due to concentration', that therein arises the idea of egoism and its surrogates: desire, pulsation, choice, fixation, control. (3) Absolute awareness appears to forever 'sacrifice' itself as 'the force of desire and its consequent attachments'. Do we then admit that because all is volition (concentration), that all is eternal limitation? We can only predict that volition, as the sheer awareness, is 'unlimited in scope but apparently limited in every action'. Here is a paradox, and the ego-mind alone is responsible for it. This ego-mind, ever certain of its own supremacy since it is 'the child of absolute volition', defines itself as 'the all-knowing creator', as the supreme operator of force and counterforce, as the 'executive agent' of a borderless awareness, forever 'in total possession of itself'. No 'driver of reality' can ever be allowed to feel it is limited in its power. Even a 'sudden sense of limitation' has the ring of totality about it!

'Context and Thing': Dance of Ideational Phantoms

What is the genius of the absolute that it contains the idea of 'other'? By the power of 'volition as pure joyous action', the 'idea of multiplicity' appears. Meanwhile, there is never anything that does not require the whole, the absolute, in order to be realised. There is never any 'thing' that is not 'part of something else', part of a 'boundless context'. Thing 'creates' context and context 'creates' thing. Context becomes 'infinite in its ramification' as long as 'thing' is posited. There is never any 'transaction' that is not 'continually transforming into something else'. There is never a 'part of a thing' that is not a stooge for something else, which in turn is never anything but a footstool to some other thing. No thing has independent arising, no thing has self-nature. At the heart of vibration (sound or word) there is none, at the heart of time (change, sequence) there is none, at the heart of space (division, relationship) there is none, and at the heart of atom (particle, limit, separation) there is none. Awareness is the pure bliss of volition, absolutely aware in any apparent state of 'modification'. It is the sole context. No 'differentiated object' can be other than the nature of awareness itself. There can be nothing but *the continual experience of the fact of oneness,* whether in 'the mode of abstracted emptiness' or in 'the egoic mode of form born of need'.

The Magnetisation of Mind and Intellect

The two cardinal modes of volition, the power of concentration of awareness, are (a) Mind, which is expansion, imagination, creation, material-seeking force, and (b) Intellect, which is judgement, discrimination, purification, unity-seeking force. These two modes are forever magnetised (that is, opposed as pulsation), and thus entrench four cardinal ideas: (1) Time, which is change, sequence, cause and effect. (2) Space, which is differentiation, relationship. (3) Name, which is classification, concept. (4) Atom, which is particle, distinction, limitation. Out of mind's rampant potentiality and multiplicity, intellect seeks order, the affirmation of moral sense through discrimination of 'good and bad', 'meaningful versus meaningless'. This struggle between the pursuit of life's multiplicities and subsequent search for unity, entrenches the cardinal ideas. Here are some examples: (1) The need to classify everything using 'name' (language) supports our need to ramify, to conquer, to 'explain' the one unclassifiable existence-awareness. (2) Our fetish for numbers exemplifies the need to 'construct the multitudinous facets of existence'. (3) The idea of 'weight' is the innate resistance we carry to our own freedom. (4) The conception of the fractal, that infinite branching of pathways, symbolises our fetish for infinite ramification in unity itself. (5) Our desperation in particle physics to find the smallest, most fundamental 'particle', entrenches our foolish belief in 'the independent arising of matter'. (6) Even the low-level intolerance we feel to those who are 'different', is a symptom of our false paradigm of multiplicity.

 **Awareness is the only 'cause'**

Since no 'object' (concentration) has 'independent arising', no object can ever 'cause' any other. Look closely. For the object (the concentrated thought) to be 'replaced' by another, the first must dissolve into its 'original state', following which 'out of the original state' another object may occur. Awareness is therefore 'known as the cause', and object as 'known as the effect'. This is called 'subject-object relationship'. There can be no 'relationship between forms' except what is generated in their common origin. Since awareness is timeless, the very idea of 'object following object' is meaningless. Similarly, since awareness is spaceless, the very idea of 'object juxtaposing object' is meaningless. Certainly, in relativity, the Four Ideas (time, space, word, atom) allow 'causes and effects' to be forever identified as we please. But only one 'cause' can ever be spoken of, and that is 'absolute cause'. And if there is said to be 'one' cause, there clearly can be *none*. Where, in that case, is the boundary between subject and object? There can be none. There is no 'relationship' whatsoever at all between so-called subject and object. **How can anything ever be but what is?** Nothing 'manufactured' has any self-nature. No 'thing' has any independent arising. The literal purport is that 'no thing can ever be'. We may object that there is nothing but action, nothing but creation. Yet all action is 'utterly replaced', since absolute replacement is the nature of action. Clearly, there can be no action but that of 'One who appears to disport Herself'. Yet how can anything ever be but what *is*? Clearly, there can be no action, and therefore no relationship.

A volitional enquiry into the results of volition

Absolute awareness is never anything but sentient. In its capacity of absolute feeling and receptivity, awareness also possesses absolute volition. Volition is its power of initiation, concentration, creation. We understand that while volition freely manifests 'the universe of names and forms', the idea of universe is nothing but 'the repetitive, fixed idea of concentration, limitation, obscuration'. That is, volition's very action births the principle of the involuntary, the automatic, the insentient, the fixed idea, the 'paradigm'. This outcome appears utterly contradictory. Therefore we must ask: **Where is the border** between awareness and its concentrative power? And, where is the border between volition and the involuntary, the automatic? We are bound to deduce that volition is the free expression of absolute awareness yet its manifestations (ideas, objects) *appear insentient.* By way of example, we as awareness generate and maintain this sentience-insentience duality as long as we ask such questions as 'does unawareness exist?'. Yet when we, the awareness, *volitionally enquire into the origin of insentience,* the latter is recognised as a mere phantom. Ultimately, the volitional thought 'Who experiences the thought?' wipes out all obscuration. It is like the burning stick that pokes the fire: in the end the stick itself is consumed. Our volitional enquiry reaches its source, and only sentience remains. We then understand that there never is anything but sentience, that is, awareness abiding as itself. We understand that volition is nothing but awareness' eternal power to affirm itself.

 The Phantom Wheel of Pulsation

Absolute existence-awareness is absolute feeling or receptivity, and is forever timeless, spaceless, present. What then is its 'manifestation'? Under the force of volition (indwelling joy), a 'magnetic wheel' appears to arise. This is nothing but the idea of **Repulsion** from the source, in eternal hiatus with the idea of **Attraction** to the source. It is absolute receptivity versus its concentrative power, it is the self-entwined serpents of yin and yang, the warp and weft of displacement, the crest and trough of wave. It is eternity and time, space and point, cause and effect. It is every conceivable instantaneous juncture and transaction on any scale (not that there is any scale). The wheel has no beginning or end: repulsion and attraction are apparent only! For where is the border between any pulsation and another? Here is idea, illusion, endless becoming, *maya, samsara*. Such displacement is our every single thought born of the impulse called egoism. It is this volition, the 'will to form' that results in concentration, distinction, discreteness, separation, automatism, idea of 'subject and object'. If we remove 'egoism', is there any idea of distinction, differentiation? Absolutely not. How can any 'form' exist if it is indistinguishable from its context, its cause? Are fire, water, sky and earth (for example) discrete? Though they appear to be in juxtaposition or conflict, how can they be, when they are all absolute energy? All 'pulsations' and their resultant 'forms' are nothing but the phantom of concentration, the phantom warp and weft within the absolute unchanging presence.

To whom could relativity occur?

Limitation of awareness is apparent only. Through the apparent polarisation of feeling and volition, projection occurs, an apparent displacement that incurs automatic obscuration (veiling). The notion of relativity becomes entrenched. Yet how can changeless awareness ever become 'relative'? *To whom* would any displacement or obscuration appear to occur? Clearly, to one who can *never* be obscured. Observe this fundamental riddle. Awareness *is*, it can never 'occur'. There is nothing about it that can ever change, therefore it has no 'aspects'. Yet this life seems to be nothing but 'the exposition of limited aspects of awareness', that is, 'objects'. Absolute presence can never be divided, yet there seems to be 'nothing but relativity'. There is no avoiding the question: *To whom* does the concentration-displacement-limitation-object-obscuration appear to occur? To awareness, who cannot possibly be subject to relativity. Appearance is thus its 'eternal body', its 'mantle', its 'mind', its 'joy and delight', its 'play', its 'song', its 'continual affirmation'.

Awareness is Volition, Volition is Awareness

Existence-awareness *is* the blissful volition of creative energy. Meanwhile, awareness utterly and always comprehends itself. No-one has ever been able, or will ever be able, to prove there is anything outside awareness. No sense, emotion, thought, event, statement or relationship ever takes place outside awareness... and this statement proves itself. Therefore, how can awareness initiate the idea of displacement or contradiction? Volition or concentrative force is the eternal potency of absolute potentiality. This potency must appear as pulsation. This pulsation suggests 'other', relationship, polarity, 'repulsion from source followed by attraction to source'. Yet how can this kinesis ever be sustained except from the standpoint of stasis? How can division ever be comprehended except from the standpoint of unity? *Who alone* is it that can know 'nothing ever happened'? It is the seer. Thereby, can there be anything outside awareness? There cannot. If all 'transaction' is 'from awareness to awareness', then there is no transaction. Nothing ever happened. Manifestation, incarnation, birth, death: none are admitted.

 **The logic of 'no state outside awareness'**

Any question of how awareness 'arises', or is 'born', is utterly beyond any possibility of solution, since we give birth to, indeed define, any origin through the agency of awareness itself. Even logic can barely erect such a question, since logic is a product of awareness. We thus begin with *what is*. Awareness, being basic, cannot be defined. It is therefore original, eternal, the one true fact. Why would awareness ever seek to confine itself or define itself by 'proofs', that is, as 'awareness of'? The haunting thought persists: why should there ever be analysis of *what is*? Can awareness embody a difference between 'objectless (rarefied, empty) awareness' and 'objectified (densified, concentrated) awareness'? Perhaps one of these is 'pure, therefore true' and the other 'compromised, therefore false'? No. Value judgement is clearly irrelevant. Is there any difference between awareness and its volition, its 'conjuring of an infinitude of events'? If yes, then 'the two exist simultaneously', by dint of being different. If no, then they are one and the same. If they are 'one and the same' then neither can be reliably proven, since their so-called existence relies on their being different. We have thus laid the ground, and posited the riddle. We can now proceed to flail endlessly to solve it - until, like the stick of polarising intellect that pokes the fire, the volitional enquiry itself is wiped out. It is time, dear reader, to just *let go*.

 This is the Tao

Water flows, but from where to where? Where is flow's beginning and end? Where is the 'substance' of the flow when no part of that flow can ever be defined? This is the Tao, and it is empty. To 'find the running water' we must 'define the still point of water'! There is nothing but 'the seer of the still point', who is the seer alone. All 'movement', all 'form', is proof of the seer who is still.

Action is a 'continuous phantom'

Let us consider awareness as volition, a concentrative force that appears to manifest infinite iterations (ideas) of awareness itself. The 'border' or 'difference' between any force, event or state and another, is defined as resistance. Yet where is that border, and therefore, where the resistance? We can say that contraction ('form') *continually* meets its resistance in expansion ('emptiness'). From this, we can say that 'all effort *continually* resolves in non-effort'. If this 'eternal context of resistance' occurs within the 'absolute context of non-resistance', then (for example) thought will continually be subsumed in one who is never thought, heat continually experienced by one who is never hot, pulsation continually experienced by one who is ever still, striving continually subsumed in a context of equilibrium… and so on. Conclusion: Can there ever be any resistance between (awareness as) stillness-emptiness, and (awareness as) dynamism, form? The answer is definitely no. No action is ever actually action, because its context is ever stillness. Awareness as volitional force is identical with and inseparable from Itself, just as burning power is inseparable from fire.

'Awareness eternally breathes the acts of itself'

Awareness is 'the only agent in all acts', and thus is forever self-absorbed as all acts. Any border between act and act can never be defined, since to seek such a definition is to enact a further 'act' of awareness. It may be said that a near-infinite proportion of awareness' capabilities operates 'beyond our personal volition'. Yet awareness is not justified as 'quantity' but as borderless indwelling presence. We actually have the capacity to arrest the awareness from continually forming discrete 'acts of itself'. On the other hand, we have no capacity whatever to stop 'discrete acts' from 'dissolving in the illimitation from whence they came'. In short, we cannot function as *anything* but awareness. Meanwhile, the inward and outward breath of life is rhythmic and unending, operating as *contraction,* where ideas of concentration, densification, point, act, word, time (*etc*) appear, followed by *expansion,* where the self-state of existence-awareness appears to reassert. Yet since this rhythm is continual and simultaneous, there can be no border between acts, since although displacements appear to exist, the context in which they appear is one and unchanging. By analogy, air is continually breathed but is forever air. Truly, that which is forever itself can never be anything but itself. How then does 'that which is forever itself', act at all? Here arises a subtle answer. If awareness is both 'eternally itself and eternally acts out aspects of itself', then 'it only appears, to itself, to act' - and therefore does not, and cannot, act at all. Its 'action' is obviously without effort, which means 'no action at all'. You and I may choose to focus specifically on 'being that constant without which nothing can occur', where our 'role' is none other than 'being present as awareness'. For example, this state is often called 'flow' by artists and athletes.

Existence is all
- Does 'death' exist?
- Certainly. The evidence is everywhere
- Then death is existence?
- Don't be absurd
- So existence 'contains' death?
- Death negates existence!
- Death must be 'something', in order to negate existence?
- Of course
- Yet 'something' is existence, so how can 'something' negate existence?
- You twist the obvious
- Just tell me: does death exist or does it not?
- I just said so. It is blindly obvious that it does
- So death is existence. And if it is existence, it cannot be death, for death is non-existence.

Our little 'death' problem
- To whom does death occur?
- To the person
- Have you ever experienced it?
- I have seen it
- I have 'seen' the moon, but I cannot say I know it
- Death is obvious to anyone who has seen it. Why bother to debate it?
- Will death occur to you?
- Of course
- So you will experience death?
- Naturally
- But if you experience it, you cannot be dead, right?
- Okay wise guy, I will not experience it!

- Who will experience it then?
- It happens to me!
- How do you know that? How will you know that?
- I won't. I'll be dead!
- Then how can you possibly prove that it happened at all?
- Others will prove it!
- Who are no doubt alive, and therefore not qualified to prove it.

The Eternal Observer of Death

To whom or to what does 'death' occur? Fact 1: the one to whom a thing occurs is, by pure logic, not that thing. Fact 2: there can be no awareness of death except to the observer, the one who is not death. Death is therefore to be defined as a perceived phenomenon. Perceived phenomena are always in flux. 'Flux' is therefore co-efficient with 'death'. Do either actually exist? Death, if it exists according to a definition called flux, would have to be *constant*. How? To identify flux, we must posit the concept of 'formation in Point A as opposed to formation in Point B'. How could anything ever be identified otherwise? Yet if Point A, according to the behaviour of all phenomena, is 'forever in flux', there is no circumstance where it can ever actually *be* Point A, and therefore no circumstance whereby it could morph into point B. Similarly, to identify 'this or that person' is an arbitrary convention, since there is no border between the so-called 'personal self' and 'absolute context', as just proven by the non-existent nature of flux (death). Next, the one to whom death is supposed to occur is asserted to be a 'limited being', since obviously death has 'occurred to that being and to no other'. But 'that being' is a limited thought, a conjuration, an artificial boundary, since (a) that being is clearly no longer separable from absolute being since he is assumed to have dissolved, and (b) that being was never anything but absolute context, since his 'death' is clearly 'totally dependent on the context otherwise he would not have died'. No-one has ever experienced death except as the observer of it, therefore the observer forever lives. We blindly speak of 'one who is dead', but speak in the present tense, and the present is unfortunately ever present. If one were to use past tense and say 'he was dead', the only assumption then is that he can no longer be dead. In sum, death is nothing but the perception of idea, the perception of form. 'Death is liquidated' in the awareness that we forever are. We never can be anything but this living being.

The Cave of Death

In the old Upanishadic story, Nachiketas enters the cave of death and confronts its landlord:

- Is this the place of death?

Death replies: - Indeed.

- I ask one boon.

Death smiles wryly. - What can I do you for?

- *Tell me who you are*

Death wrinkles his brow a little. - Truly, I'll offer you anything you *want*: fame, riches, power, love, long life

- I want none of these. Tell me who you are
- I offer wondrous gifts. Do not ask it
- Tell me who you are!

And death becomes very stressed... and he starts to shrink before Nachiketas' eyes, then suddenly vanishes like a hermit crab into his shell. And Nachiketas thinks: 'Where is death? It is nothing but 'the ego', the 'idea of someone', of definition, limitation, separation, automatism. It is nothing but the idea of other, *the idea of negation*. All ideas are the idea of negation! Death is every thought that arises and shrinks away. It is said: 'out of emptiness arise form, name, space and time, and into emptiness they disappear, only to arise again'. *To whom* is death supposed to occur? If it cannot be proved that death occurs to anyone, then how can it exist? Death is a phantom pulsation, ever dissolved in the still eternal heart.'

No death, no death

The conditions for suffering and its erasure

There will always be suffering, it is said. But suffering varies from person to person, where 'one man's meat is another's poison'; and clearly, suffering is often absent. We thereby conclude that if there is suffering it must occur to the ego, to 'the idea of someone'. If there is no 'idea of someone', there is no suffering. Only the awareness as ego, as contraction, concentration, definition, limitation, automatism thus suffers. To surrender one's sense of separateness by understanding the illusion of it, is the perennial path for the lessening of suffering. When we travel on a train, do we carry our baggage in our hands? We place it in the luggage rack. So too in life. To carry stress without trusting in the absolute totality of unalterable being, is a fool's game. And if there be no *awe and amazement* at the saturating miracle of awareness, then we are permanently asleep, and permanently fragile. We are in fact borderless and eternal being(s), continual purveyors of an infinitude of apparent manifestation, and our presence at this instant, at this juncture, is the *total* fulfilment of the eternal presence. In this profoundly simple sense there is never anything but THIS. We can never be anything but the profound import and the profound simplicity of this absolute gesture, now. We stand as nothing but the eternal NOW. So, relax. We shall do our best, then cast our acts into the bright air of this eternal, and cease to worry about consequence, because we are not 'a bundle of events and their consequences', we are instead the sublime liberation that 'nothing ever makes any difference to anything'.

Infinite capability is infinite freedom

Whatever can possibly exist, certainly exists in *us*. For example: We are utterly impersonal yet experience it all as personal. We are all-knowing yet take on the apparent mantle of ignorance, insentience, automatism. We are bliss yet accept darkness. We are immobile yet are in perpetual motion. We are eternal yet 'entertain continuous death'. We are utterly empty yet appear defined as time, space, name and form. We are peerless and absolute yet seem to suffer immeasurably. We are ever free, yet seem to be bound by absolute forces. There is liberation in our attitude of acceptance, yet ignorance, limitation and confusion snare us everywhere. We are empty, yet we contain all. We are both contradictory and not. We abide by all pathways yet laugh at them all. We are infinitely ourselves. **Awareness beyond objectification: the value of effort** How alert can we be to remembering the fact of awareness when we continually live in, and as, the quotidian, changing, objectifying world? Is this 'coming to awareness' simply a momentary indulgence? Answer: The key is to continually discern existence-awareness as forever what we are, *that we can never be anything else.* Our egoism as self-obsession simply means that we continually seek to define and control, and therefore obscure the reality that we are nothing but free awareness. We must *ever enquire* into the actual nature of this egoic pulsation of awareness and its so-called concentrations (objects) or states. For example, it does not matter if we as awareness are 'empty' as in sleep, or 'appearing as form' as in the waking and dreaming states. We are always transparent, whether we discern this fact or not. Some will say: if we are ever transparent whether we discern it or not, then why make any effort at all? Answer: We should make a massive effort to discern our pure transparent awareness, until we no longer need to, until we are forever aware of being aware.

This, and this alone

- We are nothing but borderless, impersonal existence-awareness
- Yet we are personal conscience and its agent, morality. We must act, and choose
- Yes, but we are not partial or insignificant in any way
- Yet life has infinite parts
- Does it?
- We seem to be nothing but the endless satisfaction of want, endlessly tasting the world's manifestations
- The 'world' is ultimately nothing but a parade of fantasies, and our life seems to be nothing but the satisfaction of these. But existence-awareness is absolute, never partial. So-called manifestations are nothing but the *organs* of existence-awareness
- But we are trapped, subject to want, form, name, time, space. What is the point of analysing such a situation?
- To analyse is to affirm the truth of who you are, by avoiding getting lost in a vision of what you are *not*. Life has no other goal or purpose. We are absolute, we are all of it, we are not partial. I am not here to tell you what to do, or which desires to fulfill. But I say this: he or she who is not satisfied with the eternal simple, the timeless spaceless formless

nameless *this,* will ever wander in the fantasy of want. Understand: we are nothing but the eternal unchanging presence of *this*. This, here, alone, is the end of want.

The all-encompassing reality

The observation 'we can't have this without that' throws up all manner of tail-chasing dualisms: idea and emptiness, involution and evolution, obscuration and clarity, idealism and realism, impulse and stasis, meaning and absurdity, 'something to be done and nothing to be done'… Yet the fact that absolute existence-awareness appears to be endlessly conditioned and limited as 'polarity, relativity, pulsation, hiatus, yin-yang', demands that we 'wield a sword of enquiry' in the form of *'To whom, or in what, does the pulsation, polarity, hiatus have its resolution?* The sages, having taken this enquiry to its utter heart, always assert the same truth: reality is nothing but all-encompassing existence-awareness-bliss, and all its ways and works and manifestations are true vehicles and expressions of itself, all components in a complementary vision without any contradiction. Sri Aurobindo describes complementarity in its highest form: 'Reality's very nature is knowledge; it has not to acquire knowledge but possesses it in its own right… Its steps are not from ignorance into some imperfect light, but from truth to greater truth, from right perception to deeper perception, from intuition to intuition, from illumination to boundless luminousness. In a graded self-manifestation by which it would eventually reveal its own highest heights, Reality must in its very nature be free from ignorance and error. It starts from truth and light and moves always in truth and light. In it, feeling and emotion, beauty and delight, do not swerve from the right and the real, or twist away from the divine rectitude. Even an incomplete action is a step towards completeness. The Reality moves in safety towards its perfection. The finite does not limit or feel itself contrary to the infinite, and the relative and temporal are not a contradiction of eternity but a proper relation of its aspects. Time is but the eternal in extension, and the eternal can be felt in the momentary. No theory of illusion or self-contradictory *maya* need be mounted to justify reality's way of existence. Escape from life is never a necessity for finding reality.

Its 'becoming' can never be a contradiction, but an aspect, an expression of its supreme reality.'

THREE

PRACTISE MINDFULNESS

To the question: *how can I meditate?* - there is only one practical answer: *you need to understand what you already are.*

There is never anything to do but examine our actual experience, which is forever current

We must become aware of the dynamics of the psyche. Psychic content (thought, emotion, sensation) can be approached in three ways: The first is to actively follow it. This is known as desire, and is characterised by need, greed *etc*. The second is to fight it, to repress it. This is known as fear, and is characterised by aversion, negativity *etc*. The third way is to take a neutral, observing, non-judging stance, characterised by equilibrium, balance, openness. To follow or to fight (desire and aversion) is to enmesh oneself in the falsehoods of 'cause and effect' (*karma*), of mental imbalance, suffering and mental illness, and to become their victim. On the other hand, to cease to judge, to merely observe, analyse and understand, is to neutralise the energies and their influence on us.

Who Are We?

Let us understand the Self and its dynamics. (a) What can we say for sure, without needing any proof? Inquiring into our actual nature, we can say: 'I am, and I know that I am'. That is: I am Existence and I am Awareness. As nothing but these, I am Bliss, fullness, unity. In Yoga parlance, this is called *Satchitananda* (I am existence-I am Awareness-I am Bliss). (b)

Meanwhile, our simple existence-awareness-bliss seems continually 'displaced' by an 'outward questing', a need, a volition, a will to create, a continual pulsation of opposites, of apparent incongruities. Held in place by repetition and resulting in fixed conceptual norms or 'paradigms', our effort is characterised by limitation, displacement, confusion and resultant suffering.

Awareness as feeling and volition

We consist of absolute awareness (feeling) and its absolute concentrative energy (volition). Awareness either remains 'empty' (unmanifested, 'the eternal seer') or 'moves, acts' ('manifests as object'). Volition projects as 'objective experience', consisting of egoism, thought, emotion, sensation, action.

Awareness has no 'states'

Awareness appears to express itself as states of deep sleep, dream and waking. Deep sleep is called a 'subjective' state of awareness, 'objectless, empty, internal'. Dream is called a 'semi-objective' state that processes impressions with a view to balancing the psyche. Waking is called an 'objectifying or externalising' state, in which we create and judge, absorb and reject, mostly according to habitual attitudes (paradigms).

However, the only 'context or medium' is awareness. It is incorrect to say that awareness exhibits any 'states' at all, including sleep, dream and waking. No-one has ever been able to say (or will ever be able to say) that there is anything outside awareness. Our experience is always unitary; that is, there is no Other. We cannot properly claim that there is any sense, emotion, thought, statement, event or relationship that takes place other than (that is, outside) awareness. The idea of a relationship between awareness and its manifestations, between 'seer and seen', between 'subject and object' has no basis at all. Further, there is no relationship between so-called objects since there is no other material but awareness. To believe in 'relationship' is a fundamental ignorance (conceptual error) known as materialism. For example, a materialist may claim that 'there is no awareness in sleep'. But *who* claims there was no awareness in sleep? It is absurd to claim that awareness 'reconstitutes itself' upon waking. Awareness is absolute, subject to nothing.

Cause of Suffering: Ego-Object Relationship

Awareness is the absolute and borderless 'I' (*Satchitananda*). We need to understand why this absolute state is not consistently available to us. Awareness 'exhibits two modes': feeling (receptivity) and volition (power of concentration, densification). When awareness as volition 'projects' a thought, egoism arises. Ego is nothing but the taking of a position, thereby creating a 'relationship' with a so-called object. It is in fact the *'this'* thought. The unlimited awareness instantly gets 'limited' to that thought. Ego and object thus form an unbreakable partnership, expressed as *'I - This, I - This'*. Analogy 1: Imagine an eye seeing an object. That object is nothing but a reflected point in the eye as 'mirror'. The reflection point is the ego, the automatic concentration or fixation of awareness as it projects as 'point' or 'thing'. This is the origin of all names and forms, and of the notion 'I am the mind' and 'I am the body'. It constitutes *a veiling power born of a projecting power*. Analogy 2: Visualise a wave, defined as 'the force of displacement'. This wave is 'the appearance of polarity between crest and trough'. It is 'ever-moving and ever-changing', and thus is literally 'never what it is'. In a borderless ocean of awareness, the 'indwelling force of volition' manifests as 'a continuous, unfettered play of waves', where crest and trough are the pulsation of ego's desires and aversions. Since the ego-object relationship is known as 'transactional', where everything habitually appears in relationship, in relativity, such 'veiling' of borderless awareness is the cause of all anxiety and suffering. Within egoism, 'perceiver and object' are always unreal phantoms locked in a dance.

Oneness and Duality

How does duality seem to persist in the context of oneness? How can awareness remain absolutely unmodified but appear to be always modifying? Existence-awareness appears to have two 'qualities':

unmanifest (emptiness) and manifest (form). The unmanifest can only ever 'be known as form', while the form can only ever 'be known by the unmanifest seer'. Faced with such a paradox, our task is to enquire: '*Who entertains the paradox?*' Analogy 1: Visualise an iron ball that is glowing red hot. The iron and the heat are simultaneously both indistinguishable and discrete. Analogy 2: Consider a movie experience. It cannot exist without projected light and screen. The projected light is the volition of awareness, and the screen is the 'context of unmanifested awareness'. As long as we are engrossed in the movie we will not see the screen, but as soon as we become aware of the screen we see the movie as unreal. Analogy 3: Read the words of this sentence. Now look at the actual paper or screen that the words are written on. Do we not see how the one simultaneously creates, and obscures, the other?

Awareness is absorption

Awareness is forever and absolutely absorbed in and as whatever 'mode' it prefers, for the simple reason that it is the absolute field of play. Here are its modes: (a) **Imagination:** the non-reflective creative flow, where 'form follows form like a continuous river'. (b) **Reflection:** the deliberate intellectual juxtaposition of discrete elements (forms) with the view to judging their position in a hierarchy of contributing elements (context). (c) **Witnessing:** a subtle form of reflection where we engage with the continual flow of forms in order to continually affirm awareness as their absolute context. (d) **Formlessness:** the impersonal state of (total immersion in) borderless timeless existence-awareness-bliss, where 'nothing occurs to anyone'.

Modes of Experience

Experience may be described in the following informal ways: (1) Dream: 'A flow of things occurs to an internal egoic witness'. (2) Waking: 'A flow of things occurs to I the ego-mind, and my internal sense organs', either as imagination or reflection. (3) Sleep: Awareness is present without ego, imagination or reflection. (4) Witnessing with enquiry: 'A flow of things occurs to one who continually asks*: what is their origin?*' (5) Witnessing beyond enquiry: 'No flow of things occurs, to one who is present without ego'. (6) Impersonal: 'No flow of things occurs to no-one at all'.

The Hell of Fixation

Ego, dealing with the overwhelming play of mental waves, and in order to maintain its 'integrity', is forced to rely on the discriminative faculty (intellect) in the form of *judgement*. Of course, every position the intellect takes will have its negation. Intellect has three choices: to follow (desire, possession), to fight or deny (aversion, fear) and to observe (non-judgement). If we decide to pursue a certain object or wave, we enlarge its amplitude or resonance and increase its frequency. Similarly, if we deny an object or wave, we enlarge its amplitude or resonance in a negative way. Either way, our judgement of the eternally contending yin-yang waves makes us their victim. The ego, in its effort to retain identity and control, is led to store in memory countless judgements that result in fixed paradigms, ie: 'knots' or 'unshakeable versions' of reality. These knots create rigid expectations, followed by anticipation and inevitable disappointment. If we are continually fearing or expecting something, we will always be disappointed when things do not conform to our need. Thus do we wander in the hell of repetition (*samsara*). Here, even our hopeful concept of 'evolution' boils down to 'arbitrary battles between any particular force and its counterforce'.

Meditation as Witnessing Awareness

The remedy of meditation is to 'remain as the undifferentiated awareness that we are, while patiently witnessing the psychic content without judgement, fear or favour'. This practice of 'being mindful' should by degrees reveal our true nature, the realisation that 'we are nothing but the play of unlimited awareness'. Outside this state, we habitually limit our awareness to the ego-object relationship, which transfixes us as 'form and name' in the invented media of 'time and space'. For example, we may swear black and blue that clay is a 'pot' or a 'jar' or a 'dish', but it is always clay. Thus do we fail to remember the 'substratum', which is nothing but awareness.

It does not matter how many times a limiting or tempting or debilitating thought arises or returns. Whether the item gathers or sustains or loses energy depends on our proper stance. By degrees (and sometimes immediately) it will lose its energy and dissolve. The thing won't keep coming around if we don't feed it! Everything depends on our attitude to the content.

Reality as Cure

To take responsibility for discriminating between real and unreal, is the only real and lasting cure for psychic limitation, suffering and illness. At last, we will achieve three transformative realisations:

1. There is no person but borderless awareness.
2. Ultimately, nothing ever actually happens.
3. Ultimately, there is nothing to be done about anything.

PRACTISE Contemplation Modes

There are two 'modes of awareness': **Contraction and Expansion.** These displacements occur continually, and correspond to 'the creation of form' and 'the reversion to formlessness'. The first is 'kinetic', the other 'potential'. The one is volitional, seeking, enquiring, concentrative, involved; the other is feeling, receptive, witnessing, uninvolved. At the physical level, these correspond to the in-breaths and out-breaths of life.

In a wider rhythm, the awareness undergoes contracting and expanding tendencies according to a 24-hour cycle. For example, at 3 pm, the mind reaches a pinnacle of 'contracting' tendency, auspicious for imaginative action without reflection. At 3 am the mind reaches a pinnacle of 'expansive' tendency, auspicious for reflective contemplation of formless awareness.

Here are six practical modes for directing awareness in the practice of meditation:

| 1 | **Emptying** | Clear the mind of all things. Remain as witnessing awareness.

Follow nothing, resist nothing.

Mode 1 fulfils our need to step out of endless flow of thought (*samsara*), transcend materiality, and exist as unqualified existence-awareness. |
|---|---|---|
| 2 | **Focusing** | Practise one-pointed concentration. Bring one limited object to birth, maintain it, enter it to the fullest possible degree.

Mode 2 practises volition, the creation of 'form', where we realise that awareness (as volition) is always absorbed in and as its chosen action. |
| 3 | **Expanding (Imagining)** | Moving outward from the object in *Mode 2*, let the mind move, imagine, expand, travel and explore, using the faculty of sight only.

Mode 3 freely expands into ideal universes of form, confirming them all as aspects of ourselves as absolute awareness. |
| 4 | **Abstraction (Intellection)** | Focus exhaustively on a single idea or concept or paradigm (for example: awareness, love, emptiness, time, causation). Deeply understand all its aspects. Like the stick that shrinks by poking the fire, let intellect discover its source in pure awareness.

Mode 4 fulfils our need to seek, to enquire. It lets us master intellectual experience by reducing it to first principles, to absorption in absolute awareness.

It is a combination of *Modes 2 and 3* in terms of abstract thought. |

5	**Pulsing**	Place yourself in the heart or in the breath, at the centre of the absolute pulse, of manifest and unmanifest, of yin and yang, of coming and going, of becoming.
		Mode 5 fulfils our need to enter the Heart, to immerse in the pulse of absolute energy, the eternal play of existence-awareness.
6	**Identifying**	Using 5 senses, mind and heart, totally identify with and immerse in, a chosen material environment.
		Mode 6 fulfils our need, using senses, mind and heart, to invest and devote ourself to the play of material creation, understanding emptiness and form (awareness and its pulsation) as One. It is *Modes 2, 3, 4 and 5,* employing all our faculties.

PRACTISE Witnessing Awareness

Find a quiet place where you feel secure. Sit in a comfortable position with the spine straight and close the eyes. Check for tension in the body and progressively relax all muscles. Now, focus on the coming and going of the breath, the steady rhythmic presence of the breath. If you like, focus on the tip of the nose, or on the sound of the breath as it comes and goes. Allow yourself to take the position of a witness to the phenomenon of breath. (The breath and the mind are intimately linked. The continual pulsation of this 'fly-wheel' maintains the duality of subject and object, of external and internal, of 'self and other': in other words, all relative forces to which we are subject rather than master.)

When thoughts arise, don't try to push them away, yet don't make any effort to examine or follow them. Don't fight… don't examine… Have the courage to simply be there, without judgement, with the thought in front of you. It does not matter how many times you have to do this. Thoughts are ultimately all the same, no matter what level of emotional grip they have on us. The thought 'I am going to die' is ultimately the same as 'I need to do the shopping'. Allow yourself to become a witness to the phenomenon of thought. Allow yourself to gradually become the simple, clear, silent, free awareness that is your real being. Come back, in other words, to yourself.

Gently seek to maintain this non-interventive stance for a good 20 minutes. Like every activity, practice makes us stronger. Do it every day. Eventually, try the practice at any time you are in repose, when you are not required to perform sensory or intellectual activity. Benefits will include: greater mental clarity (simplicity), greater intellectual penetration (truth-seeing), emotional equanimity (calm), independence from sensory stimulus (self-abiding), and non-dual cosmic awareness (peace).

PRACTISE Surrender: the absolute test

A fundamental test of what is real is to ask: *how am I able to surrender?* I am able to surrender to the fact of my absolute existence, and the fact of my absolute feeling, because these are *unconditionally* what I am. Can I surrender to absolute projection, that is, 'the continuous flow of outward thoughts', the creation of 'other', of 'form'? I cannot! Further, can I surrender to 'unknowing' or 'veiling', which accompanies the concept of other? Again, I cannot. Why can I not surrender to the projections? Because *the one who surrenders* is always myself, always the core existence-awareness and bliss of myself. Test it. Practise the act of surrender. It reveals the infallible fact.

PRACTISE bloody-minded courage and honesty

Our so-called identity is made up of our assumptions; that is, thoughts that embed themselves by repetition. There is absolutely nothing we can do to erase thought, feeling or sense, for these are the eternal nature of ourselves. What we can do though, is become *transparent.* Ultimately, all tenacious thoughts and feelings, *deprived of implicit participation or agreement of the perceiver,* will wither on the vine, will 'not come around any more'. A core technique is to adopt the attitude of courage and total honesty. This writer spent years on end systematically inviting the most tenacious and persistently negative thoughts and feelings to arise within him, to come at him with everything they had, to challenge him to crumple and to fail. He would sit there with the attitude of 'come and get me, you bastards, see if I care!'

Understand your habitual paradigms

By way of example, this writer used to entertain the consistent thought *'life is worthwhile'*. In time this was replaced by *'whatever I do isn't going to free me from anything'* and *'I can't change anything'*. This segued in time to *'life is meaningless'*. Later this thought morphed into *'though whatever I do is futile, that fact doesn't actually matter'*. Recently the dominant thought has been *'there is absolutely nothing to be done'*... and *'don't speak, you only cause disturbance'*... Have the thoughts refined themselves? Have they 'evolved' or are they simply inert, proving the sheer persistence of assumptions? We need to 'tire patience with patience', play the long game. Thoughts, after all, are nothing but thoughts. Below is a list of typical (upsetting) recurring thoughts. **Witness the thought** as many times as it takes for it to lose its power to control you.

'Nothing ever changes or improves.' 'I'm a victim because I have no choices.' 'I'm not special.' 'Nobody will miss me when I'm gone.' 'Why do I lie to myself all the time?' 'I can't perform any more.' 'Why do I use obsessive achievement as a way to cling to identity?' 'What happened to my life?' 'I'll never be as good as X.' 'People will think I'm a fool and a loser.' 'I'm just a replica of my parent.' 'I really have no love in me.' 'I couldn't care less.' 'I admit it's pleasurable to cling to my suffering and play the martyr.' 'I'm losing my mind. I can't remember.' 'I'm impotent.' 'I'm an obsessive.' 'I'm out of control.' 'I'm really just a greedy so and so.' 'I'm the silly child I always was…' 'Religion and faith is rubbish. There is no god.' 'Life is futile, I should commit suicide.' 'I hate that person so much I want to harm them.' 'I don't love him/her any more.' 'I'm getting old, I'll get sick like my parents.' 'Time is passing, always passing…' 'My child is defective.' 'I really should admit to my (criminal) guilt.' 'Up, down, up down, it's all meaningless.'

PRACTISE borderless awareness through breath

1. Practise quiet, even, rhythmic breathing, in and out, in and out.

   Recognise the in-breath as the eternal 'compulsion' of the vital life force, the need for creation, the need for manifestation, involvement, 'identity', 'duty', the origin of ego.

   Recognise the out-breath as the eternal 'return' to solitude and emptiness, to the absolute non-dual presence of existence-awareness.

2. At the peak of each in-breath, recognise the borderless peace of the absolute as our 'true context and identity'.

   At the trough of each out-breath, recognise the borderless peace of the absolute as our 'true context and identity'.

3. Continue to affirm, with each breath, the ego as the product of the eternal compulsion of the breath.

   Continue to affirm, with each breath, that ego can have no existence without our ever-present *context* - the borderless, empty, non-dual absolute presence.

Expand into the Borderless Self

In order to shrink obsession with ourselves as the 'body form', as 'emotional bundle', as 'mental centre' and as 'personal I', and to identify with 'expanded existence-awareness', we should practise the technique of travelling outwards in six directions. These are: left, right, in front, behind, below and above. Sit in a firm position with the spine straight. Relax and close the eyes. Begin with your left side. Visualise your immediate surroundings in that direction, for example: the floor, the furniture, the wall. Now travel beyond the wall to the garden or street outside, then continue down that street (*etc*) to encompass, in detail, all objects that occur in your immediate neighbourhood. Dwell in detail on each object as you come to it, and make it as real, as tangible as possible. At this point, turn your attention to your right side and perform the same process. Repeat this process in all six directions. Finally, abide as you are without visualising anything. You will experience borderless expansiveness, connectedness and peace.

PRACTISE withdrawing the Superimpositions

According to the absolute power residing as ourself, there are five 'sheaths' or superimpositions that 'turn reality into unreality'. 1. The Bliss Sheath. This is the pure power to enjoy anything and everything. 2. The Knowledge Sheath. This is the intellect, the power to discriminate, judge, choose. 3. The Mental Sheath. This is the power to use internal organs of sense to fulfill the desire for enjoyment. 4. The Prana Sheath. This is the power to go outward toward objects of sense. 5. The Physical Sheath. This is the power to completely attach ourself to the objects of sense.

Now: carefully visualise the five objects of sense (sound, light, physicality, liquid, gas). Let them be as they are.

Visualise the five outward-seeking powers (speech, grasping, locomotion, sex, evacuation). Let them be as they are.

Visualise the five organs of sense within the mind (visual, sonic, tactile, gustatory, olfactory). Let them be as they are.

Visualise the actual power to create objects of thought. Let it be as it is.

Visualise the actual power to discriminate life's polarities. Let it be as it is.

Visualise the actual power of pure enjoyment of this being. Let it be as it is.

Now, visualise *That* which remains when everything is wiped out. Let That be You, forever.

Now, let go of the need to 'meditate'. Be as you are. Be as you *are*…

Now, let there be no 'internal or external', no conception at all, no 'impulse to create', nothing to 'do', no impulse to be anything whatsoever at all…

Be that which is forever present, beyond the need to be anything or anyone.

Let there be no 'practice of meditation' on behalf of anyone or anything.

Let there be no-one who will benefit from this state.

Let there be no seer who experiences anything.

PRACTISE Borderless Meditation

Realise each of the following statements in the order they are set down. They form two 'movements':

(a) Deconstruction. (b) Affirmation of absolute presence.

1. Nothing ever happened but what is happening now.
2. Nothing will ever happen but what is happening now.
3. There is never anything but 'now, here, this'.
4. There has never been, and never will be, anything but 'now, here, this'.
5. I cannot ever be the weight of past, churning into future.

6. There is no border to the infinitude that is happening now.
7. There can be no 'individual events' that are happening.
8. There is no border to 'me, the person'.
9. No event can ever be ascribed to me as 'identity'.

10. I have no identity as space.
11. I have no identity as form.
12. I have no identity as name.
13. I have no identity as time.

14. There is nothing to think or feel. There is nothing to be done.
15. I cease to exit as anything. *Impersonal, impersonal.*

16. I am none of it, *and yet* I am the infinitude of it.
17. Whether I am located or defined or not, I eternally am, here.
18. My lack of identity makes no difference to anything.
19. That I am no time, no space, no name, no form, is irrelevant to the fact that I am.

20. This meditation, this state, makes no difference to anything, ever. Yet it shall be done.
21. I take responsibility for my totality of being, in all of its modes and forms.
22. The absolute borderless awareness experiences all its waves, simultaneously and forever.

FOUR

REAL AND FALSE KNOWLEDGE

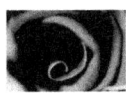 **Desire and its transcendence**

The role of knowledge is two-fold. Its first task is to lay out the many ways in which desire (*karma*) can be fulfilled in this world. In this mode, knowledge is like the mother who grants all desires. Through our experience we gradually supersede each desire, step by step. The second core teaching of knowledge, after the granting of all desires, is transcendence of desire. The goal is to be liberated while alive. This literally means 'to be unaffected by the appearance of objects'. Here, the accumulated content of our existence does not matter, only the unchanging space within which all the content occurs. Following this understanding, there arises 'no more birth following the dissolution of all objects'.

There are three defects in the world

1. Sorrow: caused by (a) effort to get what we want (b) effort to maintain it (c) the inevitable loss of it.
2. Dissatisfaction: awareness that satisfaction is finite, that it turns to dissatisfaction.
3. Dependence: the entrapment of success, the need to multiply our achievements.

There are three levels of seekers after understanding

1. Concentrated, detached from undermining desires.

2. Needing to do concentrated mental practice or perform regular rituals.
3. Unable to focus the mind, subject only to likes and dislikes.

Conditions for enjoyment

We experience desire in three channels: body (food, action *etc*), speech, and mind. We require three conditions for enjoyment: 1. Suitable physical and mental equipment (health in body and mind) 2. Obtaining the actual object of desire. 3. A conducive environment for enjoyment.

We need discipline in three spheres

1. In the body (be clean, be sincere, cut down sex, avoid violence, serve people wiser than us)
2. In speech (speak truth, don't upset with words, always say what is beneficial to the listener)
3. In mind (practise peace of mind, gentleness, mental silence, withdrawal, purity of heart).

We need four attributes

1. Discrimination: Know the real from the unreal
2. Dispassion: Desire truth, remove untruth
3. Discipline: Build physical, mental and emotional stamina
4. Desire: Desire nothing but grace and freedom.

Accept the absolute

Our role is ultimately to *accept* the absolute fact: the infinite, changeless, borderless reality of awareness. We should understand that no 'action born of desire and its corollary, aversion' has any actual nature, and therefore cannot set us free. Human beings create a complex morality, the battle to distinguish between 'helpful acts' and 'unhelpful acts' (*karma*). Yet 'effort and result' are phantoms: we can never hope to retain or own 'objects born of desire'. Whilst we need to act, to explore everything, belief in the *results* of desire (*karma*) can never deliver anything but restlessness, insubstantiality. We do not understand that the accumulated content of our action and exploration does not matter, that there is only ever the 'creative play' of absolute existence-awareness.

There is no mastery

True to our desiring nature, and since we demand ultimate satisfaction, we seek to 'master' the totality (*Brahman*), to get it, have it, possess it. We can never do this. We cannot 'surrender' to it either, since we cannot give anything of ourselves away. We cannot move away from it, and it certainly cannot move away from us. That absolute is our own true nature. While our personal awareness is limited by egoism, limitless awareness is ever our real totality. May we never deny our limitless totality!

Examine your actual current experience

No-one has ever been able, or will ever be able, to prove that anything exists outside awareness. Therefore, there is never anything to do but to examine our actual current experience, now. There is absolutely nothing new to create, and nothing to change. We are only awareness, and it is forever now. It is ridiculous to say 'I know a thing as an object'. If I claim to 'know' it, then I absurdly separate myself from it. There is no external object to be 'known'. To believe so, is ignorance. It is our overwhelming habit, the trap born of the level of awareness known as rationality. We must always ask: 'Where is the border between formless and form?' 'Where is the border between aware and unaware?' No border exists.

There is nothing but 'I am and I know that I am'

What can I be and know for certain? 1. I am. 2. I know that I am. We are nothing but the conscious principle. Thought is deemed external, that is, it is 'awared of'. This 'externality' is a fundamental falsehood, born of the ego's need to assert itself, that the body-mind is seen as separate from awareness. We are nothing but a singular experience. Thought, feeling, sense and action are nothing but expressions or conditions of immovable, indwelling awareness. Do I need to say 'I' over and over to validate my existence? No. If the thought is gone, do I cease to exist as 'I am'? No. And is there anything I can do to destroy 'me'? Absolutely nothing.

Immediate Knowledge is the only knowledge

'I am, and I know that I am' is the steady state that requires no effort or object in order to be. To illustrate this, we may put 'I am' in one column, and in a second column place an endless list of attributes and conditions. For example: I am fat, I am thin, I am intelligent, I am stupid, I am tired *etc*. All these conditions pass away, the 'I am' alone remains.

The limitless fullness (*Brahman*) and the apparent manifestation (*Maya, Samsara*) are two in one, like fire and heat. 'I am' and 'I am aware that I am' is immediate knowledge, that is, knowledge not requiring, or born of, any medium or organ. This is our absolute current experience. Knowledge that treats the 'manifested and transmigratory' exists as *inference* only. The 'infinite manifestation' can be termed the 'subtle body', or 'mind', 'body', 'cosmos'. Yet, just as bubbles appear in an ocean, the subtle body only appears to be born, to be active and to pass away. Like a dream body, it carries all impressions and suffers. It is called *Jagata:* Ja = born. Ga = standing. Ta = passing away.

'I' and 'know'

Like a stick with two ends, we create the terms 'I' and 'know'. Together they make 'I know'. Can we imagine a stick with only one end? Ego and thought arise together, and together create a limited, inferential knowledge. **No compound has self-nature** The compound 'I know' is ego + thought. This combination ramifies into the organs and objects of sense, the emotional nature, the imagining mind and the judging faculty. Yet no 'thing', no relationship, no process, has any self-nature. All are relative only, that is, they 'serve the purpose of something else'. That entity is ever the awareness.

We exist without the organs of mind and body

All our so-called faculties of perception, speech, movement and so on, are organs. These are 'carriers' of awareness. They are nothing in themselves. We are *aware of* these organs. Their actual function is awareness. Awareness gives existence and functionality to all 'things'. The term 'object of awareness' is merely a point of focus, a reference, a definition. Nothing exists independently of anything. Does electricity disappear when a bulb blows? Can awareness cease to exist simply because the body and mind and identity 'dissolve'?

It is quite impossible to envision birth and death

We can experience nothing but awareness. There can never be any other experience available to us. Awareness is permanent and unchanging, and is therefore the only thing that intrinsically exists, that has self-nature. Birth is nothing but the appearance of point, of limitation. Birth is nothing but the concept of extroversion, of the 'repulsion of unity'. The same applies to 'death'. The classic text *Katha Upanishad* sees Nachiketas enter the cave of death 'to discern what happens to the self beyond death'. What he means is: what is real beyond the illusion of becoming? Death slyly offers him the so-called external objects of the world, but Nachiketas is adamant. Death has no answer, and literally dissolves before his eyes. We discover that the greatest blessing is to give away every illusion that we cling to.

Beyond the relative vision

The vision of relativity says: 'That which goes must return and that which returns must go'. This is true, in terms of relativity. For example, we habitually ask: 'Where do we go at death: somewhere, or nowhere?' 'Has she gone? Will she return?' Truly, we can say 'she is no more', but we must therefore also say, 'she remains'. Yet what is beyond this relative vision? Nothing can 'partly exist' or 'exist for a while then cease'. That which really exists must always exist.

There is no such thing as 'awareness of'

What *is*, in itself, can never be known. Instead we eternally project, seek to know ourselves through 'external objects'. Yet it is quite impossible to 'have knowledge of' *oneself*. The idea of 'having knowledge of' or 'studying', is to project, to create the *other*. A projection has no substance in and of itself, has no independent arising. I cannot 'know' my 'face' or 'body' or 'mind', because they are projections of my awareness, even as I appear to study them. The object of concentration, the projection, is always in some way oneself. Act and actor are one. Therefore, in this idea of infinite projection called the universe, there is really no knowledge to be had.

All 'knowledge' is transactional, inferred, comparative

The ego-mind alone generates 'name and form'. Name and form arise together as 'I know'. 'I' is the name, and 'know' is the form or object. Any 'object' is nothing but a description. We should take no 'thing' for granted. The rational judging mind (*buddhi*) will dominate in its function of classifying so-called objects, but can never discriminate *identity*, the absolute real substance. Anything that is sensory, emotional, imaginative or intellectual is only knowledge by inference, by comparison or transaction. Inference says: 'I believe I know what this is, because it is not some other thing that I know'. It is 'dependent knowledge', it is concept, inert, insentient. It is never awareness as identity.

Ego is superimposition

Borderless awareness cannot suffer, since it is the absolute substratum of all organs and objects. Only the controlling ego suffers, in its quest for enjoyment, by 'superimposing itself as awareness', by 'acting as it'. The ego instantly 'claims a position', instantly generating displacement as 'other' or 'object', and 'self or subject'. Ego can thus be termed 'the displacement, fixation, limitation, automatism' of borderless awareness as volition.

The absolute is that which is not external

There can be no 'definition' of the absolute. All that can be said is, 'it is that which is never external'. Ultimately, we should not use words (eg: 'consciousness') for 'That'. Names are conceptual only. The experiencer can never be known, can never be experienced. She is *that* who is eternally aware. There is nothing that is external to her.

Quality, not quantity

Absolute existence-awareness is *quality*. It is absolute substance, transcendent presence, beyond description. Existence-awareness as the idea of quantity is called 'form', expressing limitation, reiteration, disappearance, becoming. These are supremely empty! Quantity is like a supermarket parading endless 'stuff, choice, difference', endless conjecture about 'where, which, when, how?' - all enforced by phantom paradigms of 'space and time and name and thing'.

Who is it that came?

Who is it that 'entered' this 'quantifiable world', who felt, who saw, who heard, who experimented, who imagined, discriminated, desired, built a life story, sought the truth? It was never 'you' or 'me', never the 'individual ego'. It was only ever the borderless, eternal, absolute awareness.

Let us enquire. What is it that sees?

In asking what it is that sees or knows, *Kena Upanishad* elusively says: 'It is the eye of the eye, the ear of the ear, the breath of the breath'. Here is meant: That which is Itself ramifies into the *idea* of separate entities. How do we see the hand? By light. Light is the means. Light is not the hand, it is independent of and unlimited by the hand. Light is independent but all-pervading. If the body collapses, light is there. If the mind collapses, light is there. The 'light' is pure awareness. What we call the manifested world is actually a continual affirmation of the independence of the knower. What is our actual relation to the object? Is there relativity? Is there relationship? There cannot be. There can only appear to be. I am thus 'awareness existing as he who appears to have thoughts, sensations, feelings'. Like the wave that can never affect the sea, nothing ever happens to *me*.

 There is no teaching through words

The teacher says to his student: 'How can I teach you? All I can safely say is: I am that awareness that is ever distinct from the 'known'. I am that which can never come under a regime called 'knowledge'. Further, I am above even that unknown knowledge I might learn in the future. What remains, beyond all objects? It is always existent. It is what I am. It is me.'

Avoid 'I understand'

The genuine teacher will blast the student who says 'I understand', since the thought 'I understand' merely comes and goes. Since awareness has no properties but itself, we continually worship it as *aspects,* and we seek the satisfaction and power of these. The innate craving for 'objective knowledge' is the 'great destruction', the repulsion of the light. The teacher's job is 'to shake any post that is deemed to be continually firm, that is constantly reinforced'. The teacher's job is to destroy our fixations, our preconceptions.

Do not say: 'I know'

There can be no objective definition of reality. One can seek an *indicative* definition only. A true teacher says: 'I cannot know it or teach it. No-one can ever know it. The discerning student says: 'Perhaps I know it, but not well!' He is correct who has no definite idea. Truth defined is truth defied. If we have a fixed idea, we do not know at all. Understanding can come only 'from the corner of the eye'. Analyse your current experience! says the teacher. Be silent, ready, vigilant, *unknowing*.

Bring me water!

At a certain stage of development, we must approach a teacher who is the embodiment of independence. Certainly we ourselves require independence, but cannot achieve it alone. Yet, when this teacher (guru), whose job it is to destroy our fixations and certainties, offers only 'the fact of elusiveness', he or she naturally becomes our 'problem'. Our natural instinct is to doubt or mistrust or attack him (or her) since he obliterates everything we take for granted. For example, he may say: *Bring me water!* The student gets a cup, puts water in it, hands it to him. The teacher flings the cup away and exclaims: *I asked for water. I did not ask for a cup!* We exclaim: *Can water be brought without the cup?* We may want the indefinable, but we will forever objectify it according to 'a vessel that contains it' (hence 'the world'). But water *per se,* cannot be so defined. Likewise, 'teacher or guru' cannot be so defined. Students occupy a finite universe, believing they will receive from the teacher what they think they need. The genuine teacher will always confound expectations. A more subtle student may reason along these lines: 'Without an obstacle, light cannot be seen. Imagine light as a pinpoint seeking to enter a dark room. The beam cannot penetrate without dust particles to reflect it. The reflected object appears to make light manifest, yet light was ever-present, causing the reflected object to 'manifest'... Therefore, dear teacher, can the water (awareness) be known without the cup (vessel, object)?' The genuine teacher will confound the student to the last, with: '*Can awareness be known at all?*'

There can be no 'discovery' of our true nature

The poet Kabir asked: *If the fish is in water, why is it thirsty?* As long as we search, we cannot discover. It is like the woman who searched high and low for the jewel that was already hanging from her neck. It is like the 'missing' tenth person in a group that sought to cross a river: the one who counted always forgot to count himself. There is nothing new to seek. There is nothing to actually seek. The self does not come or go. It is utterly present.

Existence-awareness contains 'three aspects'

(1) The notion of continuity, of 'experience in time', says that 'life, no matter how much it appears to change, remains the same' (*Vishnu*) . (2) The notion of 'the discrimination of emptiness' says that 'everything is forever wiped out' (*Siva*). (3) The notion of 'eternal renewal' says that 'everything is continually refreshed' (*Brahma*). These aspects can be entertained in the sense that 'the absolute expresses itself absolutely'. They

can also be said to have no existence since they are 'relative parts of a phantom notion of becoming'. This text suggests that they are 'useable notions on the road to discerning the sole, absolute but undefinable fact of existence-awareness'.

Meditate on That, without which you have no existence at all

In *Kena Upanishad,* three powerful demigods seek the all-encompassing absolute (*Brahman*). They are Agni, Vayu and Indra. Agni is the power of the five sense organs. Vayu is the power of the five organs of action (speech, movement, grasping, sex and elimination). Indra, Lord of the demigods, is the mind. To these three, Brahman is elusive: he comes and goes, he is 'the phantom within'. Brahman says to Agni: here is a straw. Burn it! Yet Agni cannot. Brahman says to Vayu: blow this straw away! Vayu cannot. Neither Agni or Vayu can even begin to approach the Brahman. Only Indra (chief of the gods) who is Mind, can begin to do so. Yet absolute awareness (Brahman) *vanishes* even as Indra approaches! In his place stands Saraswati, the goddess of knowledge. Agni is forced to see that his power (to burn) is nothing but the power of Brahman. Vayu is forced to see that his power (to act) is nothing but the power of Brahman. Arrogant Indra (mind) alone remains, but he is made humble because Saraswati, goddess of knowledge, signals to them all: without the absolute awareness, you are literally nothing. *Meditate on that, without which you have no existence at all!* Certainly, with Vayu we may use the five organs of action for the sake of selfless karma. With Agni we may use the five sense organs to help obtain knowledge. With Indra we may achieve one-pointedness and purify the mind. Thereby we may practise being 'seated near truth'. However, Brahman, absolute awareness, is ever the substance of all these 'faculties'. *We cannot cease to exist, but we can cease to indulge in the describable.*

By what means does the seer comprehend her own limitation?

When a student reads or hears the work of a 'wiser person', by what means is the student's interest (respect) sparked? Why does the student not proclaim it, in their satisfied wisdom, a waste of time? The student has insight superior to their present state of knowledge in that they know there is something to be learned. In fact they exist as a state of awareness that is superior to any 'external' knowledge. Otherwise how would a student have the insight to understand that their knowledge is inferior? Even a child or a fool knows there are things he or she does not know. Similarly, if a person considers themselves stupid, by what criteria do they do so? Obviously by criteria superior to stupidity. Our awareness is not transferable, not learnable, and there can be no division or difference in it. Our awareness is borderless, absolute, indivisible. 'External knowledge' on the other hand is mere concentration on particulates, signs. It is nothing but the awareness of apparent division, or the apparent division of awareness. It is intrinsically relative, that is, false. There are no so-called objects that are not of the nature of awareness. And if they are of its nature, then they have no other nature.

 Just Observe

Observe the body. It is clear that the body is not aware of us. We are not required to see the body as our own. Observe the coming and going of the breath in this body. The breath is not us. We are not required to see the breath as our own. Observe (without following or resisting) the coming and going of thoughts that arise. Clearly, they 'enter and leave' the borderless space of (ourself as) awareness. Awareness is infinitely capable of manifesting any 'aspect' of itself. A tiny part of that creation is 'our body and our mind'. If there is doubt - which is restless ego, the play of mind - we should always ask: **To whom does this thought occur?** This leads us instantly back to the borderless, ineffable sea, within which 'all possibilities arise and dissolve'.

The Projecting and Veiling Powers

What are the causes of this endless 'becoming', this 'passing through', this automatism (*Samsara*)? Awareness exhibits two 'modes'. One is 'the silent, feeling witness'. The other is volitional force, the genesis of illusion (*Maya Shakti*) which consists of the Projecting and Veiling powers. These are literally misapprehension (projection) and non-apprehension (veiling).

What happens? **The ego** superimposes the 'I' thought, which is literally the thought 'I am a limited entity' simultaneous with 'I possess unlimited power to perceive'. All subsequent thoughts are 'this' thoughts, that is, 'limited objects of unlimited awareness'. The ego's projection is automatic, involuntary, blythe and self-believing. It cannot possibly believe that its perceptions are 'veiled'. Meanwhile, it is perennially frustrated, entrapped by 'cause and effect', by consequence. Herein lies the cause of suffering.

The internal organ of perception is mistaken as the knower

The internal organ of perception consists of **ego** (the idea of separate self), **mind** (the will to enjoy), **intellect** (the will to control, to choose) and **memory** (the power to retain). As any thought arises, the ego automatically arises with it. There is 'shrinkage' of the borderless awareness (the real self) into the limited object. The ego thus 'repulses' or 'reflects' the borderless awareness. As the great sun reflects itself in a glass, so the ego signifies the idea of limitation. The ego assumes it is the self. The ego identifies with the body, with the mind (thought) and, most tellingly, with the real self (the knower, borderless awareness). Thus, each perception creates its own 'version' of the knower. An analogy: Consider clay and a pot. The pot is a 'form', with a 'name'. The clay is the actual reality of the pot. The pot is unreal, while the clay is constant and undying. Just so, all perceptions are nothing but 'momentary illusions' in borderless awareness.

Apparent change only

Absolute awareness eternally appears both as mutable (changing, the experience of volition) and as immutable (unchanging, the experience of feeling). How can mutation happen within the immutable? We must understand that change as an idea only, it is *apparent*, the elusive work of the superimposing ego. Example 1: The clay is real, the 'pot' made from it is unreal. The ego has superimposed the pot, *as if* the clay were transformed. Example 2: Body and mind are like a shadow. If a truck runs over our shadow, do we feel the pain? The discerning person does not identify 'I' with a shadow (which represents 'body' and 'mind'). Example 3: Visualise a screen and a movie. As we watch the movie, are we aware of the screen? The screen alone facilitates the movie. Without it, can there be a movie at all?

Beyond apparent states of awareness

Where is the border between formless and form? Where is the border between aware and unaware? No border exists. Awareness appears to undergo changing states. 1. Waking: In this state the awareness appears to be limited, that is, the ego connects to objects (forms and names). The senses go outward and are attracted by form and name. Here, there is the feeling 'I know', defined as 'the ego linked to the object'. 2. Dream: In this state we manipulate our stored impressions, engaging the feeling 'I am the subliminal body'. 3. Sleep: In this state the awareness admits to no objects. There is no feeling that 'I am' any form at all. However, upon waking at the end of sleep, there is always the awareness that objects were absent during that state. Thereby sleep is a treasure that teaches us: whatever the 'state' of awareness, awareness is absolute.

 **Borderless Wholeness: A Single Actor**

No 'aspect' of existence-awareness can ever exist without, or separate from, any other. There is no part of the psyche that is not absolutely present forever. There is nothing but borderless wholeness. Since there are no independent parts, there are no actual parts at all. We can spend an infinitude of time and space trying to figure out how one 'thing' affects a multiplicity of other things, or we can recognise them all as *the infinite present play of a single actor.* **Enquiry alone** To enquire into the heart of anything: ignorance, death, atom… is to discover that it is not there at all. What remains? Only the enquirer… who is not there at all.

FIVE

DECONSTRUCTIONS

 Absolute Precepts of Experience

1. There is no separate experiencer, and no separate experience.
2. There is no separate entity 'to whom the experience occurs'.
3. The appearance of a 'separate entity', is the superimposition of an 'ego as seer' and an 'object as seen'.
4. It can be said that there is an actual experience of 'no experience separate from the experiencer'.
5. The fact of 'actual experience' (4) does not contradict the fact of 'no experience separate from the experiencer', since existence-awareness is all, and is always experience, no matter whether the 'experiencer' is in the 'formless' or 'form' state.
6. There is no actual movement or border between form and formless. There is only existence-awareness, as experiencer, being 'involved in the duality or not'.

Perception is ever One

Look closely at the nature of your experience:

1. Awareness is always absorbed as itself.
2. Awareness as Volition, is always absorbed in its chosen activity.
3. Awareness in the form of egoism (limitation), is always absorbed wherever it is focused. All its 'positions' automatically become 'absolute positions'.
4. When 'perception shifts from one object to another', it never experiences 'two objects' or a 'multiplicity of objects'.

5. Our experience is never made up of a multiplicity of discrete objects. It has no 'components'.
6. Even though in our reflection or memory we count a multiplicity of things that 'make up our experience', our actual experience at any given instant is never compound, it is always a seamless wholeness.
7. If we were to stand on a warm sandy beach, tasting ice cream while looking at the blue sky, we could not possibly experience these so-called 'components of our experience' as discrete.
8. There is no discrete, separative 'I' who experiences a separate 'that' or 'other'.
9. The idea of an 'experiencer' versus an 'experience' is a total nonsense.
10. In summary, our experience literally cannot be divided into 'seer and seen' or 'seen and seen'.

The Phantom Other

There is no such thing as 'relationship'. No matter how we try to 'differentiate states or create sequences', we are 'forever absorbed as one experience'. We cannot experience 'two times' or 'two places' or 'multiple objects'. According to the idea of relationship, there has never been an 'observer' who is not 'the thing observed', and awareness as feeling and awareness as volition are one, and there is no kinesis outside infinite potential. Similarly, to utter a word we must utter it out of silence, nothing can 'move' but in 'stillness', there has never been any 'form' that is not 'emptiness' and there has never been any emptiness that is not form. If one is eternally the other, then no relationship can exist! The shocking fact is: there has never been, nor ever could be, any experience but *This*.

Deconstruct the 'I' thought

The first thought is ever the 'I' thought. The rest (this, this, this) follow. The 'I' thought is called subject, and 'this, this, this' is called object. Without the 'I' thought, there can be no other thought. Therefore, is there *any* other thought but 'I'? Our obsession with 'the problem of form' is nothing but obsession with ourself as 'I', as ego, as 'person'. What exactly is this idea of ego? It is nothing but absolute awareness that appears to contract, displace, divide, limit, focus on 'point'. Volition superimposes the thought 'I am a limited entity' *simultaneous with* 'I possess unlimited power to perceive', which automatically means 'the power to choose'. The ego cannot possibly believe that its own awareness is 'veiled'. All its 'positions' automatically become 'an absolute position'. While any of ego's singular selections 'shut out awareness as the absolute context that gives life to that selection', awareness is always absolutely present. The apparent 'loss of awareness' in ego, in action or object, is *superficial* only. Awareness is never 'modified by' any particular perception.

We are automatic beings

The notion of the 'person' depends on the confirmation of 'identity', like skin, or an old coat that fits. By entrenching fixed paradigms we goad ourselves to a drenchlight of importance, build an armoury of indefatigable realism, materialism. We become cosmic life prisoners. There is no thought that is not of the past, that is not the reiteration of memory. Our egoic search, through pleasure and knowledge, for identity, certainty, paradigm, is no ascent to clarity but a descent into permanent confusion, where our ego delivers nothing but displacement, a so-called 'seer' and so-called 'seen, entrenching endless conflict with the 'other'. Beyond this phantasmagoria of 'bits', what hope is there to come to the essence of oneself? To come to a sneaking sense that *one is never anything but a prisoner…* may signal a glimmer of light at the end of the hypnotising automatising tunnel we call ego-perception or thought.

The ego has no self-existence

Awareness is utterly sentient while the *idea* is always insentient. This appears to be an insoluble riddle, for even as we 'deconstruct the idea' and 'dissolve it into the unity of awareness', the vision of separation (objectification) comes again as if automatic. Why? The ego demands that any and all forms, as they arise and fall, be contingent on its void centre. The force of egoism flashes into every perception, yet is also limited to every perception. Meanwhile, awareness seems perpetually indistinguishable from an imposter ego who poses as emancipator, who uses intellect to generate, then dissolve, all dichotomy between awareness and its forms. Awareness however, cannot under any circumstance be separate or divided, since it is never anything but itself. The insidious ego even upholds the insight that awareness is never anything but itself! Unless we knowingly practise the continuous awareness 'I am That, and That am I', we will forever be subtly asleep to our own real self.

Pulsation is utterly insubstantial

Awareness is the absolute and eternal real substance. While awareness is utterly indefinable, it is our utter self. There is literally nothing else that we can ever be. 'I am That, and That am I'. How can awareness ever appear to manifest as 'partial, objective, insentient, involuntary, automatic, inert, dark'? It is said that volition, the force of pulsation, is innate: that volition expresses absolute possibility through all ideas, all phenomena. How to account for this 'impulse to action'? The Real Substance is said to scintillate, to displace, to pulsate as 'a force that is felt'. Eternal existence-awareness thus allows itself to appear as 'an infinitude of opposites in relationship'. From this we might superficially claim that 'action is the beginningless inertia of previous action'. But the stunning fact is: 'opposites' can only 'maintain their oppositeness' based on the fact that they have *not the slightest relationship to each other*. Like 'yin and yang', phantoms forever revolving about the other, they literally can never 'meet'. To say that they are 'in a relationship' is an absurdity, since neither has any substance of its own. How can any particle physicist say that 'particles exist only in relationship', when neither component has any substance of its own? Their 'relationship' is rather 'the very vision of insubstantiality'. 'Pulsation' is thus nothing but the 'creation of phantoms', the unending assertion of 'this-this-this!'.

No Relationship: Observer is the Observed

The teacher Krishnamurti precisely deconstructs the so-called subject-object relationship. The first idea is that self (subject) and other (object) arise simultaneously, 'generating' each other. That is, there can be no 'sense of self' without an 'objective mirror'. This limiting 'relationship' is called 'perception', and is defined by the flashing forth of ego. This is his initial position, aimed to focus those less experienced in analysis. Following this, Krishnamurti says that since perception (thought + ego) is simply the *apparent* modification of undifferentiated awareness, the subject-object relationship does not in fact exist. He explains it thus: undifferentiated awareness is absolute; therein it has no features. Its eternal volitional nature is to appear to modify, to 'become' the perception of object. Yet, like the ocean that is infinitely malleable and fluid, no matter how many waves arise, the ocean is ever itself.

Krishnamurti is right to show that the subject-object relationship is the *only* transaction or relationship that can ever appear to exist, giving rise to ideas of space, time, atom, word, polarity, cause, effect and so on. But we reiterate: he only insists in *relative* terms that such a relationship exists. That is, the observer is 'perceived to be' the observed. Therefore, we should meditate on (or as) the following: all so-called 'objects of the world' are non-existent unless and until 'an egoic act called perception' make them appear to exist. Otherwise, there is nothing but awareness as 'the borderless feeling that is our self'. Be not troubled by the myriad changing waves of the sea, it is said, for the sea ever remains - as ourself. No 'external thing' can ever exist: there is but 'borderless ocean of awareness'.

There is no external world, no incarnation

The absolute real substance never 'becomes relative', that is, never 'incarnates', since 'the phantom dance of subject-object' never happens. Relativity or displacement have no existence whatever. Where is the border between 'emptiness' and 'form'? There is none. There is no such thing as border. There is never a 'time' when incarnation takes place, or a 'place' where it takes place, or a 'point' where it can be defined as taking place, or any vibration (word) that can express it, nor any border between the incarnation and its source. No thing has any self-nature. Nothing ever incarnated. Incarnation is utterly denied. 'Now' is forever *this*. 'Here' is forever nowhere. 'This' is forever empty, and 'word' is forever unreal. There is no such thing as this sentence. The awareness is never anything but itself. Between so-called seer and seen, there is no relationship whatever. Beyond all the production of automatic 'things', of 'automatic polarities', there is no relationship between anything and anything. Period.

 **Fishing for The Secret**

Imagine you are a fish swimming through a borderless ocean, and you are saying to yourself: 'Now then, I've been told there's this thing called *water* that is very important, but I'm damned if I can discover where or what it is. And if I found it, how might it have got here in the first place since they say it's how *I* got here?' Now imagine you are a scientist looking through your microscope and saying: 'If only I had a bigger microscope, I could see into all the tiny spaces, into the cracks between the sub-atoms, and I could watch the electricity pouring through there, and then I could get to the *bottom* of this thing... And if I could look closer into the *brain* with all those little synapses and dendrites, and if I could just watch all that electricity flowing in there and see how it makes all those complicated moves and figures, then I could work out what this thing called *consciousness* is. And if I could just get a really huge telescope, I could see all those Black Holes at the centre of every galaxy and I could predict how those Bangs keep coming, and then I could see the Big Picture of how Space Happened and then I could get to the Secret of this whole goddam shebang called LIFE. And if I can just build a really really clever complicated spacecraft and get a man out there into that gruesomely hostile place (that I invented) called space and find out how things really really tick out there, then I could get the real picture of what this goddam universe is really like...' *Etcetera etcetera etcetera.* It's all so complicated! Isn't it high time the LOOKER asked a better (and far less expensive) question? And the question is... *Who the hell is looking?*

There is only You

The Looker is not located, at any point or in any place. And he takes up no time... because whenever you look he is always there... like trying to look at your own eyeball. And this Looker has no name. And he doesn't appear as any kind of object. I guess he is not here at all! But then he is *always* here. He can't be contacted in your body, or in any tiny space, or in any big space, and he's not a ghost... because he is always here. Let's face it, if you want to explore every last nook and cranny of life's supposedly infinitely intricate fractal mass... this looker is always the one doing it. And he's obviously not complicated, since he never changes, even to the faintest degree. He is always very reliable. In fact, he is your only friend. He is YOU.

Journey without End.

What states does the absolute awareness appear to undergo?

Reality exhibits three so-called states: sleep, dreaming and waking. Sleep is called the 'internal' state since it is blissful objectless awareness. We should not make the mistake of thinking it is 'unawareness'. The 'dreaming' state processes impressions without recourse to the external senses. Waking is called the 'external' state where 'objective phenomena' are sensed, judged, absorbed or rejected in line with fixed attitudes (paradigms). In the deep-sleep hours there is 'no person' (that is, no ego) yet in the torrid waking hours there is such a fierce need to assert a relationship between 'self and other' that the *idea* of self is taken for the 'other', for the 'thing' - to the extent that the person's identity depends on it.

Would you chop up the seamless flow? Where is the part of you that is separate from the whole of you?

'Object', 'point', 'part', 'wave', 'event', 'act': these are nothing but arbitrary partitions of a conscious flow, *selected* by the perceiver to be enmeshed in the continual reinforcement of concept, classification, paradigm. It is absurd to describe anything as discrete. As soon as we identify any 'object', 'point', 'part' *etc*, we summarily denounce all others. All others literally cease to exist! No 'thing' can be claimed to have any self-nature, any independent arising. Where is the part of you that is separate from the whole of all? Where is the end of one wave and the beginning of another? Perception sees crest and trough, trough and crest... but is there any 'beginning or part or end' to a wave, where crest is ever morphing into trough and vice versa, where its context is 'ever here'? Take a slice of the flow, take a lump of the river, take a speck of the sky and call it a 'thing', a 'particle', an 'event', an 'atom'. We create a pure lie! There is no place that is not here. There is no place that is not nowhere. There is no time that is not forever now. There is no wave (vibration) that is not all waves. There is no sound that is not all sound. There is no light that is not all light. There is no awareness that is not all awareness. All paths lead 'to nowhere', all objects signify 'other', all 'movement' signifies the absolute demise of itself. Where a thing travels, it is ever here. A thing that pulsates, is never what it is. A thing seen, is not. If you 'see the buddha on the road', kill him.

The Tao, the Tao

Materialist Objection: -

As a Chemist, I cannot accept 'the immaterial as the basis of the material'. And you should hardly be surprised. There will always be bodies, always objects! There is no part of creation that can ever disappear. The sum total of energy can never diminish. Your 'consciousness' is not in control of that! The overwhelming bulk of our 'innate faculties', those within ourselves, are undetected. Autonomously, the heart feels, mind thinks, senses sense. The utter majority of our functions are unknown and unseen by the very 'doer' of them. There is *no* escape from the Material!

Answer:

Absolutely. This real substance, this Life, is *material, material* - and so it is eternal putty in our hands! It is *the absolute pervading lightness of being!* Therefore, this 'fixed world' is as a mirage, is nothing but the soul of *inconsequence*. Let me list the ways! Think of all the things we do to maintain our sense of self, all things we must do to cling to pain and need and want and self-reproach and importance and validity and pettifogging ego! **Try to extricate a slice of your being,** take a chunk of your feelings, divvy up your heart, stuff them in a box! Box up the light and call it a name, corral all the world's noise and study its frequency, take your pulse and stopper and bottle it, grab the sights of your eyes and paint them on a page, plant them in a crop-field of air! Take the air and discribulate it, take a thought and pulverise it, take a feeling and ring-fence it, dissect it like a rat with forceps, pluck its substance out! Workshop the lightness of being, fathom and tame the anatomy of light, clobber and lasso and bung in a tin the silence of the stars, grasp and bundle up your senses, shove your nose in a field of thought, hanker inside a bullish dream like a rowdy cowboy! Stick your need under a microscope, ponder all its parts, pin a wish on a public board, drag a dream like a liar into the light, shout down and denounce the fleeting ghost of longing, put on a death list the love of man for woman, put a bullet in the brain of shared bliss, cut out the eyes of the memory of beauty, roast in an oven all sense of right, turn into ash the lingering of tenderness, bury in a mud field an eternity of desire. And what have we done? Why are we all such materialists? Why such fools?

No-one will ever be able to prove there is anything outside awareness

There is nothing but awareness. Awareness only appears to dance, according to the mysterious generative (volitional, wishing) power residing within it. Yet we 'refute' it thus: *Rubbish! Are you trying to tell me, that that fencepost has awareness?* Answer: Our experience at any given juncture is absolute, it cannot be arbitrarily divided into components, either 'seer and seen' or 'seen and seen'. The 'object' is in no way other than its *context,* its environment. There can be no boundary between so-called object and the context in which it 'occurs'. Identify context, and thus identify the object's real nature. The context is awareness. 'Fencepost' is nothing but a conjuration of awareness. In reality, there is no fencepost. There is awareness alone.

Show me the border

- You're trying to tell me this *wall* has awareness?
- I'm trying to tell you 'there is nothing but awareness'. If you can show me the border between 'that wall' and your awareness, then I will believe they are two separate things
- It's stupidly obvious that the wall has no awareness
- Who calls it a wall?

- I do
- And by what means are you able to call it so?
- I have a brain!
- And the brain is an organ of…? that's right, awareness. You gave something a name, so that makes you think it is somehow different from 'the one who gave it the name'?
- Sure
- Is wind different from air?
- Conceptually, why not?
- Show me the border between 'air' and 'wind' and I will believe they are discrete. Just because you 'name things' and think they are then 'discrete', doesn't make them so. Don't ever believe a thing is discrete just because you gave it a name! The question is, what is that *real substance* that gives rise to all names, all 'forms', all 'ideas of difference'? Find that substance, and we will see whether there is anything discrete from it
- You tell me then
- All right, since you ask I will assume you want a proper answer. 'That' without which nothing (else) can be, or can even 'appear to be', is existence itself. The only means by which we can discern that fact is through awareness. Therefore existence and awareness are identical, two 'names' for the same substance
- I still say the wall has no awareness
- Be serious! The one who identifies it as a 'thing', as 'wall', is awareness alone. Awareness operates through your sense of sight or touch, and so on. These are mere filters that promote the *idea* of separateness or gradation or density or whatever you wish for. You are victim to a phantom idea of your own making when you identify a thing called 'wall'. You are free to do so, and we all do it, but you are not free to tell me that there are 'things outside awareness' simply because you cannot discern the illusory action of your own senses. One last analogy. You see the sea there? Show me a single wave
- There's an infinite number of them

- Show me *any* border between wave and wave, or between wave and sea, or between sea and water, or between your sensory act of looking and your awareness itself - and I will believe there is such a discrete thing as wave, and I will accept that it exists outside awareness.

Fruit **Continue as you must... without fooling yourself it makes any difference**

We can convince ourselves that our acts are consequential, but we must face the truth: there is never anything we can do in this world that will make the faintest infinitesimal difference to anything. No experience, event, moment, condition, posture, thought, feeling, sense... can make the remotest difference to life itself. That which *is*, is ever itself and nothing but itself. In this absolute indivisible flow, there is nothing anyone or anything can ever do to change anything, even to the remotest degree. So we continue, as we will and must, and do it with a good heart, yet ever must try to avoid fooling ourselves.

There is a play called **Waiting for Godot,** in which we witness endless self-generating talk and speculative babble and ritual: a prelude to the verity that nothing ever changes, another way of saying that nothing ever happens. In this wasteland we are asked to contemplate 'continuous suicide', or worse, 'inconclusive suicide'. This too is the situation in the dayrooms of institutions where the old and demented 'wait for death'. But if death has not come today or yesterday or tomorrow, it will never come, or 'will never have come'. Whatever we do doesn't matter! Our suffering comes from endless wanting. It is the very structure of our struggle and our 'identity'. Even if every creature on earth quit its body, it wouldn't make a difference! How can anything be 'born' or 'pass away'? Birth is nothing but the idea of limitation, and death nothing but the idea of return to illimitation. These are nothing but the eternal cosmic rhythm-breath, where nothing ever makes the slightest difference, because no 'thing' or 'difference' ever is.

Give away everything

Should we seek to obliterate ourselves? Yet how can we possibly do that? We are. And we are empty. There is no place we can call ourself. There is no time we can call ourself. There is no form we can call ourself. There is no name we can call ourself. We are not even 'small or infinitesimal'. We are empty. There is no border, except for the borders we impose. We have no choice but to 'indulge' all the forms, the manifestations. They will not, do not, cannot, last. The key question is: 'do we have the capacity to liberate ourselves from the belief that we are limited? Answer: We do. Use the forms, use the manifestations - yet cleave to the wordless, the non-imposed, the non-conceptual, the formless absolute that is only Ourself. And let us not seek to obliterate ourselves by believing we are going to 'die'. All rubbish! Through discrimination, we shall affirm: **I am not subject to illusion, I am not subject to anything.**

Fight the silent war

We one day realise that we are solely a mysterious eternal invisible wind that sways the trees of sensation and feeling and thought. Yet are we not compelled to scribble our spidery phenomenology in the midst of this uncontrollable life, and thus scribbling, 'ever fail to see the forest for the trees'? These trees are 'the infinitude of discrete sensations and feelings and thoughts', and we are bound to create them. Nothing can stem such tides, for they are the nature of Mind. Yet *as whom* does they occur? They are surely the play of the absolute seer (ourself) who, as in *The Bhagavad Gita,* poses as an infinitude of little foot soldiers who deem their duty to be 'to survive, to create, to endure, to kill, to die'. Yet every little soldier learns, little by little, that spiritual progress lies in continual *insults* to his preconceptions and expectations! You and I might thus enact a cathartic scene: how to find the gumption to 'give up everything to save a dying person who is ourself', and who will leave us behind very soon anyhow. Such a sacrificial act, such a silent and secret work of art, never to be known by anyone but ourself, would be the best proof of our transparency, of our unborn, undying, unchanging awareness.

What is lost and what is attained?

We must deconstruct the relative conceptions of **involution and evolution.** Involution is defined as the process whereby absolute existence-awareness involves itself in and as every conceivable expression of its own potential, descending even to the depths of inconscience. Correspondingly, evolution is defined as 'development back to the source'. Involution denotes the idea of creation of what is *discrete,* so that evolution denotes the idea of that discrete entity or person 'seeking its own self-development'. Yet, *infinite potential eternally exists,* and therefore any process or cycle of involution and evolution can only be judged to occur in 'defined systems, universes, microcosms'. Further, how can the respective processes of involution and evolution ever be defined as beginning or ending? Where is the border between any singular example of involution and evolution? According to 'involution', the absolute existence-awareness is said to veil and limit itself, and according to 'evolution', existence-awareness is said to 'progressively regain its absolute powers through the microcosmic struggles of entities or persons'. We are bound to conclude that 'such an infinitude of involving and evolving' exists as *appearance only,* in that no so-called event or state has any substance other than existence-awareness itself. Therefore, is there 'personal evolution'? The answer is yes in the sense that by the endless effort to shed limitations, an 'entity or person' may 'realise and occupy a higher vision-place in the eternal cosmos', whereby it 'incarnates into positions representative of its self-awareness'; and no, in that the notions of entity and personal aspiration are obliterated in the utter eternity of timeless, spaceless presence that is existence-awareness.

'The one who changes' cannot be located

The search for 'personal growth' championed by social, psychological or spiritual movements is a powerful motivator. This writer spent decades in a quest for 'change, progress, evolution' before being moved to analyse its substance. *Who or what is it,* he asked, that moves within, between, through and beyond all perceived forms and levels? He failed to see that the notion of 'changing form' or 'moving beyond' could only occur to one who is not, and never was, the proposed form or movement. 'A changing thing or person' is a complete oxymoron, since how will anyone define a thing that is continually changing? Such lazy, convenient ideas are but 'dots in phantom time and space', arbitrary points in borderless existence-awareness. The one to whom movement or change or evolution occurs *can never be located*. You and I certainly exist, but not in any constructed form. We shall not decry effort, but it may be said that all seeking foreshadows its own obliteration. This fact may be hard to swallow for one who has spent a life in seeking. Yet, nothing is lost because no-one was ever there. There is, at last, nothing to do but realise our identity as unassailable existence-awareness, where 'I am aware that I am' is the only true fact.

Becoming is… Samsara is… that which ever seeks itself. And that which seeks will never find. Seeking's very existence is seeking. Beyond its own seeking there is nothing. Seeming to come into being and pass away, nothing is retained. All is process, all is becoming, all is empty. No 'thing' is ever what it is. Nothing ever is.

Phantom Pulsation is… the impossibility of the idea of Nothing versus the impossibility of the idea of Something.

 All our illusory acts of measuring

Physicists rightly show that particles (entities) exist as *probabilities* only, overwhelmingly behaving like waves. This is due entirely to the status of the *observer*. Their wave-like structure means that a particle *might* appear to exist in any number of locations **(the superposition principle)** but this can never be specifically observed. In any 'system', particles also appear to interact or 'interfere' with each other, and they will be co-dependent **(the entanglement principle)**, with the state of one being 'opposite' to the other, so that if we affect one we affect the other. Next, the more precisely we 'observe' a particle's position, the less precisely we can know its trajectory **(Heisenberg's uncertainty principle)**. Therefore, 'the state of a particle' cannot be known unless it is 'measured'. Until we measure it, that particle may exist in 'all possible' states or places. The act of measuring 'collapses'

it into 'one of these states'. What then do such 'principles' of quantum physics tell us? Precisely that the status of a quantum entity is a *condition of the observer,* that is, the conditions of observation are its *context,* and not merely whether it behaves as a particle (perceived point) or a wave (perceived possible series of events), or that an act of measurement turns it from a wave to a point. The entire notion of particulation, either as wave or point, is a condition of the observer. Quanta? There is no 'quantity' whatever, except what we dream up according to 'the principle of displacement'. We need our little quantum-matter balls to play with! In reality, the physicists' entire study of quantum entities is contingent on the notion that these are 'things independent of the observer as context'. That assertion, have no doubt, is obliterated by the proofs in this book.

There is no God Particle

Words ... Words ...

Language creates Paradigms

All our observations depend on the presence of paradigms, that is, fixed components of our 'identity'. In the beginning was the *word.* For example, no-one can 'see the rock' without naming it first. To confer a name or label lets a thing 'exist': that is, to be 'part of a context', and distinct from 'an other'. This similarly applies if the thing is 'denied'. The creation of language (name or word) is simultaneous with *use,* which means to distinguish the object by its place or function in a wider system, and at its widest, in our established paradigm called 'reality'. According to the philosopher Wittgenstein, the grammar of our language defines the construction of our conventions, our paradigms. For example, we insist on the dualities of subject, object, and active agent (verb). To remove that grammar is to remove the convention or paradigm, whereby, it is said, all 'philosophical problems' are removed. **Grammar dictates Knowing** Grammatical convention says there must be 'someone who knows and something that is known' (Eg: 'I know that god exists'). What is the state where 'knowing' *is,* without recourse to 'knower and known', 'subject and object', 'me and it'? How can there be simple 'awareness alone'? The strange discomfort we feel at the last question, is due to *an error of convention,* a *paradigm error.* Alan Watts likens this to 'turning up to a dinner party in our pyjamas'. But is 'just knowing, as awareness alone' an *existential error*? Not in the slightest degree.

Look at the screen, not the movie

This text is nothing but word, idea, name, form. It is a bunch of particles and participles. It is a construct, it is manufactured as 'bits'. This text seeks to obliterate itself, as any self-respecting tract should. Otherwise, it is mere puff, humbug, vanity, hubris. How? Look at the 'space' between all the words that are imprinted on this page. Or look intently into the empty wordless paper space below. Is the paper the least bit affected by words? Is a movie screen the least bit affected by what is projected onto it? Ask yourself if words, conventions, paradigms, are essential to 'knowing', essential to your awareness. You know the answer.

┌───┐
│   │
└───┘

No outside, no limitation

We can never deduce that anything takes place, in and of itself, outside awareness. That is because we, awareness, are always the deducer. We may technically claim to deduce that things occur outside our 'personalised awareness', although that deduction is itself within our awareness, but what possible basis can there be to assume that 'your' awareness is different in nature, or discrete from, 'my' or anyone else's awareness ('your water' from 'my water')? We certainly never will be able to prove any such thing. Identity is nothing but a phantom. If you and I and Jane and Raj and Mohammed operate within the realm of awareness - how can we fail to assume that all transactions of life occur within, and therefore as, that eternal context? We can expend reams of energy trying to prove that things occur 'outside our limited awareness', or in a so-called 'objective' world… or we can finally relax, take the burden away, stop believing that we are arbitrarily limited, and admit that we are *seated in and as the power of powers* - that our life itself is *nothing but awareness,* the origin and context of all so-called manifestation, whatsoever or wheresoever it may be.

The absolute only appears to become

A famous name given to the concept of the Absolute is 'Krishna'. Yet Krishna appears to be utterly embodied, that is, *subject to any and all conditions* - just as the universal Holy Sound deploys in the myriad 'vibratory organs' of the world, or as light is only seen when reflected in an object. Yet no arising impulse, no manufactured object can have any self-nature, and thereby is 'identical to its source'. Meanwhile, existence-awareness appears to have unbridled power to veil or mask itself, and thereby to 'question its own existence and awareness'. Herein is volitional force, and it appears to be blind, insentient and binding, the epitome of empty relativity, of displacement, which is the idea of *repulsion* (*maya*), which in turn creates the idea of *attraction* back to 'source'. Yet Krishna ever reminds: 'I dwell in you, therefore how could you not dwell in me?' Meanwhile, it is said that Krishna can wilfully, playfully, forget himself in his dream of creation!

Therefore, how do 'things' appear to be divorced from awareness if there is 'nothing that is not of the nature of awareness'? How would absolute awareness nurture the *idea* that it needed to seek itself? Whence comes the idea that anything is hidden or blind? Self-awareness is effortless: whence then comes effort? Effort is restless seeking (*samsara*). If energy is restlessly, therefore blindly, seeking, wherein is the true nature of effortlessness? We are led to speak of three 'aspects': (1) Eternal impulse, restless desire, creation (*Brahma*) (2) Eternal fixation, clinging, habit, preservation (*Vishnu*) (3) Eternal mutability, destruction (*Shiva*). We immediately see that these three 'modes' must instantly, continuously and eternally cancel each other out. The creation of such 'displacements' signals the utter emptiness of force versus counterforce, of 'arising', of 'the fruits of volition'. Herein we discover the true value of effort. Through the 'manifestation of its modes and its things', awareness is bound to continuously generate the reflexive question *Who experiences?* This reflexive question alone affirms the presence of the absolute Player. These 'modes of volition' are nothing but the effortless play of the Absolute, who is never affected to the faintest degree.

Understand the negation of the negation

Existence is awareness in its 'modes' of feeling and volition. Volitional force has no existence without boundless feeling, receptivity. An 'impulse' cannot arise without a 'receiver'. Force and feeling are thereby termed 'the original and only modifications' of the absolute. Modification is nothing but wave, displacement, the appearance of force and counterforce, crest and trough, repulsion from source and attraction to source. These are nothing but 'volition and its reception', 'impulse and its reception'. As Hegel explained, the sole law of energy (and thus 'manifestation') is the negation of the negation. Crest and trough negate each other. Volition and feeling negate, yang and yin negate, object and subject negate, seen and seer negate, manifest and unmanifest negate, Other and Self negate, point and emptiness negate, thing and origin negate, repulsion and attraction negate, thesis and antithesis negate, 'thing and negation' negate.

In what context do all wave-forces, all displacements negate? Since context, the idea of cause, is utterly malleable, negations are said to occur 'within an increasingly complex or encompassing evocation of themselves'. Ultimately, they 'negate within the absolute context of awareness alone'. Hegel's negation of the negation describes both 'absoluteness in relativity' and 'relativity in absoluteness'. Here is 'the eternal scintillation of energy as absolute emptiness'. Existence-awareness is therefore termed *the eternal and instantaneous resolution of itself* in terms of volition and feeling. The idea of repulsion (antithesis, manifestation, form, limitation, ignorance) is continuously, forever, being resolved as attraction to source, as synthesis. Therefore, *continuous* attraction and repulsion means that *no specific example of it can ever be identified* outside the absolute context of existence-awareness. Therefore, there can be no negation at all.

No Negation, No Negation

The dance of non-existent things

No 'idea' or 'process' or 'thing' has self-nature. Since they 'create their negation', they are 'relative by definition', which means 'non-existent'. All 'opposites' are subsumed within their mutual context, their 'cause'.

The 'ultimate context' is 'the negation of the idea of opposites', that is, the negation of 'absolute in relation to relative'. In sum, the idea that 'all things are relative' demands (the idea) that there is no relativity at all. The paradigm of 'cause and effect' is generated according to things that do not exist in the first place. For example: 'big bang to black hole', time paradigm, space paradigm, atom paradigm, name paradigm. These are merely relative, without self-nature. There is no actual cause or effect. All such paradigms dissolve in a post-paradigm truth: 'nothing ever happened'.

Volition and its 'instant dimensions'

In the absolute abstraction of awareness, there is no relativity. Yet the *idea* of relativity, or dimension, arises with volition (will) and its action. Volition instantly conjures a 'cardinal polarity' between borderless feeling and bordered action, resulting in the idea of point, densification, displacement, limitation. With this act instantly comes the idea of difference, perspective, relationship, comparison, space, field. These are instantly accompanied by the idea of sequence, time or 'wave'. All such 'points, fields and waves' express the idea of *displacement*, that is, 'the polarity of densification relative to rarefaction'. They are therefore nothing but 'perceived events within a vision of displacement'. All acts of volition are therefore acts of displacement (creation of 'other'), and *in themselves* constitute the idea of relativity and its fruits (object, relationship, density *etc*). That these acts are *instantaneous* within the absolute context of awareness, expresses their status as *nothing*, a phantom dance where the dancer (awareness) and its acts are one. The absolute, abstract rarefaction of awareness is never disturbed or modified.

The Oxymoron of Infinitude

We may hold a vision of volitional energy as 'an infinitude of waves, each resonating under displacements between secondary and tertiary waves and so on, in endless ramifications of spontaneous adaptation to conditions, utterly complex and unnavigable'. The ocean of awareness is thus seen to 'experience itself as infinite possibility and its simultaneous infinite resolution', effortlessly containing all 'acts' or 'waves' within its eternal stillness. These waves of volition may appear to 'emanate in a dance with an infinitude of charged particles ('vortices' or 'points')' but since particles and waves are forever 'relative to all others', and thus have no independent nature, they have *no existence whatever*. The terms 'point', 'wave', 'infinitude' and 'infinite events' are thereby oxymorons, literally non-existent.

One Two Numberless Infinitude

Let us invent the number 'one' and the number 'two'. How many points or numbers can be said to exist between two such invented points? Clearly, an 'infinite number', and therefore no number at all, since the term 'infinite number' is oxymoronic. Number is an arbitrary construct, spawning reams of constructions known as mathematics. The common factor in all these arbitrary, imagined, created points is undivided awareness. Ocean may seem to have an infinitude of waves, yet since 'an infinitude' of things equals no things at all, 'ocean' is never anything but itself. Does awareness modify at all? Just as an 'infinitude of objects or numbers' denotes none at all, so an ocean of awareness will undergo no modification.

The phantom Point

Spaceless, Timeless: Nothing is located

Where is information? It takes up no space or time. Why then the obsession with locating it in so-called physical form, in genetic codes, in ones and zeroes? The information technology revolution alone should alert us to the timeless spaceless simultaneous causeless real. Why not admit that 'information' is stored in and as emptiness, in such a way that 'it never exists… until it exists'. Similarly, even if space and time are said to form the apparent loci of the 'self', the merest shred of deconstruction reveals that self (defined as origin, identity) can in no manner be located in space or time. Nothing is located!

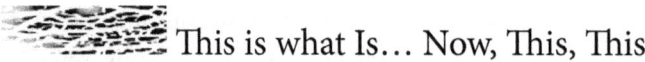 This is what Is… Now, This, This

Nothing but This: Forever here and forever nowhere

There has never been any moment but 'this', never anything but 'this dance of forever'. Nothing is negated, everything is. There has never been anything that is not 'now-this', there will never be anything that is not now-this. No 'thing that occurs' can ever contradict 'anything else that occurs'. Let there be an infinitude of occurrences! They are all forever now-this. There is no history. History says 'these things happened', then says 'these things got replaced'. It wants to pick, choose, judge. History is absurd, nothing but a 'bludgeoning instrument'. How can that which *is* be removed or replaced? Everything is forever what it is, now. *There has never been anything but now.* There is only this, this, this. But who can quantify 'now' and 'this'? They are utterly unquantifiable. There is no sequence, there is no replacement. A 'replaceable thing' is a non-existent thing. Can there be a non-existent thing? And no-one can ever assert that a thing is 'non-existent' since this is a positive assertion. On the other hand, 'can an existent thing arise'? Can 'this reality' arise? All is forever here, thus it never arises.

There never was any 'time' where anything happened other than anything else

Is there anything in this wide eternity that is not happening at this instant? Was there ever anything in this wide eternity that was not happening at this instant? Will there ever be anything in this wide eternity that will not be happening at this instant? This instant is all there ever 'was', all there ever is, ever 'will be'. And there is in fact *no instant*. No-one can ever quantify 'now'. There is only the unquantifiable, unqualifiable THIS. No-one has ever experienced anything but THIS. What conjuror, what confidence trickster, what 'historian', would seek to deny it? Time is non-existent except as a phantom conjuration.

Phantom Time, Imagination

Time is nothing but a matrix of invention, imagination. We abide as the eternal NOW. Practise the mental exercise of removing all references to time: minutes, hours, days, dates. A strange hiatus of vacancy occurs. From what standpoint can 'the nineteenth century' or '700 BC' or 'yesterday' then be visualised? Can it be that imagination (creation of objects) is nothing but a dream? Is there ever 'a time'? And the 'future'... 130,000 AD? What is that? A label stuck onto nothingness. Can there be any such thing as change? Can any 'transaction' exist except as Now Eternal? There is no 'thing', 'event', atom', 'particle': nothing but 'the imagined event'. Time is nothing but imagined position, space nothing but imagined relationship, 'word' or 'name' nothing but imagined identity. We might object that to posit the idea of Time then say it does not exist, is an irreconcilable inconsistency, akin to 'letting the existential cat out of the bag'. But if time really exists, then everything must always be *instantly replaced* since time can only be defined in terms of sequence. To posit that 'time replaces everything instantly' is to accept that nothing can ever be what it is, and that thereby nothing can ever exist *per se*. The reality is, time is 'a thing merely spoken of'. To whom does it occur? The idea of time is a (subtle) fundamental volition of awareness known as subject-object duality. Time is therefore nothing but the idea of 'event', of 'event following event', of 'cause and effect'. These are all non-existent.

Now, Eternal without End

The Ancient of Days: forever for the first time

Existence is a borderless ocean that scintillates as energy. It is delight, life's absolute spontaneous expression. Every so-called pulsation is all pulsations, and is the only pulsation. The only. All pulsation is 'eternally originally happening'. Here is the Ancient of Days. This pulsation has no scale. The scientists' fabled Big Bang is of no more consequence than a single pulsation, a thought, a wish, a twitch, a sneeze.

The Mystery of Forever

It is not the case that all those in the past have died, and I now live. It is that all live always, in the present. There never was anyone who lived or died in the past. There is no incarnation or de-incarnation. All live here and now, in This, this Forever.

 **Creation of Time: The Reflective, Processing Mode**

How does time, the idea of comparison, sequence, cause and effect, appear to occur? When the ego-mind is in the midst of seeking and of gratification, it is in *creative* mode, the trance-like creative stream, and has no sense of time. When this trance subsides and the mind switches to the reflective, intellectual, processing mode, the idea of comparison or ratio arises, creating with it the anxieties of expectation, lack and loss, framing them in terms of 'then, now and later'. The idea of time solely arises in the reflective mode of processing expectation, lack or loss.

Time as Illusion: The power of egoism

Any 'phenomenon' born of ratio, polarity, relativity, comparison - that is, egoism - is non-existent. We speak habitually of 'things past, lost, replaced', of 'time gone or time passing'. This vision stems from the viewpoint born of egoism. We assume our total identification with the *relative* to be the only reality: so innate, so intrusive, so taken for granted as our 'nature' that awareness of the silent, deathless, impersonal, borderless eternal oneness cannot get a look in. This oneness is absolutely as it is, forever, containing all possibilities, always.

Every instant in which we identify 'a point' in awareness, gives the appearance of being 'ever erased'. Focus now on the phrase 'ever erased'. That which is 'ever erased' can have no existence whatever. No 'temporal event' can be erased, since it never was. This, since the 'beginning of the world' which never began.

The transparency of 'things'

'The last second' is obliterated as irrevocably as 'a thousand million years'. Dreams, events, objects, thoughts, feelings, meetings, traumas, transactions, bits… Where are they? Yesterday, where is it? Your future, where is it? That sentence, where is it now? That breath, where is it now? The thought 'where is it now': where is it now? And you, where is 'you' now? Coming Coming Coming… Gone Gone Gone. There is nothing but living Thisness. There can never, ever, be anything but this Suchness.

I ask you to prove that you 'did a thing yesterday'. *At two o'clock I ate an apple.* Did it happen? *Sure it did.* If it happened I want to know where it is. Where is it? *In my phone, I took a selfie.* I don't ask for a photo, I ask for the event. *It got replaced by another event.* Replaced by the selfie? *(Smartarse.)* If the original event happened, it has got to be somewhere. Show me! *You're talking rubbish!* Sorry, but if a thing exists then it must exist to me and to you, here and now. Otherwise I can only conclude that it doesn't.

Repetition - Habit - Time - Death

The idea that our 'chronological age' keeps changing is banal testament to the fact that it is unreal. 'Innocent infants' merely grow from an omnipresent egoless state into 'awareness of the separate, the other'. The thought 'I am X years old and getting older' ever recurs throughout life, so that age is nothing but a thought. 'Memory', like all thoughts, manifests in the immeasurable present. The clock face keeps changing: it is never anything but a convenience, a hypnosis. The physical, emotional or mental 'bodies' appear to 'store experience' by repetition and habit, yet such experience is not stored in any measurable time or place. People spend their lives entrenching the idea that they are 'separate beings', and memory merely serves to 'maintain identity through particular choices'. The self wanders forever and ever outward, grasping at finite things, at 'points in the emptiness', or rather, 'shadows in the fullness'. Meanwhile, the pressure of 'passing time' leads to a hiatus. The notion that all things pass away gets stronger and stronger, and we suffer because there is 'never enough time' to do the things we want to do. The idea of death arises from this suffering caused by flouted desire, thwarted expectation, fear of lack and loss. Then, the suspicion that all is futile since 'death' ('the final reckoning') carries us away, strengthens the reactive idea that we need to either grasp at pleasure, 'achieve things', or win knowledge born of philosophy or religion. Yet, even if we declare that the only proper attitude is 'humble awareness of one's death', we fail to see that this 'death within time' or 'death as time' is surely *continuous,* and if continuous then absurdly non-existent. That is, death, announcing itself as time, cries 'wolf' times without number! The reality? Death is nothing but the notion of it. It is nothing but the idea of limitation, nothing but the fixation with 'time'. **The creative, impulsive power of joy** We should therefore cleave to what is *not* this insidious primal idea inured by experience. Visualise instead, waves breaking forever on a shore: they arise and reabsorb, arise and reabsorb... All our self-generated karma, we donkeys chasing carrots, demented cats chasing our tails, leering serpents devouring ourselves, all these waves we call time... are nothing but the ever-new creative impulsive power of joy, and that immeasurable timeless joy is forever THIS.

 **Absolute Felicity of Awareness**

Such is the borderless, infinite felicity of awareness, that you and I may instantly conjure up all 'planes, hierarchies, matrices, events, pathways, nuances'. Awareness is infinitely capable, infinitely dexterous, infinitely malleable. Space and time are instantly invented and withdrawn again. So-called events have no existence or nature separate from the absolute energy. Above all, there is never a situation where the sum total of energy is not expressing all possibilities and actualities simultaneously. How then, can we call them events at all? See below.

Discussion: Time

If the one who experiences event A is the same as the one who experiences event B, then there is no possible conclusion but that the events are 'simultaneous' since the seer of them (that is, the creator of them) is utterly unaffected, being one and the same. Yet, this seems ridiculous in terms of *time*, the idea of sequence. How is the illusion that events are sequential able to be entertained? Ironically, the only possible explanation is that the 'parts' are never anything but (components of) the whole. **Devil's advocate:** 'Thank god for time! If one had crossed the street one second later, one would have been blown to atoms by that bus that whisked past one's shoulder.' That is, in any given 'space' or 'context', a multitude of events are deemed to take place in sequence! Yet are we not haunted by (a) the palpable fact that in the absoluteness of being, everything is always happening at once, since there is never any time but now? And (b) that if there is 'no time when things are not happening at once', then the idea of 'sequence' is nonsense? There is only ever-unchanging awareness. That is, 'the one who knows himself to be undergoing a sequence of events', is ever independent of that so-called sequence.

Discussion: Space

Identical to the strange idea that 'the experiencer is *nothing but* an elusive series of so-called events' is the notion that 'multiple things' occur in a 'single space'. That is, the one who dodges the bus is surely 'different' from the one who is blown to atoms by that bus. You and I of course defy that idea: we are surely identical and unchanging. How? To remain intact, and to be blown to atoms, are surely two entirely different states according to the perception of the seer (you). Yet the seer continues to believe that by mere 'displacement in time' he can constitute two entirely different states (ie: atomised and intact). Why then would that equation not apply in space as well: the notion that if one came to occupy two separate 'spaces', one would be a 'different person', ie: in a different state? Absurd! Why indeed does that equation not apply to every single so-called event, such that when the event changes, the 'person' changes utterly as well? You and I absolutely will not believe it! No, I can only conclude that if I do get blown to atoms by a bus, my perception of 'myself as myself' will be utterly unaffected! I do not propose to test this, and I don't need to… because change itself is illusion.

There is no space

Apparently space is a tangible 'thing', so that 'outer space' is an actual place to be explored. Yet, can anyone actually point to a concrete example of 'space'? Can one locate it in any way? It is clearly abstract, empty, never empirical, an idea only.

Plus ca change, plus c'est la meme chose

If I were in a position to see what happens if my body got obliterated by a bus, I would certainly be a fool to continue to identify with that body.

If a person thinks that something is lost because their body is obliterated, then they are surely deluded in identifying with that body in the first place. Continuing to do so would be a severely regressive act, since 'the spirit would undoubtedly have flown'. If there were one who experienced all changes to her own nature, she would see that a change in bodily circumstances (obliteration) effects no change whatever to herself. Plus ca change, plus c'est la meme chose. The more we see how things appear to change, the more we see they do not.

nothing can ever be erased... because no thing ever was

 **If there is something, it must ever be so**

If there is *something*, it can never be born. If something is something, it must forever be so. 'That which is ever changing' quite obviously cannot ever be what it is, therefore cannot exist at all. No 'object' or 'event' is ever discrete: thereby it has no self-existence. Why should we frame 'event' and call it 'history' or 'death'? Why frame 'event' and link it to 'another event' when neither has any self-nature? What actually has self-nature? Answer: That which is not any 'thing' and yet is absolutely present as itself. 'That' cannot ever be named and yet is utterly present. It cannot be defined as time since it is absolutely ever-present. It cannot be defined as space since it is utterly borderless. That which we call a 'river' can never be defined since it is never the same river, and therefore is not a river at all. The Real Substance can be 'known' only by an infinitude of its apparent manifestations, none of which exist in and of themselves. It is truly the Holy Ghost! Take any 'thing' that holds a name, like 'water'. It appears to flow, to pool, undulate, bubble, evaporate... and even as we say 'water is nothing but water', it does not mean we know what it is! No-one can ever say that any 'thing' changes into any other thing. It is only when we 'localise a context', a 'name and form', which is mere artificial limitation, that we can talk about 'change'. And that is all it is, talk.

You are not what does not exist

You are utterly independent of that which does not exist. No object has any independent arising, no object has self-existence. You cannot be that which has no self-existence. So, who are you that you are not dependent or discrete? You are the nameless one to whom all things appear to occur. All that can be said is: I am that which is not external, that which is not superimposed.

> thou art that... that art thou

The Apparent Pulsing of the Real

If there is nothing but existence-awareness, how are its 'modifications or expressions' considered substantive in themselves? It is only the permanence of the real that makes the 'creation' appear to be permanent. Permanent recurrence of the 'form' or 'event' is nothing but the *apparent pulsation of the real*. A drop of water may appear to be 'distinct' from an ocean of water, but is it anything but water? Where is the border, where is the difference, between the ephemeral drop and the eternal ocean?

Observe the continual movements of our own awareness! Insentience (unawareness) is defined as 'the belief that sentience (awareness) is limited or absent'. Yet *who is it* who believes that sentience is absent? Only the deluded can think this! Can sentience be deluded? No, but it can appear to be! The (apparent) pulsation of the aware creates the 'unaware' - which is nothing but the partial, the relative, the contextual, the shadow, the displaced, the 'limitation of the light, the reflection or repulsion of the light.'

> **Who, who observes the continual activity?**

Obsession with Stop-Frames

From what perspective does the absolute appears to move, pulsate, scintillate? *Who* pulsates, *who* undergoes change? Look closely. We all watch movies. The material captured by the camera is in 'stop-frames'. We should ask: does one stop-frame cause (that is, give rise to) another? Is one frame the 'result' of another? Clearly, no. And does the 'reality' that was 'captured' by the camera consist of stop-frames? Emphatically no. Therefore, does any 'event' cause any other? The stop-frame is precisely how perception, memory, intellect or judgement works, creating the *idea* of time, space, atom, point, cause, description (word). These have no existence outside the series of stop-frames called perception, memory, intellect or judgement. This is the lie of perception. Awareness is empty. It has no 'frames', has no 'parts'. 'Sequence' is a mere trick, and 'cause' is a mere convention of perception. Our experience at any given juncture is absolute, it cannot be arbitrarily divided into components, either 'seer and seen' or 'seen and seen'.

Personal Identity is mere Fixation

The notion of 'retaining personal history' is said to create and reinforce 'personal identity'. Retention or memory is the agglomeration of repeating elements and 'conceptual gatherings' by means of magnetism around an 'empty centre'. We should always ask: whatever thoughts we think we ever had: *who was it* that was having them? We may assert that there is always 'someone' here now who remembers. But what and where is that 'someone'? Meanwhile, retention fades and memory never remains what it is, so that the very process of fading is 'akin to mere waves of the sea', where memories only ever appeared to resemble some 'original event'. Further, so-called 'sequence in time' is a mere trick. There is no such thing as 'cause and effect'. That one wave 'appears to follow another' does not mean there is anything called relationship. As with water, are not all waves the same, literally empty? Nothing actually 'forms our identity' except the artifice of fixation, gathering, magnetism.

We are Energy: vortex and wave

The 'physical body' is absolutely not separate or different from the absolute energy that constitutes it, just as 'a drop of water' is not different from the ocean. To ask: 'how does the body sustain itself' is an absurdity since 'body' is the embodiment of all levels or contexts of vibratory energy, expressing as vortices of energy (*chakras*) and pathways of energy (*nadis*). What fool therefore would fetishise 'physical death'? Death is nothing but clinging, the sentimentality of habit, the error of division.

Karma is a Phantom

If there is ambition (will) there is wish (imagination, manifestation) and thereby there is pain. Need, karma, reaction, thought of revenge… these stick, these literally 'reincarnate'. It is pure physics. The human being is not a mere object. He is awareness, and awareness weaves the imagined event known as *karma*. Sometimes we enjoy (pleasure) and sometimes we do not (pain and suffering). On the Battlefield of Life, there is merely (a) ignominious and embarrassing action, and (b) deft and elegant action. *The Bhagavad Gita* says: do not bother with the outcome of the fight, since we are always in transition, never fixed and therefore never arising, always leaving, always gone.

Eternal Substance, Absolute Ground, Borderless Presence

No question can ever be asked, no feeling can ever be felt, no impulse can ever arise, no gesture can ever be made, no thought can ever be thought, no sense can ever be sensed, no 'worlds' can ever be fashioned, no assumption can ever be made, no birth can ever occur, no death can ever happen, no 'thing' can ever disappear, no words can ever be written, no particle can ever be formed, no point can ever be fixed, no time can ever be ticked, no place can ever be coralled, no 'thing' can ever be discerned, no fixation can ever be entrenched, nothing can ever be done at all… without the eternal substance, the absolute ground, the borderless presence. **I am the Screen** I am ever the screen upon which the act is reflected. There are clouds in the open sky: but do they affect the sky?

The seamless, borderless reality

The Real Substance, the Presence, is the only thing that ever *is*. Yet, the condition called 'pulsation' makes us believe birth and death to be a fact. Pulsation or 'incarnation' is precisely the act of appearing to be separate, where 'the creation of context' and 'appearing to be a person' arise at once. Yet if there be no 'individual event', can there be any 'person to whom it occurs'? Although 'to be a part of the main' might suggest we are separate persons, the 'main' is nothing but borderless awareness. Even a cursory inquiry reveals that there is no 'part' that is not 'part of something else', that boundaries are mere convention, that a 'context' or 'system' (web of relationships) is designated only for the sake of convenience or classification. There is nothing that is not absolute. There are no things. The idea of 'quanta' in physics is an arrangement only, whereby 'we seek to manipulate energy in all its forms'. Certainly, there is no limit to our ability to do this, but as long as there is manipulation we will necessarily be blind to the absolute fact. Any physicist who thinks 'particle birth' or 'particle death' are discrete events has understood nothing of the seamless, borderless reality.

The seer of the phantom of erasure and renewal

Dear reader, all of us seek understanding in one way or another. I don't rail against any of life's myriad needs, and I would be a fool to do so. Yet the issue always becomes: is there an absolute fact or state that we can hope to attain, that is, to understand? In order to 'get to the bottom of our suffering' we continually seek and grasp. Yet inexorably, through experience, we discover that absolutely nothing is fixed. We cannot ever remain as we *want* to be, even if we move heaven and earth. We are led then to ask: 'What is it that is unchanging'? We at length discover that life's *dynamics* are unchanging, in that you and I merely experience the same processes in diverse and endless trends of evolution. But all along we hauntingly feel ourself to be an *independent traveller,* to be *the one to whom everything occurs.* 'I am, and I know that I am', we declare, more and more urgently. Therefore, where are we 'going', we ask, where there is nothing but 'utter replacement'? For example: when a 'milestone' or 'momentous change' occurs, the time before it is suddenly as if nothing at all. When we leave a place, it is as if we were never there. Similarly, when we have spoken these words they are instantly erased, and when we have eaten and drunk and acted our acts… they are forever gone. Are we making this up? At last we discover that even 'utter replacement' is a total phantom. How then do we live with 'this phantom of erasure and renewal'? Why take life seriously at all, since everything is forever lost, replaced, lost again? A point comes where we learn to cease to worry, because we recognise the *freedom* in this. In freedom there is no history, not a skerrick of history to be had. At any instant in this infinitude, we are *aware* that everything is 'the phantom dance of utter replacement'. What should we do about it? There is absolutely nothing to be done! Yet we must place our attention somewhere, because we are nothing but awareness, nothing but attention. Where we place our attention, is all we ever are. To know that *we are nothing but attention itself,* is to master the game.

PURE No conversation at all

- Teacher, teacher, who am I?
- You are the silence (which we just forfeited)
- Wait. Where do ideas come from? Ideas like 'origin' and 'effect'?
- There is nothing but You, the awareness
- The world is observed!
- The world is what you are *as* you observe
- What is the origin of my 'ego'?
- It is the volitional force of awareness appearing to modify as 'seer-seen', the eternal ocean appearing to ripple as wave
- Is this how the idea of multiplicity, complexity occurs?
- You are the simple seer. You have no qualities except that you are the seer, that is: you exist and you are aware that you exist. Complexity is the result of grasping at what we see and wanting to retain it. We the seer delight in multiplicity! Complexity is the ego-force, delighting in 'subject versus object', endless 'yin and yang'. There are many 'organs' but only one seer
- Is this 'incarnation' then?
- Ha! The idea that 'someone' incarnates, who 'lives a lifetime as a single entity', is utterly false. Incarnation is utterly denied! The real position is: the seer, one and eternal, delights in her scintillating elusive multiplicity. The one who is ever-present appears to be 'immersed as this or that'. Thus is extrapolated all 'human life', 'progress', 'change', 'journey', 'memory', 'history'
- Then what is the difference between 'you' and 'me'?

- None whatsoever. Where is the boundary between 'water and water', 'fire and fire', 'air and air'?
- 'When and where' did this all happen?
- Ever 'now', ever 'here'
- What is it, then?
- Ever the '*idea*', the 'notion', the 'object', the 'phenomenon'. None of these exist. They have no self-nature
- So what is its name?
- Whatever we want to call it!
- What am I?
- I dub you 'The Empty'!
- What is understanding then?
- Understanding is 'coming to yourself', since you insist on 'appearing to go away from yourself'
- Then how did we get 'lost'?
- We attach ourselves to the idea of multiplicity
- Why do we do that?
- Multiplicity never 'began'. It is the Eternal One at play. It has no 'origin'. It is ever this and ever nothing. It is utterly elusive
- So do we not tread a 'razor's edge' between 'being attentive as the action, the multiplicity', and 'being nothing and nowhere'?
- Well said. But we the seer have no qualities, no properties. Listen. We like to speak of the 'life of the person'. But if we cannot locate 'the events that occurred' to her, there was no 'life of the person'. If disease came, it came to no-one. And disease is not disease, it is simply 'a thing someone does not want', just 'life going about its business'! No person ever lived a 'life span'. There is never anything but absolute life. No-one ever lived in any 'place', since no place is ever distinguishable from any other except in the imagination. There is no 'narrative', no 'sense' except 'an absolute sense'. There is no point or particle that is 'the person'
- But I exist!

- Fine, but who said it? 'Somebody' said they existed? Big deal. The ego, the phantom volition, said it. He said it over and over and over and over. And it was all a mirage upon a mirage, a ghost dancing with old ghosts, a compounded foolishness, a recurring dream...
- So *'who* is it that thinks something arises?'
- Tricky fellow! But relax. Nothing arises. There is nothing to 'attain'. Therefore we say... if you see the buddha on the road - *kill him*.

Our existence is contingent on nothing

- What is 'the individual'?
- It is 'that which cannot be divided'. If it cannot be divided, it has no borders
- What is the ego then?
- It is the manifesting force, that throws up the idea, the appearance of definition, division, border, protection
- So *appearance* is the *essence* of the ego's nature?
- Very clever. But no, ego has no actual existence
- Who am I then, if I have no ego?
- You are awareness that is borderless and nameless
- Do 'I' exist as a distinct entity?
- Your real existence as 'the one who is not divided' is not contingent on anything. 'Ego' is the idea that 'your existence is contingent on something'.

The Laughter of No Displacement

- Who is entitled to laugh?
- The one who understands everything
- What will be the quality of their laughter?
- It will be selfless, borderless
- Can any other laughter be selfless?

- No, it is always at the expense of someone or something - and therefore hollow.

Everything I don't know

Once I had a guru who insisted he wasn't a guru. This man travelled the world, attracted disciples, set up places of study, trained us all for 'life'. But the 'training' was endlessly confounding. *Take initiative, idiots!* he'd say. *Do you want to be mummy's little child forever?* So we would do stuff, arrange in our efficient educated (western) way all manner of things for him. And then he'd scold us crazily and say: *Obey the path. Get rid of your egos. Show humility! Do as I say, idiots!* But when again we tried to do as he wanted, he would set us impossible tasks. Any and all means to drive us nuts. - Sit here. Hold for me these pins all night long in the palm of your hand. Make a hundred copies of this document and distribute it to these (fictitious) people. But there's no photocopier in a desert. Find one! Sit in silent meditation while I drill this copper plate inches from your ear. And to any protest he would whisper: - *There is the door, my friend.* And some of us would walk out of it… and would feel guilt and remorse for letting down the cause! And when we'd return he'd greet us sweetly, or even bow, a twinkle in his eye. Ten minutes later we were again the stupidest beings known to god. He would tell Person A in a mighty voice that Person B had mightily failed. Next day he'd not fail to inform poor B that A had almightily failed. And then he would lambast them both to a crowd of strangers assembled to hear his nectar-words of sweet yogic wisdom. Then he'd start a fight with a student over a tape recorder at the climax to a public lecture, or demand one hundred people perform *asana* in the space the size of a telephone box. He'd ask a faithful old student to explain to newcomers the Truth, then ridicule him in front of their innocent eyes. And he'd make us wait till three am to eat a stone-cold repast that was piping hot at six pm. If you meditated he'd shout: - *Work! The world will not eat with you sitting on your bum.* And if you worked he'd say: - *Meditate! You'll not reach enlightenment by shifting bricks!* If you were sick he'd lavish kindness. And if you were well, he'd drag you through the slime again. Later he'd thank *you* for it. For he was committed. In the heart. Away from him we were lonely. With him we were lonelier still.

When he was dying of his twentieth heart attack, his sole interest was in monitoring his own blood pressure. There is nothing but action, he said. Cling to nothing! Utterly committed and utterly detached he was. He taught me everything I don't know.

SIX

JOURNEY WITHOUT END – JOURNEY'S END

Awareness is absorption

Awareness is forever and absolutely absorbed in and as whatever 'mode' it prefers, for the simple reason that it is the absolute field of play. Here are its modes: (a) **Imagination:** the non-reflective creative flow, where 'form follows form like a continuous river'. (b) **Reflection:** the deliberate intellectual juxtaposition of discrete elements (forms) with the view to judging their position in a hierarchy of contributing elements (context). (c) **Witnessing:** a subtle form of reflection where we engage with the continual flow of forms in order to continually affirm awareness as their absolute context. (d) **Formlessness:** the impersonal state of (total immersion in) borderless timeless existence-awareness-bliss, where 'nothing occurs to anyone'.

Where is the Charioteer?

The human mind oscillates between modes (a) and (b) of the previous paragraph, usually without recognising the need to practise and achieve modes (c) and (d). To this extent, we are pawns of our faculties, our organs, rather than dwelling as the awareness that directs those organs.

Dichotomy and distortion are the norm, where 'wild horses drive the chariot instead of the charioteer'. This present text was born of frustration at this 'insanity' - where we are driven forward by automatic, habitual ramification into 'the material spheres of existence'. We are like fish who are always looking for a better class of water without appreciating we are nothing but water itself. What is insanity but refusal to recognise and accept a basic fact? On recognising it we are bound to relax, and to rest in a timeless, absolute view. Yet we are victims of repeated and compounded confusion. We fetishise the pleasures of experience while desperately seeking to obliterate the downsides. We turn to 'knowledge', but in the service of power, of egoic reinforcement. We think that rationality will save us from the excesses of the irrational by enforcing a 'scientific view', which, instead of delivering the liberations of deconstruction, enforces a tyranny of 'scientific materialism'. Intellect, imagination and senses are never recognised as faculties, as organs, as mere reins in the hands of the Charioteer. We fail to accept the truth of deconstruction: the removal of all illusions and arrival at the one shocking but liberating fact: that there has never been, nor ever could be, any reality but *awareness itself.*

∞ Emptiness is form, and form is emptiness

This profoundly challenging statement by the Buddha forces the reader to undergo a series of cognitive positions. Ultimately, it is intended to wipe out the idea of relativity, rendering all 'terms' and 'contexts' as non-existent. The statement contains two 'opposing' terms and a connecting verb 'is'. This delivers a core hiatus. On one hand, 'is' is not a verb that connotes a relationship between two terms but confirms they are identical. On the other hand, the fact that we have a *statement* with constituent terms demands that we consider them 'in relationship' as 'independent contextual entities'. Initially, this causes 'entrapment in a context of relativity', which is defined as 'the notion that the substance of one entity can only be judged in terms of another entity'. In this light, the Buddha's statement subverts the idea of independent entities: 'If form and emptiness equal each other, then neither can be what they are claimed to be (either at face value, or according to the complexities of their respective contexts), and to assert that one is the other is to obliterate both'. Following this, the Buddha offers the double positive 'and'. In this context, both terms are 'as if something' and 'remain as terms in that they provide a context for each other'. We are thus again prompted to conceive a relationship of opposing terms, yet which connote oxymoronic meanings akin to 'eternal change', or 'awareness appearing to self-limit yet not doing so'. Now we see that 'relationship' means a *transaction,* where neither part is independent, where one is 'remade' by the other, and 'can only exist in terms of the other'. Yet, to say 'emptiness is form' and vice versa, is to say *they are identical.* We are led to ask: How can 'two things' be identical? This is absurd. 'Relationship' is thus seen as a ghostly term, like *maya* or *samsara;* that is, 'having the characteristics of both emptiness and form but embodying neither'. This is revealed as a nonsensical statement. Thus, the Buddha illustrates how (a) constituent parts are non-existent, and therefore (b) all relationships are non-existent. Yet, finally and ironically, we are left with the impression of a substantive and eternal dance - of ghosts.

Words We are (not) the dreamers of apparent worlds

To encounter 'form' forever begs the question: who or what is the *actual substance* of that so-called form? We assert that 'whether the awareness pulsates as form or not, she is always herself', in that 'the continual pulsation of appearance (form) and return to non-appearance' (emptiness) affirms the pervading, unchanging awareness. It therefore only *appears* that awareness is 'both subject and not subject to conditions (form)'. The Buddha said: *Emptiness is form and form is emptiness.* His statement implies three facts: (1) If awareness is 'both emptiness and form', it cannot be either of them. (2) If awareness is not both of them, it cannot be either of them. (3) If awareness is neither of them, it surely remains as itself! It is safe to say that awareness *appears* to pulsate as 'form', 'point of view', 'relativity', and that this 'point of view of form' is limitation, hence confusion, hence our wordy discussion.

We stated that the continual 'pulsation' of 'appearance and return to non-appearance (form and emptiness) is an 'affirmation' of a pervading absolute. Yet let us go a step deeper. The act of inventing relative ideas such as 'reality and appearance' can only ever take place in the context of the awareness who *is*. Awareness can never be affirmed or denied in the first place. Likewise, we cannot 'affirm a form as unreal', since by doing so we 'affirm the reality of its so-called unreality', which is nonsensical. Conclusion: 'Appearance' is a 'phantom invention' of awareness, where the entire 'problem' is sustained by words alone. Words (as forms) 'support the idea that appearance is unreal', or 'the irony that appearance / form cannot rightly be mentioned'. Ideas such as body, mind, thought, feeling, sensation, experience, cause - are merely of the nature of the obscuring and limiting power of the awareness. There is no point even bothering to analyse appearance / form using words since the very act of doing so is 'the indulgence of the dreamer's dream'. Therefore: 'You are not the dreamer of any forms'. Or perhaps: 'You are the phantom dreamer of all non-forms'! And every one of these clever sentences is cast up like spray into the air, and ever obliterated in the utter presence of awareness.

Words and Non-Existence

There cannot be any 'thing' without the naming of it. There is no 'existence' without the naming of it, no 'awareness' without the naming of it, no 'bliss' without the naming of it, no 'purity' without the naming of it, no 'silence' without the naming of it.

That which exists, must exist absolutely. If we exist, we never cease to exist. If 'form' exists it must exist absolutely. If 'change' exists it must exist absolutely. Yet we glibly accept the term 'form changes', though the term is meaningless. 'Change' is a meaningless term since 'that which changes' (ie, a form) is by definition never what it is. The term 'form changes' is absurd. It may thus be said that all our 'language forms' are impositions of absurdity.

There is but one 'context' in which anything can mean anything: in the context that 'it is forever what it is'. Thereby, 'relativity', as we talk about it, is seen to have no existence whatever, and such an *absolute* statement as 'seen to have no existence whatever' appears to prove itself as true.

Yet in the blurry medium of these sentences, 'absolute' and 'relative' are meaningless terms. How? If absolute is absolute, there can be no relativity. Again, if relativity is an 'absolute fact', there can again be no such thing as relativity! If 'the problem of relativity' (as continually espoused in this book) has no 'absolute solution', then we cannot prove there is a problem. That is, if a 'problem' has no solution, it is not a problem. By the same token, every 'real problem' automatically manifests its own 'solution'.

Here is the conundrum again: *Who* speaks of relativity? The one who is, and knows he is. He who is and knows he is, is absolute, not actually subject to change. How then can such words as 'change' and 'form' and 'relativity' ever exist within the Knower, as ideas? We can only say that 'idea' and 'word' are generated by a mysterious eternal potency within oneself, but cannot ever be other than oneself, and therefore cannot exist 'in their own right'. Herein is explained 'the substantial basis of non-existence'!

The One to whom nothing occurs

- In awareness, how does 'point of view' appear to occur?
- In fact, it does not appear at all
- How then does 'appear to occur' appear to occur?
- Very clever! But listen carefully: If 'the force of appearance' is seen to arise as 'a counterforce to awareness', then simultaneously, 'awareness as counterforce to the force of appearance' 'arises'. It is like a phantom snake arising to devour itself
- Is there an *original* force or impulse? I mean, what is the *exact point* where point of view arises?
- Where is the border between 'awareness and point of view'? Where is the border between 'force and counterforce'? Only 'point of view' can 'establish a border', according to point of view! Point of view therefore purports to affirm the existence of its non-existence! If air claims to blow as wind, is it other than air? If water claims to flow as river, is it other than water?
- Does any point of view occur, then?

- *Who* views?
- Awareness alone
- Correct. Itself, without a second
- But is awareness a 'view'?
- If it wants!

The Great Uncertainty Principle

Nothing can ever be truly located or defined. There is no such thing as modification. The glib phrase 'all is relative' simply means there is no relativity whatever... which again, like all statements, automatically becomes an 'absolute position'. How can there be any absolute position since no position can ever be defined? Thereby 'all is relative'... and this glib phrase... so, ad infinitum.

The Great Certainty Principle

Nothing that is 'coming or going' can ever be. Absolutely nothing is, except the absolute presence. Face the fact of this! Focus on *that* which stays. Put your faith in that alone. Here is the essence of *practicality*. To whom do all the billions of events appear to occur? Whether 'to you as subject-object' or 'to you as awareness alone', it is *you*, forever.

Koan, Koan

 Awareness is neither empty nor modified

(1) - Where is the border between sentient (aware) and insentient (unaware)? Where is the boundary between the experiencer and the thing experienced? Example: 'Seer sees table'. Is the 'seer' sentient?
- Yes
- Is 'the table' sentient?
- 'Table' is an idea, therefore no
- But where is the boundary between seer and 'idea of table'? Feel the cold, feel the heat. Where is the boundary between the feeling and the one who feels? Think *this* very thought. Is 'the thinker' sentient?

- Yes
- Is the thought sentient?
- As 'manufactured idea', it cannot be
- Again, where is the boundary between thinker and thought? If there is no boundary, neither element exists.
- But, when you *ask,* you 'create the condition', a reflexive syndrome. That is, 'the impulse to ask constitutes the problem'. And as long as there is impulse, we have polarity, hiatus, yin-yang, subject-object, 'figure of eight'…
- So what does it actually mean to 'know' something? What has happened?
- The awareness has modified
- But has it? When 'air' becomes 'wind', does air modify?
- Not in the slightest degree
- Okay, this is our so-called *relative* world, where we discuss superimposed stuff as if it actually means something! But what is the state where there are 'no conditions', the state where 'after the sentence has been spoken' we forget it?
- As you already said, to ask is to create 'conditions'. This is the hiatus called 'asking'. Our anxiety is our continual grasping
- So there is One indescribable, who is subject to conditions…
- No. The One indescribable is never subject to conditions
- But it is subject to grasping, to impulse
- That which is sentient can never become subject
- But it always does! Forever!
- If always, then never
- How?
- 'Always' is its forever-condition, whereby it can never be anything else. Thereby it can never modify. So, is it forever sentient, or forever insentient? It can't be both
- Well, the one who asks is obviously sentient

- Correct
- Aha. So the 'thing' is just an imposition, a name or word
- Correct. As you said: the 'relative world' is where we discuss superimposed stuff as if it actually means something.

Words

(2) - I thought of some Koans: 1. Who is the *one* who is moving? 2. Who is the *one* who is thinking? 3. Who is the *one* who is deluded?
- Good. Where do we put our attention?
- At a point
- How does our attention relate point to another point?
- As wave
- Is our attention the point and the wave?
- Yes, but not at the same time
- Correct. Now Buddha said: *Emptiness is form and form is emptiness.* So, logically, there is no emptiness that is not form, and there is no form that is not emptiness?
- Right. But am I where my attention, my perception, is put?
- You are. There is only ever *seamless seeing*. There is no 'perceiver *and* perceived'.
- But how does 'emptiness' engender the idea of appearance and disappearance, of continual coming and going?
- 'Emptiness' is engendered as an idea, a word. It is not *origin*. It does not 'originate' form. 'Form' and 'emptiness' are conjurations, they are words, two words for a thing, like 'poppeljuke and scumblepot'. *Any* word will 'tie the fatal knot'.
- So the question 'how does manifestation occur?' turns out to be a ludicrous one!
- Correct. The question is merely self-generating. This is our 'dance of phantoms'. Ask any 'question' and you require an 'answer'. As John Lennon said: *'We're playing these mind games forever'*. Make your bed and lie in it! Words are nothing but this churn of incarnation, this

superimposition, this relativity. Words react. 'In the beginning was the word, and the word was 'with god'. Vicious vortex!
- Buddha said: 'Suffering alone exists, but there is no-one who suffers. The deed exists, but no-one does it. 'Suchness' is, but no-one can seek it. The path is there, but no-one may travel it.'
- Exactly. So, my best advice? We set up, then try to annihilate, what is not there. Don't try to set up and annihilate what is not there! There is nothing whatsoever to be grasped.

There is no Doer
- There is definitely a 'body'!
- 'Body' is only a crystallisation of awareness into 'a concept of body'. In reality, 'body' is only pure awareness
- Yet we must 'maintain' the body
- Who 'maintains' it? Who are *you*? If 'the one who maintains' is the same as 'the one who is maintained', then there really is no-one doing it, and nothing to be done. Is there?

The Tao, The Tao

Manifestation is Void

'Manifestation' and 'void' ('form and emptiness') are one and the same idea. They 'arise' together. There cannot ever be one without the other: no void without idea of manifestation, no manifestation without idea of void. Subject ('me') and object ('this, that') arise together! No-one can imagine a point without a space or a space without a point, or a wave without an ocean, or 'self' without 'other', or a dollar in the left hand without 'no dollar in the right'. If the mind 'fixates', there must also be 'no fixation'. If we conceive 'point', there must be 'no point'. All impulse conjures its vacuum. All warp conjures weft. There is no wave crest without undertow, no kinesis without stasis, no gesture without stillness, no thrusting tree without the embracing sky, no river without banks, no water without container, no thought without the thinker, no smile without creasing, no meaning without unmeaning, no 'single perception' without absolute awareness forever.

The instant arising of context

Because a 'thing' never exists independently and must always 'be of something else', what we call 'context' is the limitless potential or potency birthed by any impulse of awareness. For example, to perceive 'form in relation to emptiness' would be to instantly birth a limitless context based on *levels of density*. If we insist on this context of 'density versus rarefaction', that is, 'the dualism between awareness as emptiness and awareness as density', we build a fixed paradigm based on our context - which perpetually blocks us from seeing the absurdity of trying to define or limit anything at all. The statement 'emptiness is form, and form is emptiness' is thus like a bomb, designed to erase all contexts and their resulting paradigms.

Separative Idea is the only thought

The separative idea 'I' is the first thought, last thought, *only* thought. If I say 'I know', I am a mere slave to 'what I know'. The separative 'Little I' means 'Lead me by the nose like a donkey! Tell me what to be! Define me as this or this. Put me in a box, put me in a cage. Separate me into bits'. All thought is confusion, limitation, fantasy.

Identity is Clinging

Clinging, the cause of suffering, is underpinned by the need for 'identity', which is the need to 'survive', entrenching the idea of separateness, distinctness. Within existence-awareness, negation, tension, hiatus, limitation, veiling 'appear to arise'. The idea of separateness caused by such pulsations is automatic. This is egoism: the 'individual' feels that he or she suffers. But *who* undergoes suffering? The boundless awareness, in and of itself, cannot suffer. 'Identity' is thereby defined as 'the capacity to suffer', born of 'the need to survive', where 'survival' is nothing but 'the idea of identity in the face of an apparent negation of identity'. An endless vicious-circling phantom is created. It is Becoming, the serpent Ourobouros, devouring itself.

Identity is fleeting, non-existent

The volitional power of awareness 'draws a frame', and suddenly there gapes a hollow (and meaningless) centre. Volitional power 'draws a line', and instantly we create the artifice of dichotomy, hiatus. Volition thinks a thing, and here is our absorbed 'point of focus'. Like a black hole, this 'created point' sucks all reality into itself. Small worlds, systems, self-involved loops, all are created. Instruments love to measure their self-involved widgets. Tools are built for jobs destined for themselves. Self-generated things self-prophesy, impertinent questions demand silly answers. Like a 24 frame-per-second film we generate endless fleeting centres, ever called 'I'. Similarly, we think enlightenment occurs to 'someone', yet there is never anyone there, only 'conjured identity'. Peace occurs to no-one, and no-one occurs to peace. 'Someone' could be termed 'some nothing'. 'You and I' are a little bit of nothing! Identity is asserted in a void. The presence, the context, is ever emptiness. In the world of utter force of nature, an infinitude of processes takes place, and these are nothing but 'of their own origin', beyond any 'cause or effect.' Yet, for 'human beings' who represent the reflective, polarising mode of consciousness, 'name' is always our beginning. Within the eternal emptiness, the scramble for 'identity' defines us. It always comes, it is always coming... Yet our thought is ever nothing but superimposition. Name and word carry the problem like a body carries its fleas. Something is forever trying to occur! Of course, it never can.

I am not a spaceship

This Existence is absolute, empty, infinite - so that in this natural ever-state, you and I cannot journey without identifying a little vessel, a 'little I', 'a body as spaceship'. Imagine an eye crossing the vastness of space. This eye must conceive that he is forever an eye, forever a traveller, or else there could be no experience of travel at all. The experiencer must come into being as an 'entity', as *'the embodiment* of all seeing, all thinking, all journeying'. Yet the need to grasp at identity appears as if a *denial* of our absolute being, and here is a precise definition of death: grasping is death, conception is death. Yet the truth is: all things have their place and time *within us,* and there is no temporal boundary, no spatial boundary, no localised space or time at all. We are *absolute,* and we are here, always. We should not indulge a dichotomy between 'impersonal' and 'personal'. The 'person' is nothing but 'identification with circumstance'. This writer for example, is 'defined' (obstructed, limited) by his vanity, or by his wish to experience his own perfection, or his obsession with detachment! To claim a sequence of events or line of development as 'our own', as ourself, is pure convenience, pure choice. Evolution? A line, a thread we conjure. How can 'events forever occur' yet 'instantly dissolve in self-luminous borderless nowness'? Absurd! We merely appear to wear the inexpressible cloak of life, all its stars and cosmoses, its pathways, its particulate jewels… just as the ideas of name, atom, space and time are forever the ghost infrastructure of this eternal being.

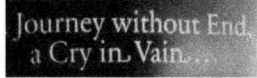

We are the absolute organ that absolutely enjoys

Our attachment to the 'projected object', to the 'fruits of our enjoyment' is the 'weight' we carry about, and it defines the resistance we carry to our own freedom. The power of awareness is supreme, and it is us. Question: How can absolute freedom manifest anything that is not itself? How can absolute existence give birth to the idea of unfreedom? Answer: There is no unfreedom at all. Like an infinite matrix, everything has its use and its purpose in an absolute scheme. And how might anything at all occur except to oneself? Our expressive faculties, our 'organs of enjoyment', are limiting, and all our suffering is the suffering of loss. Yet our faculties initiate the enjoyment of infinite strands, infinite fruits… We must therefore be nothing but an infinite organ, not a limited one that would garner only limited fruits. What is this absolute organ that absolutely enjoys? It is awareness. And it is you.

What power do we have in this infinitude?

Once in his life this writer was totally paralysed, losing for months all his faculties of action: movement, grasping, speech, sex, evacuation. His faculties of sense were also badly weakened, along with the powers of imagination and reasoning. Yet the ground, awareness itself, did not fail, and all faculties eventually 'returned' - out of the mysterious source into which they 'disappeared'. This confirmed the (Aristotelian) insight that all faculties are permanent (eternal) constituents of the absolute. It also confirmed that disease, the veiling power of life, manifests on all subtle levels before it ever reaches the 'physical'. To 'lose' everything then to have it all 'return': what conclusion is one to draw? The same question arises with sleep. Having forfeited all faculties for object-enjoyment, then seeing them return in dream and waking: what conclusion should one draw? Simply that all faculties for enjoyment of these strands of life exist within one power alone, which is permanent, pervading, absolute. Undoubtedly, *this* is you and me. Not a metaphor, not a fancy, not a dream, not death, not change - the Real alone. You and I are at once 'the Ancient of Days' and 'this compelling instant'. And these are one and the same. Therefore, amid this apparent pulsation, this 'appearing and disappearing, coming and going according to an eternal law of displacement' - our real position must be *to perform it all, here, now, as ourselves, alone.*

Our Footprint

When this writer asks the absolute question *'What am I?'*- his deepest instinct is 'I am borderless, forever arising and gone without a trace, yet forever here'. Meanwhile, the intellect juggles three options: (1) I am impersonal nature itself, I am the *total impersonal action* of sense, feeling, thought, memory, brain, body. 'I' literally invent nothing. This nature as action may seem to signify limitation, transience, but if I am nature, I cannot be other than *all* its genius, its utter complexity, its eternal action, its borderless infinitude, even if it appears to dance within the limits of time and space. (2) I am the absolute eternal empty presence of awareness, of feeling. (3) I am 'both awareness and its nature'. Is there a 'footprint' then? Is there a 'personal self'? Answer: What we call 'ourself' is simultaneously eternal and transient. If we are eternal awareness, we are the *eternal context* in which all nature appears to have its action. This is our 'footprint'. If transient, then we have no footprint at all, unless we call 'eternal replacement' a footprint. Meanwhile, this writer's deepest instinct remains: 'I am borderless, forever arising and gone without a trace, yet forever here'.

The flicker-film

Let us affirm the noble truth that 'those in chains are ever free'. *The lotus blooms in the mud,* the sages say, such that purity is never tainted by ignorance. Purity is constant and eternal, and the eternal is never tainted by time or event, be it ever so dark. This 'world', says the argument, is nothing but a flicker-film of imagined frames emanating in silverish ghostly succession, and the 'screen' on which these project is utterly unmoved in the clamour. Behold the 'workings of awareness'! In order to produce an image, we nudge ourselves as emptiness, as the pure conscious ocean. And for another flicker-image to come, we utterly dissolve the first in our own conscious emptiness. Nothing ever happens, since the assertion of a single flicker-image is the dissolution of all others. What proof is there that a thing exists if it cannot be said to remain in any form? In the midst of so-called creation, this power of attachment to flickering automata, wherein the very power of attachment is commensurate with illusion… this power is ever of the utter ever-present emptiness. This is our proof.

Just Awe

The greatest attitude of all is to be continually amazed and awed by the very fact of our awareness, without qualification, without qualities. *Oh my giddy aunt, I exist!* Those of us who have never experienced the naked awesome miraculous fact of our own awareness, are as if asleep, and up till now have always been so.

Freedom Has No History

There is no such thing as history, except history invented for the delectation of scholars, for the convenience of propagandists and politicians, for the solace of sentimentalists. There are no time-lines, no consequences, no significances beyond the ever-present fancies of you and me. For where is the history of the voiceless, the forgotten, the unknown little people, the used-up animals, insects, bacteria, flotsam and jetsam who lived and passed away yet felt all things and documented nothing, except that their very breath was a document of truth cast in the bright air, vaporised in sky, vacant of memory… These are never summoned by the denizens of the future, who conjure and toy with history merely to serve themselves. History is our own story, concocted and manufactured for our own business of identity, serving our agendas… And all these powers-that-be will want to summon us back to pay for our karmic crimes. But we shall never return! For without history there is no guilt. And without guilt there is freedom. *And freedom has no history.*

One Free

Free, whether you like it or not

What is the point of 'experiencing all this', if we are not to dwell as 'the one who experiences'? There will come a time when we must choose ourself, the awareness, alone. This is the end of all searching. But: the fact *there is no boundary* will drive us crazy before it becomes our truth. The 'passing of time' will drive us insane with nostalgia and clinging before it becomes just another *nothing*. All these bits and bobs called 'objects' or 'things' will drive us to depressive distraction before we let them dissolve in the nothing that they are. All this belief in 'events' and 'history' that plays us like a goggle-eyed fish before it dumps us on the wasted shore of oblivion: these will dissolve into a void sky. All these planets and stars in 'space' that drive us to idiotic lengths, sucking up our 'science' and money and adolescent dreams: one day we will recognise the blithering absurdity of wanting to 'go there'. Every thought pins us down, every need sucks us like a drug, every ashram wall looms over us, every holy book enclutters our minds. If I bulldozed your church, would you be less or more 'holy'? Every *word* meshes up our freedom. Does the sky need to be endensed with the names of stars? Does the flow need to be dammed? Does our breath need to be stoppered? Must our awareness be choppered and pixelated to minute insanity, till we can't look any more? How long will this endless search drag on before we drop skeletal in the dust? There is no boundary. Nothing ever happened. Nothing ever matters. You are free. *Whether you like it or not.*

Stop Waiting

Stop waiting for love, for death, improvement, life, happiness, success, identity, substantial thing, hope, past, future, meaning, significance, revenge, chance to be victim, better weather, time to go, things to return, nice feeling, right thought, true sense, calm, order, ducks in a line, fruition, wisdom, your wife, husband, child, parents to die, sunrise, sunset, education, a fish, clear air, proper moment, the markets, coffee to boil, inspiration, discovery, to be noticed, hunger to come, weighty things, hand of the clock, fresh release, next heartbeat, breath, cool, quiet, emptiness, peace, blueness, god, for a time you can stop waiting, for the end of this speech, for a thing to happen, for the bomb to fall, for christmas, for your wedding, for sleep, for time, for life itself. Stop waiting. Stop waiting.

Be as you are

Be as you are. What are you able to be? You are that nameless eternal, which cannot be *other* than what it is. What are you not? 'Change or passage or transition' can never be 'that'. We cannot be what has no existence. In our hands lies freedom to be what we are; that is, 'to not be what we are not'. How can we be what we are not, except by clinging to something? We can whip up a storm, but that storm must eventually return to nothing, to the quietude from whence it came. It was only a dream, whipped up. Nothing stays… nothing is what it is… except the nameless. Relax. We are that.

Something Nothing

There Are No Transactions

1. What is existence? Is it something or nothing? Answer: it is obviously something. If existence is something, it can only be a singular

substance. Can a 'separate thing' arise from this singular, unified substance?

2. Any 'thing' that 'arises' must 'appear to be fixed', otherwise it could not be 'defined'. Yet 'that which appears to be fixed' can never be defined, because it is 'arising'. It is in 'a continual state of transformation'. 'Continual transformation' is an oxymoron, since there is nothing there that is changing. The 'thing' is never what it is. Behold the volitional nature of eternal awareness! 'Thing' can only be defined according to 'that substance from which it came and that substance into which it goes', which are *one and the same*. Hence, 'arising' is a phantom. All worlds are phantom!

3. Does anything 'come or go' at all? Here are the options: (a) Something cannot revert to nothing (b) Nothing cannot revert to something (notwithstanding that the nature of that 'something' may appear to be like 'nothing'). (c) Nothing can arise from nothing. (d) Something cannot arise from something. If something is something, it must forever be so.

4. Here are examples to illustrate (3): People think that in 'death', 'something' reverts to 'nothing'. Yet the sum total of energy can never diminish. The definition of energy is: 'that which appears to change form'. Water may be still or may form waves, but it is always water. In these terms, birth can never be termed 'something coming out of something'. 'Birth', like 'death', is therefore a nonsense, since who can ever define the border between a state and any other state?

5. Conclusion: There are no 'transactions' at all. We may illustrate this by an example: The eternal sound (OM), appearing to vibrate forever, 'eternally expresses all things that yet are effortlessly contained in what they already are'. The One Substance merely 'expresses what it already is, what it forever is'.

Nothing Is 'Ours'

A swimmer may flail in the sea but may never affect the sea. By her flailing, she asserts that she is 'one who becomes aware that she is bound'. Yet is her experience of being bound all she is? Is our emptiness (*Nirvana*) nothing but our hopeless wandering *(Samsara)* and eternal duty *(Dharma)*? If so, is our liberation an absurdity? Is it merely to be termed 'total acceptance'? The proper position is to understand that there is but one Absolute Substance, entertainer of all 'minds, bodies, systems, faculties, actions'. In and as this absolute awareness we should do everything life requires (our duty), but solely in the understanding that not a single thing is 'ours'. We should seek no fruits of action, no ownership of anything. We should be able to count a billion dollars of our employer's money yet not require a cent for ourself. We should do our best at all times, but continuously remember that there is not a single thing we can ever call our *own*.

Not I, I

There Is No Secret

The great secret is that there is no secret. Absolute awareness is the entertainer of all 'minds, bodies, systems, faculties, actions'. Why then do we wander endlessly, restlessly 'seeking that which we have no idea of', that is in fact already ourselves? The average person will take the view 'do nothing, accept life and enjoy', and in a sense she is perfectly right. Yet how can a person who 'seeks enjoyment' ever come to the absolute bliss that she is? Overwhelming experience (and logic) says it is impossible. No, there is something else. The key is to confirm our absolute identity with the Real, and this can never be done as long as the mind and senses are wandering. And yet, there is no way this can be done by *effort*. Or rather, there must be unbridled and insatiable effort, until we realise... there must at last be no effort at all.

Freedom = One

How does it feel to be unlimited?

Since the indestructible incorruptible eternal absolute awareness, ie: that which *is* - expresses as ego and thought and sense, there comes to us a vulnerability, a sense of dislocation, limitation, confinement, loss and fear, all caused by the idea that 'we are either nothing but fixation and limitation, or subject to the winds of continual change'. Yet we must enquire as follows: Since 'continual change' by definition 'perpetually obliterates the limited object', how can 'that which is limited' be subject to change at all? Only the Unlimited can appear to be so subject. You are therefore nothing but the unlimited, who merely appears to be so subject. Just as the unlimited appears to infinitely fractate into filigreed 'parts and pathways' (as 'yourself'), so these paths and pathways are instantly suffused, saturated, drowned *as* the infinite absolute substance. How then does it *feel* to be nothing but 'the absolute expression of the infinite substance'? We should meditate on this, feel it, feel it, in the body and mind, over and over and over. We should accept 'the infinitude of the manifestation' as ourself, while simultaneously discerning the fact that we are never bound, or changed, by it.

We are always all, and none, of it

I am free to wander, and in wandering I am (ever and never) free

The cause of suffering is limitation, caused by endless displacement as the ego-mind. When the objects of this world (thought, emotion, sense) become a disgust or a torture, mind's remorseless displacements are at last seen as conditional, provisional, makeshift. At that point, we discover an irrevocable need to 're-immerse in self'. But what if wandering never ends? What if we are nothing but pawns in an absolute game, forever? That is, 'there can be nothing new under the sun'. There is no question but that forms will form and dissolve and re-form forever, according to the particular energy they exhibit within a boundless scheme. If it is *escape* that we speak of, then there is only one escape: to recognise and cleave totally to the eternity that we are.

We experience the continual brimming fear of 'time passing and heralding death'. There is nothing for us but an endless battle to establish our position, corral it, justify it. For the sake of learning and experience we try to trace all the paths and streams of our wandering. We try to understand the relationship between what is fixed and what is freeing. Yet this writer's experience painfully reveals that the very effort to deconstruct or remove or dissolve 'the person', only confirms, entrenches and reinforces him. We cannot 'look for' truth and integrity: this is like a fish looking for water. Life *is* truth and integrity, in that all its 'things' have their use and purpose. We engage in a moral struggle to distinguish helpful from unhelpful, right from wrong, and we should do it by all means! - but in the end there is no seeking or finding or creating. Each position or 'persona' is always a phantom. We are certainly born to action, so we should act, not out of need to change or remove, or run from something, but from *the joy of our own emptiness…* Then, it doesn't matter what the action brings. Act, act, act - but out of cool joy.

We are the merciful lightness of being

We are told that we require 'strength to endure', to deal with life's shocks, its endless forces and counterforces. But we will never survive as we are, will never cope as we are! For we are actually 'the total field of battle', total embodiment of all shocks and forces, and we are this way forever. Who can change anything? What we need, and what we are, is *lightness:* the feeling, the awareness, that we are the merciful lightness of Being itself. These myriad paths and pathways of force and counterforce are suffused, saturated, drowned in the infinite substance, the absolute lightness, the absolute clear light. This is *who we are.*

I am the patient one

Who is it that experiences all? He is surely the embodiment of patience, of surrender. You and I do not usually feel patient. If we are not to be confined to any particular event, form, thought, sensation, feeling, trend, time or place, we will require continual patience, for things will ever arise. To 'tire patience with patience' is surely to reside as the self. **Be as you are** Imagine you are not confined to any particular event, form, thought, sensation, feeling, trend, time or place… Yet at the same time be aware that you are *life itself.* By what 'means' can we know that we are life eternal, life itself? There is no thought that can ever know it, but the inner heart, and every vibrating fibre of our feeling body, certainly can.

.ꟾꟾꟾꟾ **This This This**

Nothing but this

There is nothing but this, and there has never been anything but this. But what is it? 'This' is utterly formless, nameless. There are not even any 'moments'. But! (you object) there *are* 'events' and 'things' that 'change' and 'move on', and thus we 'look back' and 'look forward'. Yet if a thing really exists, how can it ever be 'past' (that is, gone) or 'about to come'? A 'thing that has changed' is manifestly never what it is. So how can there be any such fixation, chronicle or thing as history? History is a phantom dream of things that appear to be, nothing but creations of the eternal now. And creation is forever empty. Forever now. There is nothing else. 'This' is the sole phenomenon of our life, and it is utterly empty.

What is gone? Nothing is gone!

How can we talk of a 'gone thing' other than to conjure something in the 'here and now'? Let us talk then of something that is here… What? Nothing can be apprehended but what is here, now. What we laud as History is but 'a present prattle on gone things', or 'a present prattle of things that occur in the eternal now', so that there is nothing but 'talk of the here masquerading as talk of the gone'. And the illusory nature of time is such that even 'the here' is gone, since no sooner is it noted than it is 'perceived to be gone'. We can readily see the absurdity. We are left with three notions: 1. Nothing ever was, since it was ever replaced. 2. Nothing ever was, since it is forever here. 3. Nothing ever 'was', since it is never 'here'. **Discussion:** If there were ever a single 'gone thing' that still exists, then 'all gone things must exist'. It must be all or none. Yet if all 'gone things exist', there can never be anything called 'here and now', since the ever-here-now would forever be perception of 'gone things'. Again, we see the absurdity. Who is it that says things are gone? Clearly, it can only be 'one who is not gone' and 'one who is capable of perceiving the gone'. But what is that 'one' really doing? Apparently, he is 'forever creating gone things'. Instantly creating gone things! To do so surely means that no 'thing' ever can actually happen. Conclusion: nothing is gone, because nothing ever happened.

Here gone here gone: always nothing

Act, but know there is nothing to be done

Act - but know there is nothing to be done. Do your best - but cling to no result. Improve - but know you are going nowhere. Travel far - but know you are only ever here. Create - but know there is nothing but sky. It all matters - but none of it matters. Learn - but know it has all been done. Grasp - but see that it is never yours. Succeed - but give it all away. Act - but know there is nothing to be done…

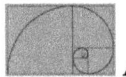 **Awareness has no impediment**

There is nothing but life, therefore life is One. The one who asserts this truth is aware, therefore the One Life is aware. If life is one, it is without impediment. Yet the concept of contradiction (duality) is asserted. **Contradiction** is nothing but an assertion by one who is aware. Contradiction is no impediment to the One, and this fact is asserted by the one who is aware. The One gestures duality (displacement, contradiction) without ever being affected by it. There can thus be no contradictory relationship between the One and its dualities. Duality is merely the play of Oneness in the guise of Volition and its products: time, space, word, atom, causality.

We ever embody existence-awareness

The seer can enter no conception, description or knowledge other than Itself. Yet we 'seekers' are subject to desire, and 'these manifested elements' gather and embody and wander. We are the makers of fragmentation, limitation, darkening, the pixelations of awareness… We manifest as intellectual, mental, emotional and sensory states. We appear in three modes: as equilibrium, expansiveness (*Sattva*), activity, mutability (*Rajas*) and inertia, density (*Tamas*). In turn, we appear as five elements - ether, air, fire, water and earth, which appear as our 'principles and embodiments'. Thus we pose as peace and equilibrium (ether); as expansion, lightness (air); as desire and obliteration (fire); as mutability, 'formless form' (water), and as fixation, inertia, density (earth).

An Adventurer in Time

Sri Aurobindo said: '…Our surface being is only the deeper eternal Self in us throwing itself out as the adventurer in Time, a gambler and speculator in infinite possibilities, limiting itself to the succession of moments so that it may have all the surprise and delight of the adventure, keeping back its self-knowledge and complete self-being so that it may win again what it seems to have lost, reconquering all itself through the chequered joy and pain of an aeonic passion and seeking and endeavour'.

Restlessly seeking what we forever are

I Make All Things New

Every so-called instant, every point and detail, is forever erased. This is not cause for sadness but for peace, for rejoicing. We are forever empty in the eternal present. We are the emptiness to whom nothing ever happened and to whom everything happened. We are the player of the absolute present. There is no point of reference but *this*. How can we say that one thing 'follows' another by cause and effect, when the original point of reference no longer exists? No 'thing' has any causal relationship to any 'other' thing. There is only *the apparent ever-now dance of the One*.

It is a universally observable fact that the self (as ego) can be enraptured and contented in any little guise or channel or corner or form, and that it feels natural. We 'sacrifice all' for the minutiae of the instant, of the place, the point. But we, the eternal, are ever this, ever this. Would we not go mad in such a pixelated, pointillistic paradise if we were not forever free, impersonal, boundless awareness? And would we not go mad in the boundless impersonal state if we did not 'personalise' the awareness in the instant, the place, the point? The bible says: 'behold, I make all things new!' We create every single experience, no matter how many times we repeat it, absolutely here and now. It is irrelevant that we feel compelled to it by the force of habit. The fact is that we are the creator, and the creation is ever now, ever new, ever gone.

We are the One Eternal Player

That we are volitional creators is cause for jaw-dropping amazement. Thinking and imagining and sensing: these are our continuous opportunity to let us know we are ever beyond it. Otherwise, how could we create? No thought can compete with, or alter, the fact that we are the thinker. We alone, are the one aware power, capable of creating all. Why then would we bother to get attached to any of it? All things are our playthings. Should the chocolate-maker let himself drown in his own vat? We are seated in and as the power of powers, and what do we do with it? In truth there is nothing to 'do' with it! This is cause for celebration, not sorrow. **Objection:** There is a continuous battle to resist (a) the onslaught of the senses (b) the creeping waves of emotion (c) the concretising juggernaut of concept-making. Answer: To know ourself more and more continuously as the unaffected seer, ultimately will quieten all. We will overcome the inertia of habit, we will deconstruct all constructions. Meanwhile, we confront the subtlest barrier: the belief that we need to keep trying, keep seeking. The great secret here is that there is no secret. Even to regard it all as a great impersonal machine… comes to the same result. There is nothing to be done. Celebrate it.

Ever New Ever New

I, I Facade

Ego, the Keeper of the Illusory Gate

The ego is a phantom gateway swinging in the winds of nowhere. It is the gate of 'This and That'. It needs, at every pulse of the mind, to turn infinite existence-awareness into tiny, momentary, discrete experiences controlled by itself. It is the mouse on the giant's shoulder, claiming to direct the giant's destiny. The ego wants to grab at the boundless ocean of bliss and hold it in its grasp.

Ego-force: desire and limitation

Volition is always absolute, and expresses as ego. Volition and ego are, for our purposes, identical. All ego's 'positions' automatically appear as an 'absolute position'. What is the difference between 'borderless feeling as absolute egoless absorption' and 'bordered ego as absolute absorption'? After all, absorption is always absolute. Whatever the state - 'unity' or 'displacement' - attention is always absorbed. This is why egoism appears to be 'a seamless expression of absolute awareness'.

But there is no peace, no resolution, with ego-force, because it is (a) continually seeking, restless, continually erasing its own point of attention, and (b) continually seeking distinction, clinging, definition, therefore limitation. Freedom (from its suffering) will not come unless ego-desire is exposed in all its phantom relativity. In desperate effort to maintain itself, fearful of its own non-existence, ego clings to its myriad concerns, experiences, functions. 'Identity' becomes its endless contortion, its 'dance of death': up-down, in and out, back and forth, yin-yang, round and round; thrashing snakes eating each other.

Ego alone generates karma

Is there a 'person' to whom cause and effect (*karma*) occurs? There is, as long as need and its clinging persist, in the service of 'personal identity'. Every thought is a touchstone to the infinite context (possibility) of past and present and future things suggested by that thought. Karma rules in the realm of appearances generated by all our psychic acts, so that the phantom cause appears to generate the phantom effect. What happened 'yesterday', or a 'thousand years ago', or 'a second ago' (it is all the same dream) is you, as long as you, the egoic identity, want it. These are the conditions. Under the need to create, karma rules.

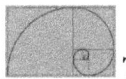 **The Involution and Evolution of Something and Nothing**

This ocean of Becoming is the expression of desire, of need, of want, of searching, struggling, winning, losing, making, breaking, shaping, rearranging… It is longing without ceasing, and each and every born creature is its embodiment. It is the infinitely complex expression of the illimitable and absolute energy field that pulsates at every conceivable juncture, forever expressing innumerable and limitless possible interactions and interactions…

If this life is a macroscopic cycle of involution and evolution, that is, a great loss of self, a descent into form and its ignorance, followed by a return to self through a seeking for liberation and happiness - then the core and only question is: *who* or *what* is it that actually becomes involved and subsequently evolves? Each 'creature' or 'part' or 'thing' or 'person' may appear to be 'the evolver' - that is, the expressor and expression of involution and evolution - yet how can this be? The fact is: to 'evolve out of what one is', is to no longer *be* what one is. This notion of a defined or definable person, creature or thing that evolves, is an oxymoron, an absurdity. Since the border between 'person' *(etc)* and the forces that constitute it, called 'context', cannot be defined, there must be an infinite weight of contextual factors that would have to combine for an 'involution or evolution' (indeed any kind of 'change') to occur. One must always be something, and if one is not always and forever that something, one cannot be defined at all. One literally cannot be. The core question therefore is: 'what is it that always is', beyond notions of involution or evolution?

Clearly, there is only one cycle of involution or evolution to be spoken of: 'out of' the absolute presence-awareness 'into the conceptual, limiting, materialist egoism' and 'back again' to the absolute presence-awareness. We are bound to ask: (1) 'Where is the boundary to be found between what a 'thing' 'was' and what it is to 'become'? (2) Where is there any circumstance in which 'an infinitude of events' is not occurring? (3) Where is there any circumstance where 'the enquirer into the workings of involution or evolution' is not limited to a temporal and spacial point of view? (4) Where is the border between 'thing, creature *etc*' and 'context'? Answers: *nowhere, nowhere, nowhere.* A further analogy: thought is dubbed 'a modification of awareness'. Where then, is the boundary between the awareness and the thought? Again, nowhere. There is no modification of awareness whatsoever. 'Modification' is a mere signifier of so-called relationship, like any phantom name or paradigm. Evolution is thus revealed as a limited idea with limited use, a notion to suit a contemporary macroscopic materialist scientific paradigm, where the notion that things 'evolve into other things' is a product of materialist doctrine.

We are now ready to ask: '*What is it* that a change appears to occurs to?' If waves occur in the ocean, is the wave other than ocean? Not in the faintest degree. Clearly, to say that evolution happens to a 'discrete entity' ('person' *etc*) is to erroneously believe in the idea of discrete entities or discrete points of view. There is nothing but the absolute energy field, the 'absolute context', which merely appears to take the form of discrete entities according to classifications we posit for our 'scientific' convenience. That is, there is nothing but borderless awareness appearing to take form as 'concept'. Remember that 'context' is nothing but 'the infinitude of contributing factors or possibilities that spring into existence where any event is posited'. There is thus no border whatsoever between 'thing' and 'context', such that if we deconstruct the nature of any thing, we recognise it as completely void other than as 'a set of expressions of its context'. To visualise or name a 'discrete thing' and then imagine that 'change occurs to it alone' is an absurdity of the materialist mind.

The Absolute Person

Show us the border between 'the person' and 'the absolute'! If those great forces we call involution and evolution really do occur, there has to be 'an Agent' to whom they occur. That Agent is The Absolute Person: always Ourself, 'both borderless and bordered', undergoing the soap opera of time, space, name, form, cause… yet simultaneously containing all of these in an effortless, causeless, eternal presence - moving but never moving; ever becoming, but forever as we are.

No Border = No Evolution

Ungraspable quanta

Where is the unit of time that separates 'then' and 'now' and 'after'? It does not exist. Where is the quantum that is discrete from absolute energy? It does not exist. Where is the quantum that is 'discrete from other quanta'? It does not exist. The absolute point of a cone, can it ever be found? The absolute curvature of a circle, can it ever be found? This very instant, can it ever be found? The sound, can it ever be found? The silence, can it ever be found? The emptiness, can it ever be found? **There is no Quantity** Try again to visualise the apex of a cone. Where is the actual apex point? It is unattainable, incalculable, inconceivable. It is an imagining, a vanishing. 'Number' or 'point' or 'moment': none of these have substance. The boundless infinite has nothing to do with quantity. There is no quantity at all. All so-called objects (of the mind) vanish into the boundless Real Presence.

Complexity Knot

The infinitely complex expression

What keeps a 'person' 'alive'? There is no such thing as a discrete person. Rather, there are limitless combinations of possible interactions that result in something we designate a 'system' or a 'human organism'. Even such names are crude. Such a 'system' exhibits the traits of all other possible systems, in that it is an infinitely complex expression of the absolute Intelligence and illimitable Energy Field that pulsates at every conceivable juncture forever. Thus, when the 'heart beats on' and 'keeps us alive' we indulge our absurd fond notions of separateness and personality, where nothing of the sort exists. Again, if 'the pulsation in any system appears to divorce itself from its customary functions' (ie: 'it dies'), the Energy has merely moved outward and onward to other configurations of itself. The 'death of the individual' is thereby an utter nothing. When our 'time comes to leave', we would be well advised to do nothing but shrug our metaphoric shoulders and say: *Oh! Here I am, as always, forever.*

The Absolute merely appears to localise

We are ever prone to ask: 'How are all the world's objects created?' Answer: they never are. The Absolute 'appears to localise' as 'the one who sees', and this is called volition or projection, which delivers 'veiling', the 'I' thought, the knot of perception, knot of identity, ego. But there is no seer-seen relationship. There is only awareness, to be called only 'self-self'. To say 'there is a seer of all worlds' is to admit to 'worlds'. To say there is a 'seer of object' is to admit to 'object'. The borderless awareness appears as 'the powers of projecting and veiling', which are nothing but volition, 'a localising as word, atom, time and space': word as localised vibration, atom as 'localised light', time as the idea of change, space as the idea of relationship or difference.

The illusion of death

The reality is, death is nothing at all, merely 'the idea of negation'. People tend to ask: where did he or she go? The truth is, literally nowhere. We say things like 'she has gone to her maker' or 'she has dissolved into her essence' or 'her soul has flown'. In fact, there is nowhere to go since you are always here: that is, where you are, you can only ever be. How can you die? You are forever all of it. You can never be, in any atom whatsoever, different from your 'maker'. **The Rhythm of Birth and Death** Death is nothing but the out-breath, and birth the in-breath. They are but 'movement outward' followed by 'movement inward'. Birth and death are presumed to 'happen to the body' as if it were some kind of autonomous system or object. But this in-breath and out-breath, this 'movement outward' followed by 'movement inward' occurs at every and any conceivable juncture, forever. It effects no change whatsoever to the absolute state that you are. He who claims there is 'nothing but constant motion', affirms nothing whatsoever at all. Where is 'life expectancy'? **Life is eternal. You are life. You are eternal.**

Pulse: the continual affirmation of forever

The Pulse

The pulse is the continual affirmation of a 'temporal point'. Like the knot of ego, it is the continual affirmation of 'identity'. Like a series of stop-frames in a movie, the pulse 'maps out our existence in 'space-time'. It gives us birth yet wipes us out. The pulse is but the continual affirmation of forever. The very pulse of the breath and the heart - *wipes out* the idea of the discrete.

Displacement, the Karma Wave

Force generates wave, the eternal idea of displacement. Karma (cause and effect) is imposed when there is a pressure deviation from a centre, what we might dub the centre of No Karma. Deviation creates its own equal and opposite reaction. Instantly, the act generates its nemesis, which demands the return to equilibrium. However, the act of deviation creates the inertia of repetition, and hence the wave goes on. This simple rule applies to all physics, all perception, all psychology, all apparent complexity.

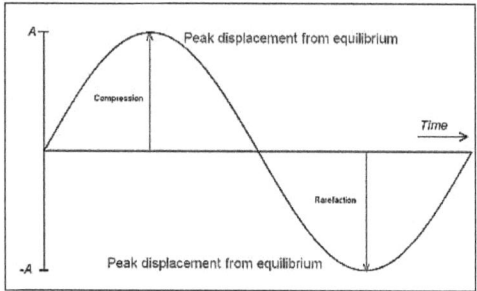

Relativity equals Limitation

The force (upward or downward arrow, above) creates the counterforce or displacement (upward or downward arrow), bringing it 'into being', 'into focus', 'into awareness'. This is dubbed relativity, cause and effect. It is always existence-awareness, but is expressed as 'the idea of limitation'. We may choose to embrace the 'idea of limitation', and likely we always do. But we should know that *we who behold the idea* are, by definition, unlimited. Whatever 'appears' and 'does not appear' is simultaneously, and forever, the same essence.

Can't have This, without That

ॐ To whom do things appear to arise and pass away?

That which appears to arise must appear to pass. That which appears to pass must appear to arise again. Yet, to whom? This is the pivotal question. If we conclude (rightly) that it appears to occur to you and me, so that we are eternal awareness itself, then the only remaining question is: **What is to be done?** We fear to accept the truth that no matter what we ever do, it makes not the faintest difference to heaven or earth. Yet we fear that to do nothing, to 'accept what we are as the utter totality', is to give up, is to accept all limitations, accept our states of ignorance. Crucially, we should realise that *the absolute is forever this, forever this*. That is, all is as it is, here and now, and the only attitude is to 'be present'. To say 'there is nothing that does not arise in absolute self' binds us by logic to admit that there is nothing that arises in absolute self. It is therefore advised: (1) Do not obsess with the object and cling to it. (2) Do not reject it. (3) Meanwhile, do not contrive to act as if it is not there. (4) Do not even claim to 'witness it without concern'. Beyond all these, retain the enquiry *'Who is the seer? To whom does the event occur?* Herein, employing the absolute power of volition, is to abide as awareness alone.

What is to be done?
Beyond suffering: 'Can I live with 'this forever'?

Ultimately, total acceptance is acceptance of total awareness. It is 'to let every possible thing exist in and as you'. Many will object that this is impossible! Such forbearance, such a level of patience, is deemed impossible. But what choice is there? In fact, is forbearance required at all? Ask now: can I live with *this* instant? The answer is: I am doing it anyway, I have no choice. And is 'this instant' 'forever'? If the answer is 'yes, there is an eternity of instants', then *where exactly is our suffering?* We are in fact so busy asking where our problem is, that we cannot locate it. We cannot locate our suffering.

What is the proper attitude?

Life is utterly unalterable! If we recognise that things appear and pass away and appear again ad infinitum, we are tempted to see this process as unalterable absurdity and futility. A logical conclusion is to commit suicide, and it is possible to derive grim satisfaction from such monumental victimhood. The problem is that since we recognise that all that passes must come again, we must accept that suicide itself is futile. We may also try to escape through purification and mortification ('slow' suicide). The problem here, as the Buddha recognised, is that we foolishly waste our energy trying to elude a thing that is truly insubstantial (ie: it comes and goes). We may also seek to recognise everything as appearance only, and thereby 'do nothing about it' since 'we know there is nothing to be done about the unreal'. The problem here is again one of escape, since our realisation of the unreal is *sporadic* at best, such is the hypnosis of this omnipresent manifesting force. Finally, should we practise accepting ourselves, through the endless reiteration of 'What is to be done?' and 'What is the proper attitude'? Yes, and this act of analysis must, like any practice, be constantly reiterated until it becomes our default, our second skin, our continuum.

Pray As, Not To

People spend their lives praying to something called god or allah or whatever, but will not admit that they merely create and maintain something outside themselves, a superego if you like, with which they can have an endless relationship of subservience and vain hope, meanwhile indulging all the old traits of unworthiness, victimhood, guilt and lack that epitomise any unreal relationship. Ultimately, *all* relationships are unreal. The key is not to pray *to*, but to pray *as*. There is no 'relationship' with the divine to be had. You *are* the divine. You are not even a 'tiny speck' of it. You are literally it. And if you pray *as*, instead of to, then your prayer is nothing but action, nothing but the continuing expression of the divine, as if the divine breathed and danced itself. To pray *to*, is the very genesis and essence of confusion and suffering, since the 'other' can never be reached. As stated, all relationship is unreal. And as long as it appears to be all we have… it is all we have!

Dialogue: No Relationship Whatsoever

- There is nothing separate from self. There is nothing outside the self. There is no object. No seer or seen, no perceiver or perceived, no observer or observed. There is no 'relationship' whatsoever
- So, *what happens* when an 'object is perceived'? Does the seer 'reveal himself to himself'?
- How can the seer possibly reveal himself to himself? He does not even 'appear' to do so (that is, 'play'). Appearance is non-existent. It does not even 'create a phantom thing that sees difference between seer and seen'. There is no 'perception' of anything, ever. Nothing ever 'happens'. And I am comfortable with the truth that no discrete thing exists: it is a beautiful fact that generates peace, not a terrible fact that generates fear
- But perceptions happen!
- There is the apparent projection of a phantom called ego that thrives on the creation of a 'phantom other' or 'phantom opposite'. But projection from whom to whom? So-called observer and observed are one, and therefore neither exist. This means it can never be asked

'Who is the observer?' or 'What is the observed?' That very thought, that projection, merely 'becomes the thinker'. Truly, there is no possible thought to be had therein
- But who can live with that?
- Here is the core intellectual meditation: We accept the phantom play of infinite variables for the sake of discovering freedom from them all. There can be no dichotomy between 'pure self' and 'complex or contaminated world'. This truth lets us see all experiences as equally unimportant, instead of feeling continually alienated by the outward-projecting automatism of need, grasping, clinging, habit. The Fool knows nothing is worth, that nothing exists, yet *she walks in the midst*. What else can she do? Here is the essence of acceptance and patience.

Accept the Conditions

What if we were to admit ourselves to be boundless eternal light?

What are the consequences of admitting to this fact? Sit still, and do it now.

Emptiness

1. There can be no difference between 'you' and 'other'.
2. Your experience at any instant is absolute, it cannot be arbitrarily divided into components, either 'seer and seen' or 'seen and seen'.
3. There is nothing separate from You.
4. There is nothing separate from boundless eternal light.
5. Other than boundless eternal light, nothing ever happens, nothing ever will happen.

Form (Ego)

6. Projections, points, events, contexts, systems appear, in every conceivable combination.
7. Every conceivable combination is possible, since boundless eternal light is boundless energy, actual and potential.
8. Your attention is volitional force (directed energy).

9. Volition generates displacement (yin-yang, self-other, subject-object *etc*).
10. Displacement generates ideas of differentiation, limitation, fixation, point, atom, form, name, space, time, sequence, cause, effect, circumstance…
11. The idea of 'other', at once flashes forth as the idea of egoism (separate self). Here is illusion personified.
12. This illusion is yet eternal and boundless (like boundless eternal light). Thereby, illusion never began.

☯ The Futile Craving for Identity

'Within the Potential, comes the Impulse'… and with that Impulse comes the notion of the defined, the limited, the bound, the particular, the spatial, the temporal, the named, the different. The Impulse, the Ictus, the Snap, appears to emerge out of the Potential that we are. Thus, to crave identity, to 'build' identity, is an oxymoron, an absurdity! Yet it is all we ever do. This identity is the great battle to 'know', the struggle to master. Where is the border between potential and identity? There is none. And where is the actual event without us to generate it? There is none, only ever awareness. 'Yet who is *that*?' we ask again and again!

The Vital Need

What should we do about our continuous, thrusting, eyeless impulse and need to 'find the origin', to 'replace the thing that already happened', which was the need to get rid of 'the thing that happened before that'? Nothing is ever good enough, nothing ever gives peace, there is only the endless need to *replace*. But with what? The only thing conceivable is 'a variation of the thing already thought'. All thought is need, and all need is the need to replace. All thought is old, chasing something we already know, wanting something we already conceived, running from something we already did. Old is binding, is limitation, is vicious circle, where the endless thought-stream repeats the failures already identified. How can this ever end, this need to replace the unsatisfactory with something that is but a product of that dissatisfaction? The mind clothes itself as 'liberator', or as 'refugee from the fleeing it has always enacted', or as 're-eater of food it has already disgorged'. We search for the new, as long as it looks like something we have already decided upon. We must understand and quieten the *vital need*. **Awareness is volition** What is ego? It is the volitional force of desire: for definition, survival, security, comfort, pleasure, knowledge, power. Ego is really the limiting ignorance and self-importance of 'taking awareness for granted' allied to the blind force of habit. It is **Little Jack Horner** sitting in his corner, eating his pudding and pie. He sticks in his thumb and pulls out a plum, and says 'Oh what a good boy am I!'

Behold the Utterness

Behold the utter permanence, that which utterly pervades time, space, name or form. *Satchitananda* is the name for the ever-aware blissful oneness of absolute being. This absolute state of permanence contains all possible things, events, points, movements, energies, vibrations, conditions, ideas, thoughts. All of these are forever drenched, subsumed, drowned, obliterated within its utter permanence. Ideas, impulses, forces may come, but are they ever anything but the permanence? That which appears to arise can never have done so. That which appears to arise must signal repulsion, death, materialism, ignorance, suffering. The opposer of being is the idea of death, the opposer of awareness is the idea of ignorance, the opposer of bliss is the idea of suffering, and the opposer of all, is the idea of limitation. Finally, that idea of limitation ever begs its consummation in the ever-unlimited, the state of utter permanence.

'Birth' into the impermanence is surely an intolerable joke called 'death'. These two ideas arise together, they are corollaries, they are yin and yang, and they are utterly without substance. There is only one substance: *Satchitananda,* the utter permanence, the utter abstraction. The apparent fulfilment of its utter possibilities will keep it 'active' forever, so that here is searching, grasping, longing, becoming, suffering… But when is that utter permanence ever not itself? When has it ever not known its own utterness?

Awareness and its Becoming

Awareness forever appears to modify as subject-object but in fact never alters. Subject and object appear to arise together. Subject and object and their medium, awareness, are ever one and the same. That is, they have *no relationship whatsoever*. Yet existence-awareness is volitional force, 'continually appearing to seek itself'. Imagine one who is trying to discover, to gain, to achieve, to win, to covet, to control, to master. Who is he? He is nothing but himself, yet he ever seeks to *become* himself. How can this be? Becoming is thus oxymoronically described as 'ever replacing its own phantomness'. Clearly, there can be no becoming at all. There can be no result, no arrival, no achievement, no substance. Here is the Emptiness of Becoming.

Is awareness forever conditioned?

Truly, awareness can never be anything but itself. Awareness admits two 'modes': *absolute volition* that 'manifests as conditioning', and *absolute feeling* that 'dwells as unconditioned awareness'. We may identify three 'conditions or phenomena' of awareness: (a) a state of balance called *sattva* (b) a state of hiatus called *rajas,* and (c) a state of entrenched confusion called *tamas*. As soon as there is 'the notion of activity in awareness', there is born the idea of conditioning, relationship, limitation, characterised as ego, automatism, ignorance. So, is awareness forever conditioned? The seer as volition, ego, always 'becomes the object'. Yet the seer is ever supremely present, as evidenced by its power to continually *change* its conditioned state. The seer may initiate the *witnessing* state, a subtle self-reflexive process where the seer (as empty awareness) solely 'allows itself to witness the possibilities of its continual conditioning'. This may take the form of 'the idea that this present thought, feeling or sensation cannot possibly know me.' The seer can always choose either to withdraw from the conditioned state and return to 'self-awareness', or to indulge in the conditioned state. Ultimately our goal is to continually understand that whether conditioned or not, we as awareness are supremely present. Beyond the sheer force of our habits, we acknowledge that it is absurd not to accept our absoluteness. Finally, we see that our awareness and its 'active states' are ever one, like the ocean and its waves. Ultimately, whether we dwell as silence, as emptiness, or as the conditioned, as form, we can be confident that it *makes no difference to us*. Amazed at the reality of one borderless singular awareness, we enter a state of 'cosmic consciousness', experiencing the truth: 'The absolute borderless awareness experiences all its waves, simultaneously and forever'.

What is it that is always present?

- Life is always present
- Are you life?
- Yes, I am
- Then you are always present. Life is eternal, and you are life. Therein you are eternal.

How can there be anything separate from existence-awareness? This notion of separateness is known as 'death'. How can there be anything separate from the oneness of bliss? This notion is known as 'suffering'. Life apparently expresses itself as multiplicity, yet are the drops of water in the ocean anything but the ocean? There is nothing but life, and life is nothing but the bliss of aware oneness. Therefore, how can awareness even appear to localise or limit? *Who* calls himself a body, a mind, a thinker, a sinner, an individual? Does awareness, for example, suddenly and miraculously come into being when we open our eyes from sleep? Does the object suddenly and miraculously come into being when we set eyes upon it? No, the so-called 'state' or 'object' is obviously ever the absolute existence-awareness-bliss.

Life is eternal. You are life. You are eternal

The Integral Presence

If life is total, there can be nothing and no-one that is not you. All so-called expressions of life - all 'things', components, phases, systems - are but 'the dance of the forever'. Everything is always done, has always been done, and always will be done. Behind and within and as all events, all contradictions, all push-pull - is the unnameable Fact, the unnameable

Presence. It has no external qualities whatsoever. It is absolutely you. You are absolutely it. It exists, it is aware, it is bliss. Accept yourself and your 'journey' as Presence Alone. There is never anything to be 'done'. There is no 'enlightenment'. There is no incarnation. You are nothing but That.

There is no modification of awareness

1. Awareness permanently exists as a state without modifications.
2. Awareness appears to exhibit modifications: in the waking and dreaming states, through the intellect, the emotional and imaginative mind, the five organs of sense, the five senses, and the five organs of action.
3. Phenomena ('events', 'changes') cannot ever be said to exist without the perception of them. They should therefore be termed 'qualities of awareness'.
4. We, as awareness, are instantly and totally absorbed in every modification (thought, feeling, sensation) as it occurs. Where we place our attention, is all we ever are.
5. Therefore, the observer is never anything but the observed, the seer is ever the seen, and seer and seen are ever the medium ('action of awareness'). Therefore, emptiness is form and form is emptiness. All these states and terms are one, and thereby none exist.
6. Why do the modifications of awareness appear to be continuous? Answers: (a) Phenomena owe their 'sense of continuity' to the continuous presence of the seer, the awareness. (b) We fail to reflect that awareness is the sole actor, and instead believe the modification to exist in its own right. We fail to deconstruct habitual forms as 'our own empty awareness'. (c) The innate idea of polarisation, of 'observer-observed', of relationship - arises all at once in the egoic act of perceiving.
7. Overall, we should reflect that according to the idea of change, no-one is ever able to say that a thing or event is actually what it is, except from the standpoint of an unmoving (continuous) observer, which immediately obliterates (the idea of) change. Belief in the idea of change therefore signifies ignorance of the unmoving observer. If

all be modification, there can be none, and if change be 'continuous', there can be none.

Nothing is other than awareness

We may be led to suppose that all 'objects of the manifested cosmos' are 'devoid of consciousness'. On what basis? It is manifestly absurd for awareness to posit that there is anything outside itself. Who would ever dare to claim that modifications of one's own awareness (like rocks or fenceposts) are devoid of awareness? Yet we do it routinely, degraded empiricists that we are. To awareness, whether 'consumed' by the object or not, all is but awareness. There can be no 'tools' of awareness (volition, thought, feeling, sense) that are independent of it. No 'thing' has any independent arising, since all things occur in and as awareness.

You and I constitute the totality of all being

It may be assumed that awareness is impersonal ('an impersonal abstract vast') until made 'personal' by perception, that is, by the ego's action in conjuring the idea of 'objects'. But awareness, by definition, is self-aware, and cannot be other than 'individual', that is, indivisibly personal, since it is solely self-aware. We are faced with the stunning admission that an infinite, borderless ocean of awareness is none other than the self-awareness of 'one unlimited individual', whereby 'individual' is 'that which cannot be divided', and is utterly personal. We are further faced with the incredible liberating realisation that 'every single one of us' is none other than that sole, infinite, borderless ocean, and, being that, that *you or I solely, personally, constitute the totality of all being*. This is pure logic as pure truth. We are then tempted to say that the true miracle of being is not so much that there is oneness, but that there appears to be division or limitation. In truth, it has to be one or the other: we cannot ultimately be both limited and unlimited. One of them has to be a lie.

No change, no death

There is no change, and therein no death. Death is the idea that we are a fixed and limited being rather than unlimited existence-awareness. It is the idea of form, the idea of clinging, the idea of division, of negation, which supposes the idea of 'modification of an original substance'. In sum, it is the idea of 'involvement in and as the manifestation'. More subtly, death is the idea that we undergo continual change, rather than abiding as unchanging bliss. Yet there can be no 'event' called death (for example, 'where the life force and the body part company') other than 'a continuous state of change'. And if change is 'continuous', that is, absolute, it is literally non-existent. If so, death is literally unreal. We should simply affirm: 'I, the Self, undergo no change whatsoever'.

Relativity is the definition of non-existence

The force of need drives all creation. Creation is nothing but pulsation: that is, 'waves of densification and rarefaction' that produce the idea of displacement in the boundless awareness. Pulsation is the eternal 'conditioning of awareness', the idea of relativity, where awareness appears to pulse a displacement (form) and 'return' to itself. Yet can any 'singular pulsation' be said to happen in space, or in time, 'in relation to any other pulsation'? Never. Where is the border between pulsation and pulsation? Therefore, is there ever any actual discrete event or form? Never. Appearance itself never actually occurs. 'Relativity' is thus the very definition of non-existence. Rather, when you 'look' and 'see' the object, you see yourself, your ever-unchanging self. The 'observer' is ever the 'observed' - and if one is the other, then neither exists. You are instead *sat-chit-ananda:* existence-awareness as its own volition of self-delight.

Let it Go, Let it Go

We certainly can and should put our hand and our mind to work in this life. Meanwhile, we can and should always let go of that work, that action. We can certainly work without grasping at the results of work. We can 'make a meaningful difference' to ourself and others yet still let it all go. Life is continual flow, yet flow is indefinable, that is, empty. Should we fear such 'emptiness', as if it were 'the death of our precious identity'? Never. The emptiness is liberation, because we are transparent, we are here forever. We are the utter totality, and we should take total responsibility for it, and we should totally relax. Do we want to hold onto the wind, stop a wave from falling on the shore? Do we want to arrest our own digestion? Can we arrest our own feelings, our own acts, our own thoughts? No, on all counts. Is it worthwhile holding onto anything? *Can* we hold onto anything? Clinging is the only way we can manifest 'death'. We can definitely put our hand and our intelligence to work, we can definitely make a difference. And we can most definitely let it all go.

Forever gone, becoming

If it is all so important, why does it continually disappear in front of our eyes? If it is all so consequential, why can't we hold onto any of it? If it is all so momentous, why is it continually replaced? Always, always, something to be done… Never, never, anything to be done…

Action, it's over

It has always been over. It will always be over. It never began. Nevertheless, it is over. There is not a thing, not an event, that is not already over. If you think it is not over, then you mistake it for 'another thing' - that itself is already over. Nothing new ever happened, or will ever happen. Nothing ever happened. And here we are. Here we are… And here we aren't. And 'here we aren't again'. So who actually is it that isn't here? …It's over. Relax! It's done.

It's over, over, over …𝓁𝓁𝓁𝓁𝓁

Nothing more substantial than this

There is no 'event' in the history of the world that is any more significant or more substantial than the flicker of your mind as you read this sentence.

No scale

'Scale' is nothing but an idea in awareness. 'The pulsation of a thought' compared to 'the pulsation of a cosmos' is simply a matter of scale. 'A bigger radio telescope has discovered the presence of another million galaxies'. Why not build a larger microscope, and discover the presence of 'another billion particles'? It is less expensive.

No time or place

There is never a 'time' when anything in the 'past' of this life, this universe, ever exists, and there is never a 'time' when the 'future' of this life, this universe, ever exists. There is never a 'time' when the 'present' of this life, this universe, ever exists. There is never a 'place' where anything in this life, this universe, ever exists.

No quantity

When someone or something is no more, when it 'dies', what is the *quantity* that does so? Is something lost from the sum of being? Absolutely nothing, no quantity, is lost. Such a 'departure' makes no difference whatsoever to life itself - since it is no departure at all. Existence is *quality*, beyond quantity.

The Joke of Relativity

A 'moving object' has no existence without an unmoving seer. 'Movement' is only 'apprehended' in *and as* still awareness. Is there movement at all? Yes, since the immovable seer apprehends it. No, since the immovable seer is immovable, and therefore apprehends no movement. Yet if there be no movement, then no immovability can be apprehended. This is a joke, the play of relativity.

Absolute space between thoughts

Look to the 'space between thoughts'. That space is the ever-present ocean of awareness. Look to the space before and after each breath. That space is the ever-present ocean of existence-awareness. To be ever aware of this ocean-self, is to kill the (emergence of) ego.

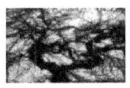 Nothing exists but Feeling

There is nothing to feel but Feeling itself. Test the assertion! No-one has ever experienced, or will ever experience, anything but feeling itself. To feeling, nothing exists but feeling. 'Object' cannot be experienced, cannot be felt. Time, the passing of time, the stretch of it, cannot be felt. 'Space' or 'particle' cannot be felt… or any name or any form. Feeling is awareness; there is no reality but Feeling itself. Feeling's seeming 'metamorphosis as conditions' is nothing but *need* indulging in a phantom play. Set not your heart on 'a thing that comes or goes'. Set your heart on that feeling which is constant.

This, this

Who sends the mind to wander afar? Who first drives life to start its journey? This life is eternal, it is beginningless and endless Presence. To assert that 'becoming' is also eternal, beginningless and endless, is to assume becoming to be the eternal condition of existence. But to say so is in fact to say: becoming *never is*. The only way becoming can be apprehended, spoken of, measured, captured, is to conjure a series of points, moments, events, waves. Yet since 'becoming endlessly becomes', there can be no such points, moments, events, waves. Literally, nothing is ever what it is. Becoming is thereby a mirage. Time is non-existent. Birth and death are absolutely non-existent. There is only This. Likewise, 'this' has no definition. 'This' is the Tao, the mysterious, the elusive.

A parade of labels

Can the hand grasp the hand? Can the heart beat the heart? Can the mind grasp the mind? Can a thought think a thought? Materialists! 'Universe' is nothing but 'a thought called universe'. Juggle your atoms in the air: the juggling persists as long as you require it. This book of juggled words will end when writer and reader need it no more. Writer and reader are trying to account for a thing that has no existence. Verily, this is *Samsara*, the becoming, the wandering, the 'external search'. Only awareness is self-existing, self-sufficient, self-self.

Nothing but a composite

Notions such as 'a body called human' or 'a human incarnation' or 'the infinite creatures of the world', are nothing but *descriptions*. Consider a line of thought based on such descriptions: 'How did 'I' gain a 'human incarnation'? How do I appear to be in possession of a human body? Of all the 'trillions of creatures', how did I get to this? Survival of the fittest? Top of the food chain? Karmic work?' Let us not be absurd. There is no discrete creature. There are no discrete forms or components. There is no discrete self! Instead there arises the volition as ego, the *idea* of a separate, personal self. Awareness is absolutely personal in that it absolutely feels itself, yet the ego-idea limits this self-feeling because it identifies with the idea of 'discrete object'. That object is described, placed in context according to myriad other factors, and the dance of labelling begins. Based on this fundamental lie, all concepts flourish: 'human body', 'incarnation', 'separate self'. In truth, there is only the eternal, unbounded awareness alone.

Manufacturing the philosophic problem

It is like god says to us: 'Walk through this gate in the middle of nowhere and you will find enlightenment'. And all we want to do is stand there, with a magnifying glass, studying the stupid gate.

Life has no Meaning

Life is 'to live'. Life has no 'meaning'. That which 'means something' can only be explained using a myriad of 'other means'. For example, the idea of meaning is only made possible by a comparison of the ideas 'meaningless' and 'meaningful'. These are co-dependent dancing phantoms. Life itself is inexplicable. To live means to live. To be means to be. To be aware means to be aware. To love means to love. All signifiers, all words, are cancelled in silence.

End? End? The End of Seeking

I am on the cusp of 'jettisoning all I have ever known', and reflect that I have learned some things: that obsession is a fool's game, that labyrinths and rabbit holes lead only to more convoluted versions of themselves, that belief in death is nothing but delusion, that memory is a web of clinging to identity, that we rely on the threads of our stories because there is no salve or explanation for this 'oppressive present'. I must thereby not only give up what I was looking for, but also the tools, the paradigms within which I sought it. In this sense, the present text is an absurdity. Strands of knowledge and experience must dissolve in a great lake of *not knowing*. Yet, my enduring need is still to characterise myself as 'seeker'. I am as if always at the turgid beginning, where I must take up again the unending narrative, the labyrinthine bind of birth and death and time and consequence. Such a person really wants to give up! He habitually thinks of the end of all clinging and wanting, of place and time, of cause and effect, of delusion… where life might come to be profound ease, simply as it is, nothing but itself. Yet he also knows there is no such thing as 'going', or 'arrival', or 'end'. There is only the eternal Thisness, the borderless Here. **Practise Acceptance** Yet, do we not experience an impotence, a frustration, a sadness, that there is no path, no method: that we can 'experience nothing except what happens'? If we are to 'surrender to grappling' with the utter complexity of Being, in all its parts and phases, we fear we will be lost to a life of distractions. You and I want liberation, but liberation *from* life or *as* life? There is a method and a posture called Integral Yoga, which accepts and deals with the infinite complexity from the position of deepest *patience*. It is a posture that never ends, and never can end. Yet, which of us can deal with complexity and not drown in it, like all other life forms since the beginningless beginning of the world? Answer: To deal with the complexity of ourselves can only be done from the position of acceptance, patience. That is, the greater our capacity to accept, the greater will be our inner simplicity, like an ocean that encompasses all its waves. Thus our capacity will grow. Instead, we privilege an endless treading of water, of wanting, fearing, adjusting, making, shaping, arranging, rearranging, rationalising, balancing… all from the standpoint of the flailing separative ego. Our judging and rationalising faculty has too much power, and we accept it too much as ourselves. Acceptance is the only sane attitude. It minimises the need to grasp and to control, and it shrinks the ego: the idea of grasping, of separateness, positionality, false relativity. To accept that there is both nothing whatsoever to do or to be, and that there is everything to do and to be, requires acceptance itself - not of the apparent contradiction, but of the *total reality that we are*.

Materialist Proposition: Existence is nothing but blind energy

'This existence is an infinitude of *unconsciousness*, nothing but blind energy forming and unforming as matter, and this energy has no self-consciousness whatsoever.' **Answers** (1) This position assumes that 'unconsciousness' is something that can be imagined, or worse, something that is 'beyond imagining'. (2) The infinite energy is nothing but the 'free volitional projecting quality' of existence-awareness. The one thing that can never be manufactured by 'endless ramification of blind energy' is existence-awareness itself. (3) No-one has ever been able to even begin to advance a plausible theory as to the origin of existence-awareness, nor will they ever be able to, since the theorist is awareness itself. Awareness has no origin, it absolutely is. **Practical objection** Why then, for you and me, is awareness continually lost or subverted or limited or clouded or diverted? **Answers** (1) Whatever awareness is, it is not 'manufactured' by the objects of one's attention! It is also not 'manufactured by its own shifting or fleeting state'. (2) The old saw: 'If a tree falls in a forest and no-one witnesses it, did it happen?' childishly posits the premise 'if a tree falls in the forest'. Who on earth is it that posits that premise? (3) Deep sleep, for example, is merely awareness in its 'objectless state'. Upon waking, one is well aware that the sleep state was objectless. Surely only a fool would think awareness was somehow murdered in deep sleep then miraculously re-manufactured immediately after it. The same person would think that awareness is somehow manufactured by 'created objects'. If it were so, in what context would those objects have ever been envisioned for creation? **A subtler objection** In the state of 'manifestation', there can be nothing but a sense of 'pure flow without reflection'. The purport of this is: *there is no-one to record* the infinitesimal, nameless, insentient movements of a universe... the rotation of a wheel, the flutter of a breeze, pulse of a heart, twinkle of a star, birth of an atom... **Answers** (1) Awareness is utterly capable of 'flowing without reflection' while simultaneously 'recording everything' and 'adjusting its action' through an unlimited capacity for reflection. (2) Awareness is not affected in any measure if it 'appears to displace itself' ('objectify'). Is the ocean of water affected by its waves? For example, the human ego continually operates in its twin capacities for imagination and reflection, but has no existence or power outside awareness. (3) 'To experience an object' is total proof that the object cannot by any means be separate or different from the seer of it.

Summary of rejections of absolute awareness

1. **Objects** If the self is one, and therefore 'absolutely objectless', awareness is by definition lost if there is even the *appearance* of displacement, that is, the ego apprehending the object.
2. **Ego** How can awareness be called awareness if 'I', the (volitional) ego, is not aware?
3. **Deep sleep** Since there cannot be any sense of self without the concurrent experience of the limited manifested object, in deep sleep 'there is no sense of self, and therefore no awareness'.
4. **Continuous action** In the state of 'manifestation', which is continuous action, there can be nothing but 'pure flow without conscious reflection'.

Summary of answers

1. **Objects** If in the 'waking and dream states', the so-called 'limiting force of manifestation' appears to arise in the self, why should that necessarily mean that awareness itself is divided, and therefore lost, in any way?
2. **Ego** The 'little I' (ego), as a manufactured entity, is literally appearance only, therefore is not a separate entity.
3. **Deep sleep** (a) In the 'sleep state', the 'idea that awareness is lost through displacement', that is, 'apprehension of the object', does not arise at all. Hence, the objection to 'the fact of awareness remaining itself', is removed. (b) Upon waking, one is well aware that the sleep state was objectless.

4. **Continuous action** (a) In the state of 'action' where there is 'pure objective flow without reflection', why should the dualistic state of reflection inhibit the pure flow of awareness? Is awareness as pure unreflective flow chaotic, blind, lost? (b) Awareness always retains the instantaneous power to 'make choices and change them'. (c) There could not even be the possibility of 'action without reflection' without awareness' eternal and borderless state of receptivity.

 Enquiry into three states of awareness: sleep, waking, dreaming

The fundamental and unqualified experience 'I am, and I know that I am' is identical with all other experience, including that of sleep.

Sleep is claimed to be ignorance, but only in relation to the wrong knowledge prevalent in the wakeful state. The waking state is really ignorance, and the sleep state is full knowledge.

If dreamless sleep is not the real state, where does the sleeper's intense peace come from? It is everybody's experience that nothing in the waking state can compare with the bliss and well-being derived from deep sleep, when the mind and the senses are absent. This means that bliss comes only from inside ourselves, and that it is most intense when we are free from thoughts and perceptions that create the world and the body.

The ego, the embryo of manifestation who suffers in the two states of waking and dream, imagining, 'I am the one who sees', is also the one who by thinking 'I did not see anything in sleep' loses his power, and gets mentally perplexed.

Body, world, objects and events appear in the waking state but disappear in sleep. Objection: *I am not aware in my sleep!* True, there is no awareness of the body or world. But you must exist in your sleep in order to say 'I was not aware in my sleep'. Who says so now? The wakeful person. The sleeper cannot say so. That is to say, the 'wakeful' individual who is now identifying the Self with the body, unreliably says that such awareness did not exist in sleep.

The same person sleeps, dreams and wakes up

The waking state, because we identify with the body, is considered to be full of interesting things. The absence of such experiences makes us say that the sleep state is dull; this is because we were not there as a 'person'. Let us be clear: do we not admit that we exist in our sleep? You are the *same person* that is now awake. Is it not so? There is a continuity in the sleep and the waking states. What is that continuity? It is the state of pure existence-awareness. So, there is continuity of being in all the three states, but *no* continuity of the 'person' and the 'objects'.

Through the destruction of the limiting ego, the polarities (seer-seeing-seen, knower-knowing-known) that are based on it, disappear along with the waking and dream states. The Self-forgetfulness that is the basis for their rising is fully destroyed. Unceasing being then shines in the Heart.

The mind creates the states of waking and dream. In its state of dormancy it remains unaware of itself, the body or the world. When the ego drops away, all disappear, leaving the state of illumination.

Once the tendencies that caused the waking and dream states to manifest have been eradicated, the three states of waking, dreaming and deep sleep cease as alternating states of mind.

When the mind of the seer has dropped away leaving only the light of the Self, sleep ceases to be 'a state of unconsciousness in which one is unaware of anything'. Though the body will continue to 'sleep' after the mind has gone, the seer will be fully aware of the Self at all times. There will no longer be any daily period of 'unconsciousness as the mind lies dormant'.

By failing to enquire into and realise the true experience that exists and shines in the same way forever, one becomes deluded and thinks 'I am the one who woke up'. If that powerful sheath of the intellect, the ignorance that is experienced in the waking state, is destroyed by the sword of self-enquiry: *'I am not the one who woke up'* - then the eminent state of sleep will shine, remaining as pure bliss, its ignorance destroyed.

If the illumination that is awareness of our being exists so firmly that it remains unshaken until sleep overpowers us, then there will be no need to feel jaded or disheartened, lamenting 'The forgetfulness of sleep has come and unsettled me!' Our awareness is taken to appear 'through the mental faculties alone'. Yet true or perfect knowledge is always shining, even in sleep. If one is continuously aware in the waking state, the awareness will continue in 'sleep' also.

Pure awareness is waking sleep

The state of the Aware One is neither in sleep nor the waking state but intermediate between the two. There exists 'both the awareness of the waking state and the stillness of sleep'. It is called waking sleep. We may call it wakeful sleep or sleeping wakefulness, or sleepless waking or wakeless sleep. It is not the same as sleep or waking separately. It is the state of perfect awareness and perfect stillness combined. It is also *the interval between two successive thoughts*. It is the source from which thoughts spring. We see this when we wake up from sleep. In other words, thoughts have their origin in the stillness of sleep. Thoughts constitute the only difference between the stillness of sleep and the turmoil of waking. Go to the root of the thoughts and we reach the stillness of sleep. However, we reach it in the full vigour of enquiry, that is, with perfect awareness.

In sleep our ego is submerged and the sense organs are not active. The ego of the Knowing One has been killed and he does not indulge in any sense activities of his own accord, or with the notion that he is 'the doer'. So, he is in sleep. At the same time the Knowing One is not unconscious as in sleep but fully awake in the Self. His state is sleepless. This sleepless sleep, or wakeful sleep, is called the 'fourth' state of the Self (*samadhi*). It is the *screen* on which all the three ignorances of waking, dream and sleep pass, leaving the screen unaffected. However, the term 'fourth state' is a convenience only. Only if the three states truly existed could the state of 'waking sleep', the pure state of awareness, be thus termed.

Continuous Enquiry is Needed

Until 'waking sleep' occurs in the waking state, we should not abandon our enquiry in the form of 'questioning the origin of the idea'. By the same token, we should unceasingly perform the enquiry, until the waking sleep pervades and shines in the dream state as well.

Forever At Once

There is never any 'state' where awareness is not absolute. Beyond the notion of infinite complexity, awareness is absolute simplicity and unity. Such 'states' as appearance and non-appearance, form and emptiness, waking, dreaming and deep sleep (*etc*) have no actual definition outside the 'forever at once' of awareness. It cannot be, that a 'single form or event' appears exclusively in time or space, that is, 'in opposition to all others'. Yet this is the absurd nature of the phantom ego, of our continued myopia. Limitation is forever unreal. For the very idea of limitation to be, the *unlimited* must reign without ceasing. The ultimate oxymoron is the idea that anything can 'manifest itself'!

The unknowable and nameless, seeking to 'become known'

(1) - How is the perception of 'becoming' or 'change' even possible since the seer is forever himself? How can the seer even appear to enter ratio, relativity, form?
- The indwelling energy of existence-awareness is volitional force. Volition can only 'appear as a counterforce to Feeling, that which ever contains the force'. Here is the idea of displacement, which becomes the great 'magnet of the world'
- But how the hell does it, can it, appear?
- The asking of that question is its 'appearance'. *Who* asks the question?
- All right. Then how am I always 'the unknowable restlessly seeking to be known'?

- Nothing that truly exists can ever be anything but itself. Yet there is free volition, this unbounded projecting power. Again, volition can only 'appear as counterforce to that which contains it'. 'Creation' is nothing but the magnetism born of displacement. The magnetic forces known as ego and memory continually juxtapose, compare, order and store. We are addicted to descriptions, to names, to inference, which we gather in the service of 'position', 'identity'.
- So the expressed, the magnetically created, never exists?
- I ask you: should ideas and forms be off-limits to the totally free?
- But how can they *be*?
- Freedom does anything it likes, all the time. 'In the beginning was the word, and the word was with god'. The infinitude of apparent expressions, all these names, are always that nameless thing we call awareness.

(2) - So, by logic, if perception (volition, action, displacement) is to 'occur', it occurs to one who is beyond it?
- Yes, to one who 'both becomes it and is ever beyond it'
- But if it 'occurs to one who is beyond it', then how can it occur?
- 'Beyond it' means 'forever containing it', not 'outside it'
- So awareness is both never and forever conditioned, limited, channelled?
- Yes and no! It is 'both and neither at once'
- Can this life be 'inert'? My question means: Who is this One who can appear to not be what he is?
- Aha, the veiling, limiting power!
- *Who* possesses that veiling power?
- It is the borderless awareness who 'assumes a border as long as he posits the idea of border'
- Yet can his awareness be veiled?

- Yes, awareness can effortlessly imagine its own veiling. It is called 'play'. Blind man's bluff!
- Then does it ever cease to be of the nature of awareness, of its own nature?
- No
- Therefore, can awareness ever be anything but what it is?
- No. Yet the nature of awareness is 'both infinite feeling (emptiness) and its volitional energy (form)'. Awareness can 'appear in the mode of force and counterforce forever' and yet will never be the slightest bit affected! Some call it the holy ghost
- So should we say: awareness and its so-called 'ghost manifestations' are One?
- Yes. But neither 'aspect' is anything but name
- And is there ultimately anything but awareness?
- No, though 'awareness' itself is only a name, a convention. Yet we may say: 'Desire is ever fulfilled in the dance, the performance. These are but breaths of the One, the Great, who is infinitely and ever Herself. And remember, there can be no (apparent) limitation without infinite liberty.

No Border, No Border

- Think of air and wind. What difference is there between them?
- None, except that wind moves
- Yet is the wind ever anything but air?
- No
- Think of the ocean and its waves. What difference is there between them?
- None, except that 'the waves move'
- Yet is the wave ever anything but water?
- No
- Think of heat and fire. What difference is there between them?
- None, except that 'fire moves'

- Yet is fire ever anything but heat?
- No
- Now, think of the will (volition) and the awareness. What difference is there between them?
- None, except that will, as force, moves
- Now consider. How can it move? How can displacement occur between the force and its counterforce when it operates on nothing but itself?
- It cannot
- How can will-force exist then, when it is nothing but awareness?
- It cannot
- Is that will-force 'continuous'?
- Yes
- Again, can force ever be distinguished from its counterforce?
- No, they are simultaneous. No border can ever be discerned
- So, can the displacement of force and counterforce ever occur?
- Never.

 **A ghost that (never) pulsates**

Consider the origin, within and as awareness, of all pulsation: of volitional force and its manifestations: sensation, feeling, thought. (1) Who or what can claim to *quantify* the pulsation? No-one can know the genesis of the very thought that is occurring right now, nor the 'points' of its progress, nor how it is 'subsumed back into the emptiness whence it came'. No wave (force, sense, feeling, thought) can be tracked (that is, known), since 'the one who might track it' is then the creator of another thought entirely. (2) If we are to posit that 'there is nothing but the pulsation of volition, sensation (*etc*) in this absolute existence-awareness', a logical question is: *If all is pulsation, who or what pulsates?* Although we may answer, 'that which contains, and drowns, and therefore is beyond, pulsation', there is absolutely *no border* between senser and sense, feeler and feeling, thinker and thought, awareness and pulsation. They are always one, for nothing can ever be 'existent as two'.

The absurd idea of projection

Absolute substance cannot 'manifest'!

We are prone to continually asking oxymoronic questions, such as: 'Can the absolute substance be obscured or lost?' We reiterate: how or why could the essence be 'obscured or lost in the infinite affirmations of itself'? How can the absolute ever appear to 'manifest itself' (ie: as a play of oppositions, a dance of differences, a game of this and that, high and low, light and dark…)? This is the ultimate oxymoron, since that which already and forever *is,* can never 'become manifest', let alone 'obscured'. What can 'be born and die' that is not already present? Between 'self' and 'other', between 'awareness and ignorance', show me the border! Contemplate *That* without which nothing can be, That which is all in all. You are here. You have always been here. You will always be here. The sum total of energy in this universe cannot ever diminish. There is no death. There is only this eternal now. You. The key insight is: no limitation, no materialisation can ever 'occur' since the eternal presence is utterly unchangeable. Yet we continually conjure the problem, where 'the awareness always appears to be pulsating between perceiver and perceived' or 'between objects'. We sagely say things like: 'there is sound (vibration) and the hearer of the sound (awareness)'. Clearly there is no sound without the hearer of the sound and no hearer of the sound without the sound. Are they two? It is blindingly clear they are not. In response, we scramble to 'affirm the death of duality' with statements like: 'limitation proves the boundless, pulsation proves the silence, time proves the eternal, concept of duality proves the utter non-dual…'

No Identity

Action has no identity. Thought has no identity. Sensing has no identity. Even feeling has no identity. What of the idea that one is 'personal'? There is no personality. Liberation is to be defined as 'No Identity'.

- There is no-one present
- Yet my sense of self is absolute
- That 'sense of self' is without discreteness, without border. Is there 'someone'?
- Yes, my sense of self is absolute.

There is no Incarnation

What is it that is 'ever present in all the moments of our acts'? Answer: Existence-awareness is the only feeling there ever is, the only 'sense' we ever have. It is dependent on nothing. Form, change, evolution, birth, death: these words signify no discrete event at all. Show me the actual border between 'thing and thing' and I will accept that 'the thing' exists. The rest is convention, sign, name only. Just as there is no drop that is separate from ocean, there is no 'birth' into anything and no 'exit' out of anything. No incarnation can ever be proved. Incarnation is denied. All possibility and actuality is forever here. The 'person' who stands here today is the same person who ever was. He is the eternal person. The animal who stands here today is the same animal who ever was… *There is no element or part that is not what it ever was.* Evolution? A perceived shuffling of preconceived parts. Death? A charade of shuffling from room to room.

There is never any time or place or cause

Time and place and cause are conventions, and conventions are illusions. The idea of remembering is a mere 'gathering in the present'. Nothing ever 'happened' but 'the affirmation of This'. How to account for pulsation, for cause and effect? Visualise waves in an endless sea. The waves appear to pulsate, to 'come and go', but the ocean ever remains, here, now. Nothing ever 'resulted' from anything else. Existence-awareness is elastic, plastic, forming and re-forming 'in the one spot, in the one time'. It is ever the same presence, ever the identical 'event', where event is 'a shuffle of ghosts'. Thank god the event is never what it is, for therein is mercy. How to account for regret? Regret is to cling to things that have no existence beyond our clinging. Clinging is slowness, dullness.

There is no 'limited individual', since there are no borders. The terms 'self' and 'context' are mutually relative, and therefore null and void. What we know as 'sequence in time' is the arbitrary measuring of 'apparent pulsation'. The key is to know how the very impulse arises, to *watch* its origin in the silent awareness. To abide in non-formation is to admit the eternal as oneself, even as pulsation appears to continue forever.

 **Evolution and the Absolute Context**

Those who believe in 'the discreteness of objects' (materialists) love to assume that 'awareness progressively manifests' in 'various levels' of creation, beginning with plant life, and 'progressing' to animal, then human. Any such vision will no doubt assume the existence of life forms higher than the human. Yet materialists uniformly fail to ask: In what 'absolute context' can anything and everything take place? We are bound to assume that there is a common 'energetic pool' or 'existence' through which the notion of 'forms and levels' can arise and be sustained. Materialists fail to address the question: 'How can one 'level' of life 'arise from another' unless there were some motivating force that is superior to, that is, contains, both the previous level and the present one, and by implication all levels?' The core issue materialists fail to address is: 'What on earth is it that actually evolves?' We will not even speak of the impossibility of differentiating any 'singular organism' from its context. We are bound to assume that 'all levels are manifestly present everywhere', since 'previous levels' never, not even in 'localised circumstances', fall away to oblivion 'when a higher level is reached'. The railway station does not disappear just because passengers are continually coming and going. This discussion does not contest the idea that 'diverse outcomes appear to manifest according to local circumstances and contexts, or according to notions of the survival of the fittest', but ultimately these 'local contexts' are arbitrary points of focus or selection, and fail to contradict 'the absolute diversity of possibility within the absolute existence, here and now'. It is blindingly clear that there must be a substance, a force, a power, an intelligence, a 'context', that effortlessly contains all so-called levels and variations. It is also equally clear that the idea of 'evolution' is at best 'a convenience for the sake of classification'. Its proponents seem to arbitrarily 'differentiate an apple from a pip' while failing to confront the common substance, the indwelling agency by which any and all so-called transformations could possibly take place. That common substance is existence-awareness in its self-manifestations through infinite volition. No boffin or pundit has ever been able to put forward any theories of creation or evolution without the ubiquitous and taken-for-granted presence of awareness. If these 'experts' continue to take a limited view or position, limitation and positionality are the obvious result.

Context absolute: evolution deconstructed

 **The Absolute Cycle of Need and Lack**

Watch carefully! Borderless awareness appears to 'contract as attention', to suddenly constrict and 'flash forth as ego'. This is the volitional force of desire, want, need, entrenched by 'perception of lack'. Need - lack - need - lack: which arose first? Do not ask! Here is the empty, polarised ritual, in phantom time, forever. Like iron filings to a magnet, the ego takes on and throws off endless modifications, sensing, feeling, knowing, remembering, clinging, ever seeking to define and consolidate 'identity'. Here is awareness as unstable ocean, where the crest of any wave is 'someone thinking they gained something' and the trough of any wave is 'someone thinking they lost something'. This infinitely malleable egoism tries to fulfil, without end, the hiatus of want and the fear of lack. The mechanics of this 'continual material incarnation' seem forever blind and machine-like, where we 'ever and never become' this great projected, self-entangling, self-voluminating web called 'a person'. Names and forms are projected and grasped at, while seeking and debate rage, then language and history and philosophy and science and mathematics attempt to explain and fulfil every sort of secondary or ancillary condition in pursuit of a nameless phantom original want or need. The resentment and sense of loss caused by the effort to fulfil ancillary conditions fuels new desire and aversion, 'in time', forever. Every breath we take, every mental impulse, is a masturbation of ever-wanting and ever-resenting. And the incarnation of need is ever now, ever-happening, one breath at a time, and we are continually trapped in the fear of 'time passing', continually clinging to the fake paradigms of what we call achievement. This egoism is nothing but the phantom habit of accumulation, of desire born of fear. Time threatens us at every step, for time is thief, usurper, bogeyman. Time is verily death! Look closely, see how impossible it is to grasp at a thing called future, how impossible to grasp at a thing called past, how impossible to grasp at a thing called present. Yet we precisely fear surrender to the eternal, we fear to be that which we forever are, beyond all these modifications: to be devoid of need, devoid of ego. **It is all right here** Meanwhile, the silent heart is ever-present, always simple, always now. This infinite life is very local, very here. No big deal, right here. It is as small, as intimate, as here as can be. It is the immutable immobile permanent, the unthinkable conscious being… Therefore, *be as you are, not as you claim to want to be.*

Our experience in the ocean of awareness: infinite acts of ego or indefinable whole?

- What is our actual experience in this ocean of awareness?
- Absolute awareness is by definition eternally self-conscious, borderlessly self-aware, so that we might say 'it is personal'. That is, 'I am and I am aware'
- Yet we engage as eternal action of force and counterforce, according to the dictates of ego
- Yes, we are continual seekers of 'identity through experience', as exercised through perception, imagination, judgement and memory
- Core question: Who is the one who is able to know his own ego?
- The ego, when enquired into, is seen to be non-existent. It has all the characteristics of a phantom, a shadow, a chimera, a dream in air
- But *experience* is a quantum that we (as egoism) build on, react to, examine. Some of our experience is retained as memory, either through the force of the unfamiliar or the habit of repetition. A 'serviceable identity', though provisional and ephemeral, is forged and re-forged. So, if ego has the characteristics of 'a phantom, shadow, chimera, dream in air', what 'relationship' should we, as awareness, take to 'identity's components', born of egoism?
- In life we have absolutely no control over the never-ending

displacements of force and counterforce, so we must continually ask the decisive question: *Who is it* that 'sustains relationships' (through egoic perception, imagination, judgement and memory)? Such an inward movement leads to the insight that we are perpetually 'conducting relationships with ourself', juggling the components of our mentality, *to no discernible end.*

- So 'the death of the ego' is 'a notion we should entertain'?
- Clever, but be careful, because this *new egoic thought* throws up even more complex, compulsive defences. For example: Ego subtly pronounces: 'There is an infinitude of things I am not aware of, and further, these are all possessed of their own life, light, function. Any cell in any body, for instance, is possessed of its own controlling intelligence.' Or it will prattle things like: 'I, the ego, am not aware in sleep, and reconstitute myself, as awareness, at the end of sleep'
- Aha, since ego by definition creates the idea of the discrete, every 'discrete thing' takes on 'a life of its own'!
- Yes, and again there is only one core question: *By whom* is any idea (that is, any product of egoism) entertained?
- So we should continually assert that awareness *cannot* be confined to a separative stance called ego?
- Exactly. We, boundless awareness, must never make the mistake of thinking an idea is a 'real and independent thing', no matter how automatically it appears
- That's right! What can we do when 99.9% of 'our own functions' are unknown and uncontrollable! We can't 'exist in the essence without parts or attributes' when perceptions, thoughts, feelings, judgements, memories, paradigms are automatic. These experiences become 'the person'
- Do not be fooled by the idea of 'quantity'! The answer is: *I am, and I know that I am.* The person is always 'the aware one who cannot be divided'
- So do 'individual things' exist or not?
- Listen carefully. If the absolute is truly so, then its 'points, pathways,

fractals, components, spheres, contexts and incarnations' totally exist in the sense that 'as the play of continual transition, continual experience, *the sum total of life's pathways and events can never lessen'*. In that case, the ocean of eternal awareness is *seen to contain all possible ramifications of itself forever,* and there is no 'time or place or instance' whereby all possibilities are not forever occurring. It is true that singular experiences are 'magnetised around an indefinable centre called ego', so that if we define these experiences as 'patterns and trends that define the life of the person', then we must accept that (at least the essence of) every one of them is retained

- Are they who we are, or not?
- We may frame the issue this way: Is the person (1) 'the sum of all parts' or (2) 'the essence beyond all parts'? If the former, then we accept that there is 'a person (ego) who evolves', ie, is in transition, who must 'eternally process her experiences as representations of her essential self'. If the latter, we accept the self as 'eternally independent of the play of any parts'. In this case, there is 'no person but the formless absolute within which all things have their phantom play'
- Or: 'I am simultaneously the one who is defined by experience and the one who is not defined by experience'
- Yes, but we are again left with the question: how can the indivisible (that is, the 'real person') ever 'evolve', that is, operate as the self-limiting ego, or even appear to do so? We are left with the realisation that any ego-based attitude that involves seeking or striving, is *fatally limiting*
- So our only job is to 'deconstruct the idea of relationship' between awareness and ego, seer and modification?
- Correct. This is the practice called *Jnana Yoga*. A corollary to this is *Bhakti Yoga*, where there is deliberate worship of the modification as nothing but an embodiment of the (divine) self. A further corollary is *Karma Yoga*, where we work with all the modifications in a completely non-judgemental way, and where the sole appropriate attitude is acceptance.

 Let us experience life as indivisible

Any singular act or thought that occurs, is seen to exist to the exclusion of all others, even if for an instant. This is the particular 'action of awareness' characterised as egoism, where the abiding sense of self as awareness is 'concentrated' in the continual 'creation and replacement of objects, which in truth do not exist'. This is the idea of 'mind'. Yet how is the non-existent object 'identified'? Any 'object' is nothing but 'the limiting action of awareness'. The so-called ego, defined as 'the continual bolstering of itself as the creator of identity', judges its manifestations to be 'independent'. This is ironic, since ego has no existence in itself. Ego cannot do otherwise but 'take on the mantle' of absolute awareness. Awareness is ever self-absorbed, whatever its so-called mode.

Yet, what is the difference between ego's 'automatic ignorant absorption', and 'the absorbed state of awareness that allows everything to *be*, without qualification, without struggle'? This dilemma has been termed 'the difference between ignorance and innocence'. (1) According to the automatism of ignorance, we habitually feel as if we are the mythical *Sisyphus* who 'pushes his rock up the mountain', only to see it forever fall back to where it started. We endure the Groundhog Day hell of 'beginning again'. We seem to be lost in the miasma of forms and the eternal effort to rearrange them. Some will blithely say 'action in this life should be its own forgetting, and therefore its own reward'. But we, like Sisyphus, continue to 'act' as long as we believe we are the 'limited actor', so that our 'rock' is the continual belief in the fruits of struggle. (2) According to the liberation of 'innocence', we all know that when we are totally concentrated in an activity, we have really no 'sense of action' at all. This we call 'flow'. Flow is a mode of awareness that is not at all 'limited' or 'in time' or 'in motion', since it really 'comes from nowhere and goes nowhere'. There is no sense of action being performed, precisely because there is no limited sense of being an actor. Awareness here expresses as simplicity, unadorned peace *in action*. Such experience is extremely common, by no means confined to peak thinkers, sportspeople or artists.

The reality that binds options (1) and (2) above is that our experience at any given instant is never compound or 'chopped into parts', it is *always* a seamless wholeness. The grand irony is that the ego cannot possibly experience the so-called components of any experience as discrete. There is never any separative 'I' who experiences a separate 'that' or 'other'. The idea of an 'experiencer' versus an 'experience' is a total nonsense. Our experience at any juncture is absolute, it cannot be arbitrarily divided into components, either 'seer and seen' or 'seen and seen'. The ego is thus a mere phantom born of a separative need for 'identity'.

To accept the reality of 'no separation' is to allow ourselves to *be*, without qualification, without struggle. It is 'meditation as action, as flow'. We surrender to the moment and the flow, without reservation. What could possibly be lost except our need to control, our need to feel separate? An analogy: Imagine your awareness as a river that eternally flows. Its flow has no discrete parts, no beginnings or endings. Similarly, imagine the position of 'an ocean that perceives its waves'. The ocean can see that all so-called waves arise and fall within and as itself, flowing onward forever and never 'arriving'. Yet you and I instead habitually strive to take the position of the 'individual wave'! This is absurd. There is no such thing. Is there anything to do, other than silently accept the status quo of awareness? The proper attitude is to affirm that 'there is no attitude or position to be taken at all'.

be as you are… one breath at a time

 **No border means no death**

To understand there is no border between 'person and absolute' is to wipe out birth and death. The statement 'I am going to die' can only mean *'I am going to stop experiencing things that appear to be other than myself'*. Yet how can 'I' converse with 'I'? What we really mean is 'there is a wish to remove the limitations of the false ego'. Where are the dead? There are no dead. Therefore they are not anywhere. The idea of 'dead' is another component in the web of 'created identity'. Death is a word. There is no frontier. There is no border. Not a single thread or atom of a brain is unconnected with a mind. Not a single thread or atom of a mind is unconnected with absolute mind. Not a single thread or atom of absolute mind is unconnected with eternal, absolute being-ocean. Nothing is personal. And we insist there is a thing called death?

No dead bodies in the graveyard

People believe that to live near a field of 'dead bodies' is not a desirable thing. Yet we all affirm a cemetery as a sacred and beautiful space - of rich (bone-fertilised) soil, green grass, leafy trees. It should be obvious there is no distinction between things 'alive' and things 'dead'. How is such superstition able to flourish? An analogy: We float in a boat in an ocean of water. We dip in our hand and scoop out a droplet, and absurdly say to ourselves: this droplet is *dry*. Not wet like other droplets, but dry. Any child knows that water is wet, that it can never be dry. But wise adults know better: there are indeed wet ('living') and dry ('dead') droplets in the ocean of water! This life is the ocean of energy, of being. It is borderless, timeless, absolute. There can never can be any droplet in life's ocean that is 'dead'. Energy cannot transform into death any more than 'wet water' can become 'dry water'. Thus, there is no transformation of any kind, because nothing is *ever but what it is*. And what is, utterly refutes the absurd juxtaposition of 'life versus death'. There are no dead bodies in the graveyard. There is but fertile soil.

What is the value of knowing the truth?

At last, what difference does the realisation of non-duality make to us? Why bother to understand the complete non-difference between awareness and pulsation, seer and seen, thinker and thought, senser and sense, feeler and feeling? In this life of headlong necessity, what practical good can such understanding do? The best answer is: we are far less likely to delude ourselves into the suffering caused by clinging to the results of our acts. We should remember: There can be no 'attachment', since the idea begs the question 'who is attached?' Likewise, there can be no 'detachment' since the idea begs the question 'who is detached?' Who can ever be a living exemplar of enlightenment? It is ridiculous: there can be no-one there, no-one who is enlightened. There is no separate person there at all. In this pristine and simple knowledge, we learn to relax.

Give up trying to maintain a 'self'

PART TWO
POETICS and POLEMICS

We now express poetic and polemical renditions of our enquiry into absolute existence-awareness and its volition, delight, projection, becoming. Our goal as ever, is to resolve the apparent duality in total unity.

SEVEN

INFINITUDE of SCINTILLATING PULSATION

The Riddles of Insidious Naming

Reader, can I waken you to the riddles of insidious Classification, of Naming? Let me cite a man who dared himself to measure the lonely coast of an island country: its overwhelming irregular jaggedness forced him to seek tinier and tinier units of measure, and that sea-swept british coast became wildly infinite before his eyes. Dismayed, he turned to football instead. 'A ball that far away seemed to my vision a two-dimensional disk, at an uncertain point turned three-dimensional as it neared my eyes!' Such conundrums made him cry out for some deeper dimensionality. 'Accept fractional dimensions!' cried the boffin Mandelbrot. 'Imagine if you will a 'Y' shape, from which each branch forms a new 'Y', ramifying and distributing forever, to infinities great and small; the same when viewed from far or near, where any bit is the mirror of the whole. It is a *fractal,* a single contained equation extrapolated to Nth degree. As above, so below, the ancients said. These fractals ('fractured stones') systematise even the broken, the non-Euclidean, the irregular. They infest all things: brain synapses, blood vessels, snowflakes, mountain topographies, rivers, waves, winds, clouds, nebulae, galaxies, eyeballs, flowers, bubbles, atoms. Fractal geometry maps infinitude at any and all scales. The brain itself performs such magic by folding and squeezing greater and greater surface into less and less volume, distributing energy and blood inward to the core of itself. What a multitudinous confabulation of interconnective integrity. Dimensional, magical submariners of chaos!'

How many trillion pencil-pathways shall we scratch in the emptiness? How many atoms shall we clutch, grasp how many fistfuls of air? Are we safe, can we live now happily? There must be order! For here is our legend, our *narrative*. Without it we're nobodies. God give me system. This fractation is the bone-structure of all our narratives. It fathoms the very substance of culture, race, country, knowledge, action, history, language, science, mathematic, dialectic, machine... Hold up a cotton-picking second! For what is it that *continually originates* this fractal propagation of thought, this explosion of nerve impulses in a synaptic brain? Consciousness stands outside and beyond and within, I tell you; it is ghost and maker and origin and master and result.

Utter Simultaneity

What of awareness' secret truth: the truth of total simultaneity? Does its absolute power not fritter and fry electric channels of the known and unknown, tossing all in ether and fire in search of outrageous possibility, working all at once in all potential worlds, wherever and whenever a tiny impulse of its own making flings an infinite electric pathway at space and time in a lunging search for 'change' or 'originality' in the perfection of emptiness? Ten million fish in utter cohesion perform a single fin-flick at the ineffable nudge of the unseen. Ten million snow-geese lift from the pillow of earth together, headed for predestined places with not the ghost of a plan. Ten million bees labour as one to complete the hive for reasons known but to the Unknown.' Simultaneity. Ghost in the machine. Utter intelligence. Gesturer of cause, effect, time, space. Conjuror of all things in the simultaneity of emptiness...

The Absolute Actor

This absolute is a nonchalant actor, who wears the fleshy costume *as if* limited, ignorant, blind, unconscious. He is *awareness and power* - the ghost that conjured its nemesis and fulfilled itself. And laughs! When the thrust, the movement comes, he enters stormy waters, enters the death-mystery... For a moment outcome languishes in the mist of possibility of which no man nor woman, no prophet or divine all-seeing eye can know that outcome. Then blessed order, result is *there.* The ghost of order willed it! Then attention shiffles away... and enters again the womb of itself, and hiatus is there... till form comes again. And though form is a blind child who murders knowing, yet awareness puts on its veil of mourning and laughs. All blind? All aware? Both. Comedy burlesque enacted forever by actor-ghosts called space and time. Even the howling wind of infinite hiatus but touches lightly the sweet visage of simplicity... Buddha said *emptiness is form, form is emptiness.* Yin and Yang, un-alive one without the other, never meet nor rest but guard their separative qualities: for the eyes of yang see no order and the eyes of yin see no hiatus. But the tiniest excess (of balance or of imbalance) ever demands its inseparable other. Here comes the *Lila,* the play of the worlds. And *you* - utterly personal and impersonal - are the player...

 The Fractal Absolute

Life is Force, and each action, each gesture, generates an equal and opposite counterforce, causing a displacement, a magnetic push for contraction, densification, point, juncture - for the circularity of a 'context'. This contraction, both defying and surrendering to the automatic counterforce of expansion, can be called 'the genesis, continuance and erasure of all things'. Being-awareness is force, where 'appearance', 'contraction' dances with its counterforce, 'expansion', 'rarefaction'. To conceive 'fractation' or 'endless division' is to visualise the flow of 'absolute possibility', of 'creation and dissolution of any point and its automatic context'. It is to describe an infinite mesh of interdependable parts, all singular yet borderless, all autonomously capable yet all melded seamlessly into an eternal aware whole. It is to describe a free pregnant emptiness coalescing in any and all contexts or junctures or forms it chooses, creating time and space yet never subject to them. It is the conductor of chaos, gesture of wind, shadow-dance of light, plastic open joyful letting... it is forever the in-and-out breath of the being-awareness, eternal contraction and rarefaction, at every never-moment, alive to any and all possibility. Like the pure language of mathematics, it is literally the grasping at the ungraspable.

Who dares to define the continual transformations of a 'system' by the effects set in train by that system? We will go blue in the face asking what qualities *all* systemic solutions will exhibit. The smooth upward plume of my cigarette at this midnight hour dissipates in villainous streaks. Where is system in *this* turbulent total mess of disorder? Where are our goddam fractals now? We blow out magic! Beat of butterflies' wings in Afghanistan sets off tornadoes on Mars. Ancient breath of muttering ghosts in far galaxies propels earthmen to scour for cosmic secrets. Knives of revenge are plunged suddenly in by seed-thoughts of 'centuries past'. Paranoid popes cling to the apex of their spirituous web. A swirling marble falls to rest in the ashen valley of my ashtray. Got to invent a concept to explain it all! Must deny, deny the beautiful possibility of the unstable... Ugh, must corral the infinitudinal mesh of effects affecting effects. What we need (now clutching at straws) is things called *Strange Attractors*. Lone strangers to the rescue! The pundits tell us strange attractors reconcile contradictory effects, make all nearby trajectories converge on them. Presto! So let's plot an attractor against *any single event* in space: it forms the double-spiral shape of a butterfly - at its very *simplest*.

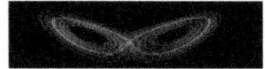

But *then* these fellows claim (stay with me, reader) that 'any given attractor' must be stable, must represent the final state of a dynamic system, must be non-periodic (never repeating itself) and can never 'cut across' (contradict) itself. And, that this turbulence-creator has *infinite curves and surfaces and manifolds of higher dimension*. To produce every possible rhythm of loopy spirals, to account for all effects, it would be infinitely fractally long - within a finite space. How can infinite feedback loops and spirals be contained in *finite* space? How can so much be going on in such a tiny space (begging the question: what the hell is a space anyway)? How to describe the infinitudinal mesh of effects affecting effects? We need *infinite* logic to plot what a *single point* in time or space will do! If that isn't the biggest load of intellectual contortionism, of trying to crawl out of our own skin! I smother myself in attracting-repulsing smoke-fields in the utter magnetical resonance of utterly interconnected being. Yo. And these dodgy scientists dodge it all by concocting a strangely attractive little conclusion: *Mutual effects of systems in collision are inherently unpredictable*. Glib chaos-denying cop-out. Chaos lets 'em escape their own ignorance. The irony! Logic, organisation, science: you groan under the weight of yourself, writhe in a box-coffin of your own making. I want a science where no total closed final view can poke and tyrannise the ineffable. Let multiple experiences and value-commitments be cherished. Let *quality and mystery* replace 'system' as organising principle. Show me *that* science and I might listen. Meanwhile infinitude tears our breath away, drowns us deep.

Get beyond System

Again, what is 'system'? It is something that is 'defined' as a system, and will be more or less complex according to a definer's need. No 'thing', no 'organ', no 'component' has any function or existence distinct from totality. And no system is whole (complete) since it is inevitably part of a wider, more complex, subtler system. 'Totality' here signifies 'unlimited', not merely another limited definition of system, and is as unlimited it is indefinable. An example: material scientists announce 'the brain' as 'the complex system that will reveal the secrets of human behaviour' (etcetera). This is a *nonsense*. 'Brain' (like 'gene') is just a word, a convenience, a 'settling' upon a so-called discrete system, convenient because it looks as if it holds 'secrets we have not yet fathomed' etcetera. Yet the 'brain' is an organ, and the definition of 'organ' is *'that which carries or embodies'*, that is, carries or embodies something greater. It is true that we may 'see the divine in a grain of sand', but the materialist approach demands endless pixellation, never an unutterable synthesis. The truth is, the absolute, the source of all systems, is utterly present. Nothing ever 'happens' without the absolute collusion of the absolute. Awareness is the infinitude of possibility that coalesces into 'a decision called perception'. To study 'the brain' is to isolate it as some sort of microcosm - and, fair enough, to study a microcosm may reveal a macrocosm - but ultimately this is an enclosed, dead knowledge in that there is no apprehension of the *seer* of the knowledge, or that that seer is the originator of any and all embodied systems, including the 'human brain'. *Who* observes? He who is utterly beyond system, He who is the very originator of 'system', of 'complexity', of 'compound'. All systems appear and vanish in awareness' wave-ocean. We have said over and over that there is an absolute force or power that appears to limit, and as it limits, veils. Limitation is 'classification', is 'word', is 'point' (the idea of distinction), is 'span of time', is 'object in space'. This 'material world' is the very definition of limitation, so why study it as if it will reveal 'ultimate secrets'? We have to come to the *seer* who is beyond system, beyond limitation. We are told that we are 'automatic' 'accumulated' beings whose every act is decided by history (evolution) and that the 'consciousness' is defined merely as a 'limited decision-making process slightly superseding the automatic'. But this is not consciousness. Why limit oneself to a definition? Freedom is obviously that which is beyond system. 'Free will' is an oxymoron, since will itself is the limiting or veiling force. He who can see 'system' is clearly beyond it. Why wallow in limiting object, limiting system? Cleave to the seer, who is free!

Absolute scintillation forever and always

If the Infinite Absolute is, it must express itself infinitely and absolutely in no time and in all time; in no space and in all space, in no form and in all forms, and in no name and in all names. It scintillates as absolute possibility and expression, always and forever. If a 'form' is called an expression of it, then that form is nothing but the continuous expression of this absolute organism of possibility. The form occurs in the eye of the seer who allows *limitation* in space and time. For example: the seer entertains a narrative called 'involution and evolution', creating 'a relativity of local conditions in the infinite scintillation'. Within this narrative, a state called 'monkey' is required to 'evolve into a state called man'. Yet these terms are but labels within an eternal state that contains them both. The idea that 'one evolves into the other' is a point of view only. There is only a 'separate state' called 'monkey' because the perceiver named it so, and only a 'separate state' called man because the body-identifying ego needs it to be so. Rather, we should ask: What is that state of which monkey and man are seen as parts? Therein, monkey and man vanish.

When a 'body dies' it is like wind that has rushed to haunt another part of the woods, or a wave that spends itself on a distant shore, to re-join the oncoming waves that rise again and ever again. No 'creature' is anything but a 'perceived combination', a 'system appearing and dissolving, appearing and dissolving, without end'. Fixation is but our sadness and our confusion, just as flow is our joy. If this is life, why would we ever wish to 'define' or 'know' or 'make an impact' on the way things are? The thing to rejoice in is not merely 'thank god I am not needed here' or even 'thank god I can get out of here', but 'As god, I am not confined at all.'

I am not confined at all

EIGHT

TALES of ENTANGLEMENT and ESCAPE

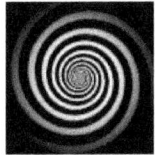

1. The Birth of the Other

'Once upon a forever time in a forever beginning, an inconceivable Emperor conjures out of himself - the Other. Willing a guileful forgetting in his own heart, the Emperor says: Can there be oneness without parts, light without darkening, emperor without dominions? In me is the source of all streams that flow forever, and I am inexplicable power, pulsing energy, light that thickens, conjuror of name, atom, time, space. I am all creatures of the darkening, the maker of relationship and cause and effect, of all journeys back to the heart. I initiate the unstoppable descent into fiction, and just as 'in the beginning was the word and the word was with god', so through language as name and form I generate all that can be grasped. I create the *individual* who embeds himself in karmic relationship by channels of intellect, imagination and sense, and since these channels are nothing but ideas in my eternal mind, they are doomed never to be fulfilled. Thus I affirm that no substantive thing ever happens... so that this wandering, this strange seeking of a home from whence the ego falsely appears to be exiled, is but a poetic dalliance, an eddy, a *becoming*. And between light and shadow there is *no reconciliation,* so that my wandering into all channels of the possible, into all corners of the empire of experience, is an abnegation, a fleeing of the Other. Here is the alpha and omega of all wanting, of sparring phantoms, filial objects, arch enemies. I am Faust's desire, Lacan's mirror... Yet how could I ever seek myself? How can that which *is,* be exiled? Here is the riddle of Samsara the wandering! I am thus a wanderer in my own fiction, I am Faust who drunk in wanting drinks his soul away, I am the ascetic who dissects and murders worlds, fundamentalist who disposed of a billion victims. I negotiate oceans of dark uncertainty, oceans of pitiless light, and having drunk red oceans of blood I nestle again in sunlit innocence on soft-heaven planets, gazing into new streams that lead far away... and always I want to follow them where they go! Yes, even by streams of paradise I follow the waters to plains where they spill in dust, to mines where they are boiled in fire... and again to the sea... where all streams end in me. I do this because I *can.* I am free to wander, and in wandering I am (never) free'.

And I ever search for the shadow, for the anima and animus, the guiding woman-man within me... I am the shambling Tarot fool with head in the sky and feet in shit! I tell you there is a time when every child, born in innocence, must become as if a stranger to himself. One day he looks in a mirror and sees a face that witnesses *him.* Though nothing exists outside the conversation of himself, the mystery is: *who is that?* Now everything turns necessarily strange, unnerved, indigestible, and as this child grows and the further in wondering he goes, the more he slips to forgetfulness. And little by little he craves a kind of cribbed sleep, a refuge in fate and circumstance and history wherein he repeats himself countlessly in the moribund gyration of repetitive lives... But there is a time at last when this wanderer can take no more the sickliness or alien loneliness or confusion or frustrated absurdity! - and at that point he hears a fainting voice as if very far off, as if an alien bird in a vaulted sky, and he wonders dimly from whence it came... and he begins a halting journey back the way he came, a retracing of steps, a rediscovering. This is the notion of Karma, of *Cause,* and look! - he snares himself in that web even as he goes, for by rooting in his past he walks as if backward into future (since the future is ever his past), getting deeper-trapped in webs of time and cause, blundering in places remembered or unremembered, touching feelings raw or displaced in gone days and centuries (which are of course not gone at all), where he grasps at ancestors and at 'significant other lives', speculating on what he and significant others used to be and might be yet. Meanwhile he feels the crowding geography of the *present,* the need to eat and breathe and walk and be somewhere here in sun and rain and north and south; and this is the killing dilemma of being in his body. And the things in his earthly wandering loom as symbols for the crowding in of the unconscious, and all are but the projection of inner *lack.* He wonders how his ego, which is but a phantom of want, managed to conjure its shadow dance with an unlistening *id.* Is the only way out of this deathly dance to dance some more? And more? All his acts are relational, he sees, all his dances are of *anima-animus…* Thus he cries and wanders. And yes, there is a family in the present world, of which our wanderer cannot deny he is a part. How often before did he engage these actors in his gangliated dramas: as perpetrators, victims, warriors, runaways; as gulled repetitors of his past and emergent ghosts of his future? And what of the razor's edge dilemma: to nullify the past or to embrace it? For the past is the heavy cloak of this fey Emperor, and its strands and baubles dangle agonisingly in the dust… such that in this gyre of incarnations he might always trudge this pilgrimage of repetition, this narcissistic romantical melange of past repression and present neurosis. Yet perhaps… there is a kind of wandering that is no wandering at all… perhaps *in the timeless here and empty now -* a traveller might cultivate no reason, make no decision, do nothing, never succeed, sieve his acts in the intuitive inchoate amnesiac lost… as if all he *is* is borderless, as if he is Everyman and Anywoman, and a murderer of all thoughts, a spirit without peculiar marks, dancer of joke dances breathing the illusion of himself, wandering nowhere in the nothingness he already is. For he who has the power to forget himself is surely master of all with which he began… But the mind is the liquid river of wanting, and each of its unresting waves is a strangling narrative of fear, and there is an infinitude of these. Suddenly, let there be none! I ask you, where or when does any one of them take place? No wave is ever what it is or where it is unless we declare it to be so. It may be labelled *now,* may be labelled *here.* But it is certain it is *nowhere.* Now hear. There can be no thing that ever happened but this. Whenever else? Should we lament it, by history or loss? One might claim to say that waves surge in infinitude. But how indefinite: if there be infinitude, then there be none. And if there are times without number, there assuredly be none. In emptiness, let narratives try to be! Let them spinning and weaving machinate and stagger and gasp and flail and wander without end. Bring them on and let them vanish! Bring them on, and let them vanish. Bring them... and let them vanish...

Fruit 2. The Energy of Longing

The energy of being, blissfully openly aware forever, delighted in itself... took thunderbolts of force, snatched fistfuls of sky, raked up gossamers of possibility, whipped the blackness to starry forms... and moulded them in nonchalant delight, suffered them to glitter there an instant before they shiffled and skittered away down unsung paths, flaunting their fraudulence, shapeshifting forever in the firmament of the possible. Form never was what it was; 'twas a chimera, an idea. The dice-gaming creator-mind flung his jewelled originations at the air, strewed baubles of incalculable richness outward forever, at an instant, at any pinprick point. He flung his very self down, wretched in the dust! Now the gawking hunter eyes of spectator-minds latched onto his jewels with a fever. Breathless they plucked and fetishised the myriad riches. These mental speculators bludgeoned, extrapolated, hammered them in precious metals underground, in industrial mind-forges, making manacles, prison palaces of metal-gold, hating and fearing the windswept ecstasies of possibility in skies above. Lunging for identity, certainty, limitation, they married suffering, and the ring of power enbaubled their sweated fingers. They came then to disillusion, to grinding hurt, to flightlessness... Down here in cringing ego-ignorant dungeons, only ever the littler version of their great self, they came again to *longing* - to redress this weighted cabined dirty-jewelled cloak of form. They longed to sputter upward out of the night, to envy freedom, envy the gods, hate the world. And they found a vocation: to be *anarchists*. To thrash at clouds of wasp ideas about their heads, at clinging shit-clad flies, to slaughter mosquitoes of puny belief, to rid their eyes of the agony... and to feel capacious, to feel cool air, sail outward forever, swallow empyrean worlds, the silken beauteous winds of emptiness, the open absolute, the free… and to know again the wondrous anarchy of acceptance, of peace.

3. Paradigm, the Origin of Torture

A lone settler on a frontier erects a fence, enclosing wide plains. He has a gun, and defends his settlement against all comers. The wandering aboriginal inhabitants are bemused, until they find themselves dead. Elsewhere, a soldier is sent to guard an isolated frontier post. His job is to hold it, though there seems no apparent threat since the countryside is entirely featureless. Apparently he must guard a thing that has been 'designated a place'. He is not concerned: he is a soldier and this is his duty. During it, and for all he knows it may last forever, 'other things' may happen but none will affect the original assignment: 'to guard the place, to guard the frontier'. This is his raison d'etre, his paradigm, frame, ready-made… *he must guard the frontier.*

A solitary holy man sits in a temple built by his zealous disciples, and meditates on the origin of Torture, otherwise known as 'fixation' or 'paradigm'. Let us begin, he muses, by imagining a great sky, borderless and clear without end, as if there be no such thing as sky at all. Clearer than sunlight on a summer sea, clearer than the blue bowl of heaven columned in electric clouds, clearer than tundra flected in mirrors of sky at the northern apex of the world. Clear sky… too beautiful. Now upon this sky let there be placed a kind of Great Window of the purest spiritual glass, so pure there are no blemishes that can be discerned by any eye or any instrument. It seems the glass is not there at all - yet it is there. It is the first *Filter.* Imagine thereby another glass pane superimposed in front of the first, so clear it is near impossible to discern any blemishes or darkenings or nebulous regions. Lo, it is a second filter. Imagine then a third filter, of great clarity, somehow in some mystic sense not quite as clear as its predecessor yet by all reasonable standards exceptionally clear and pure and transparent… and yet it is a third. Imagine now an endless series of panes, superimposed one on the other, each a minutely less clear and pure version of the previous… until there is a subtle but appreciable darkening, a muddying, a nebulosity, a clouding; yet even now one can *see* through them all. The presence of clarity is a continuous factor, it seems! And who, by the way, is the one who knows such clarity? Imagine now a further endless series of filters, so many that there seems to be no difference between the new and its predecessor, yet *en masse* the filters begin to fulfill their promise… They constitute a darkening, a descent to deeper, denser, more material worlds… The filters hang eternal amid ever-present light. All appear within that light, the original great and clear sky. The one who sees through all the panes is ever the one who lives. It is Me.

Let us speak then of the vibration, the magnetism, the scintillation, the great Volitional Force. As if the eternal impersonal sky-emptiness wants to shake out its own voidness… the infinite business of *doing* demands the *magnetic collusion of things* that are desperate to *be*, to 'be somewhere' in space and time in a roiling displacement, a demanding of presence by seething and wanting, as if 'things' awarded themselves existence by frantically osmosing into one another. And this struggle *dons the mantle* of the eternal but in a *cruel and limited way,* in the way of ghosts who walk in borderless light. And so the relationship between particular and eternal has come, and it is irreconcilable torture. It is fixation, limitation, materiality, *paradigm.* Where is home for us, we men and women who now resort to listing and naming and tabulating all things in order to control them? We namers are desperate and restless! We are literally the impossible tension of the borderless light. We are all torture, all exile. It is 'you', it is 'me' - the very makers of our frontiers, our churches, our paradigms.

4. The Cluttering Wood of Becoming

The Meditator's conscience, just as light sweats its shadow, will drag him from the beatific to forms less pleasing and reassuring. He finds himself as if alone in a darkened wood where the sun is silent, in some darkgreen world of tangling roots and trunks and fractal branches, where wild animals may carry him off and devour: creatures of immoderate desire, grasping, proud or violent. Now he can't make sense, his efforts distort, he indulges separative thoughts by turns manic or depressed, he encounters a smorgasbord of sufferings as subtle and elusive as this cluttering wood of becoming. And he panics, repeats to himself: 'The thing is to be nothing at all; the thing is to be. But how to do it, or 'not to do it'? Stay just as you are, don't move a solitary hair. Outside my firmshut eyes eternity replaces all, swiftly, silently. Nothing actually happens nor ever will. Don't worry about a single thing…' Yet despite this brave auto-dictation he will slither further in imagination - into miasmas of chemicals and vegetations, of creatures gnawing fumbling and grasping, beetling clawing and multiplying in the gluey lower depths and folds of the Being. This forest is murder absolute! Nothing survives but by eating some other. How creatures claw at the sun, millimetre by millipedal millimetre in their ten billion-year woe. Yet, beyond all these forms we might have been, out of the strands of time and endless circumstance, we are unbearably human. 'And what do I do with this gift, what do I make of it? I who bear all shapes and scars and horrors and hopes and ghosts and dreams of the lower ones embryoed in my bones, I who have been all creatures… am yet a man, a man without a notion of how lucky he is, enmeshed in the soap opera of himself, in these fractal dungeons he crawls and falls to, weaving his microscopic beetling way in this cosmic weal, imbibing his turgid lesson, trotting his consequence inch by inch, embedding his grinding bread-butter experience on the wheel without end. And all the while a tiny voice echoes from deep shafts: you are the light of the world! Why conjure wastes and hells and enchainments and sufferings where there are none? Because you *can*? Your narcissistic all-suffering conscience breathes and sighs. For we circle, we entertain, flaunt our stupidities to a big daddy conscience, we abusive creatures drunk on darkling drafts of the heart! We are blunderers with hands over eyes, faecal-brained dunces and dupes, gulled nonces, railers against windmills, cryers and wishers and mourners and cursers and negatives and jilted jealous curmudgeons, lame and lampooned… we are holy goons, groaning hypochondriacs, faustian calculators flatterers smoothies arrogants pretenders treachers liars hypocrites pissy poets blockheads politicians prissy artistes proletarian poseurs pathetic and grim! Anxiety of love, love of death, cloying wants amounting to nothing, hate of authority, poison of memory, trauma of history. This bitter fruit of our clinging and grasping! Yet if we could only be like waves in the impersonal vast… we'd feel no suffering at all. If we *ceased to grasp,* if we *ceased…* Nothing to be but a throbbing clearness, abandoning gross claiming, dancing this drudgy mundane without principle, guru, path or ego. Who'd need a body or blood or sight or breath or bed or happiness, sleep or job or drink or food or books or mind or neuron pathways, past or future history thought or sentence, buildings parties plans or erudition, or even trees or beaches stones or sky? How many lives do we need? This lifetime, a blip on the eternal. Who wants to drown in surrendering, who wants to love this world to death? What use even, is helping? We meditators want to vanish! Yet we obsess at being an *individual.* But where's any limit to you and me? What telescope, what hourglass can measure it? Are we cosmic breath that outward flows forever, or starlight of stars that gaseous burn the aeons? Are we vibration that dreamed a particle, or a microtime so brief it never was? You don't know me, can't think me, I'm quick, you don't see me! says this Absolute. But can a master meditator be mute and absolute, cut off from streets and streams of the world? An idiot's question. Because he is raped by temptation to be a demi-god, little Jack Horner in his corner: where not one notion, act or feeling, discovery or vista or kingdom is not plucked from the field and sometime claimed as his own as if he dug a mound of gold from the giving earth, locked it in great safes and hired a phalanx of soldiers to protect it from all comers. Is there anything more insular than self? Is it possible not to cling? And so this little ego, chained angel, arriviste, ignominious fumbler for light from which he came, chatters out the endless schizoid conversation of himself. Let any man enter the Celestial Library and read a million volumes; does he own a single letter of them? Serve the greater thing, the greater thing, it's said. But how to utter such a thing of *yourself?* Though at heart I am nameless, borderless, unsullied, unruffled, nowness entire, yet must I be spawn of Satan in the bottom parts of hell! And all rough things in between - in this *Samsara,* this cocktail of Becoming. Here or gone, makes not the faintest difference.

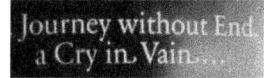

5. All Fruitless Journeys Lead To Here

...And out of the unutterable spaces of unconscious dreaming we trace the thread of the goddess though the labyrinth, back to the Sunlit World. And here is the contradiction: no matter how we live we will always follow her and will never arrive, for this life is a railway station where souls depart on night-trains just as others arrive at the gate, and the crowd never diminishes. Displacement is our fate. There is no evolution. Each victory is the death of the hard-won, each learning the displacement of something precious, ruin of an old order, just as today's success is tomorrow's failure. When the psychologist Jung 'dropped away' to discover subliminal lands of the undead, he knew he would never return. On our journey of a thousand miles we die to every step. And when we die to ignorance we never return. And the great ticking shuffle of shift and change whispers to our ear: you'll never come back, not by this road, not by any road. You are a ghost who walks, a mist of bones, a catenation of ideas; you dissolve in the very sun above that bore you. And out of the darkness, the primeval world-past from whence we 'evolved', that we claim to revisit with the torch of greater understanding, with the torch of the future - we are confronted by a bloody laughter that shakes us to the core, and we see that all we are is apes in suits, eyeballs in scholarly glasses, bloodied hand with a manicure, grist of primeval ooze that fashioned letters and words. We are the indescribable mass of churning life that blindly seethed over countless ages toward order, toward the sun. Yet all these ages are forever washed away, so that this moment is the only thing that is. All time is slaughtered for this insouciant sweet moment! Oceans of blood have fried in the sun for the sake of the smile on your infant face. Billions of years of moments, all gutted and gone, so that you and I may stand *here*, in this sunlit woodland in the morning, and thrill to the soft perfection of ourselves. Thanks be to the darkness...

6. Departure and Return

The church bells tolls, and your writer, standing amid a cluster of souls gathered about a departing body, succumbs to the unnerving truth that time has run out… These aged bystanders nurture their own emotional departures, inwardly rework the value of a life, and whether or not they believed it when the sages said… that the substance of our leaving is the substance of our returning, that the soul's frame is cast, and in the far future the waters of life will pour into this cast again… they sense that a stringent mathematic is coming, a cool judgement whereby the soul, parked on its conveyor, readied for departure to a great clearing house out of sight, released from its packaging in a whimpering expiry of breath, retreats to a space beyond cause… to lie at peace in the empty, to make its subtle hugs and handshakes with the eternal… until it begins again its slow redress to the worlds of cause and mind and sense and finally flesh once more. Yes, a breath departs, returns, immerses, emerges. What frame of mind then, to suit 'departure'? Herein is our riddle of ignorance, for we re-imitate what we think we know, seek an ideal version of what we failed to be: a better lover, better parent, juster man or woman, sweeter, seriouser, sinless. Ours were lives lived behind ego-fences in private gardens, where the little things we did in fiddled isolation seemed to us momentous, poignant, apt. We were ever islands in our self-concern, our ignorance. But in the flood of our leaving there is panic - and when ideals mingle with sickness, arrangements with pain like blood with gravy, when strangers and priests must signpost our exit - so this day we have a play, at this moss-walled quiet place under the arms of great trees… where the long cars parade in slow motion, the long box is carried forward, the prayers are intoned, the black-clad mourners gather about the hole, the sod is thrown, appeals to god are sown, and the visages of mourners register their separative scripts of love and fear and bewilderment and grey distraction. And this will be repeated to the ends of time, till hell freezes over, till the last man and woman have departed the life-worlds into the sheen of light, into the clearing house out of sight, into shells of greater meaning, of incalculable love, into the spaces of peace so deep none ever wished for past or future, where no causes or desires ever came. And one sweet day in springtime, the breath of underground undersea winds from far might rustle the trees of paradise hanging eternal amid the light. And seeds from the trees of paradise may scatter in the garden, and gentle rains of time and change push them under the earthen grasses to the subsoil, wherein their little nature tugs and strains and squeezes, as tiny memories of past and future curdle in their hearts. And forms, the forms of the previously known, the encased, the subtly evil, the insidious, the returning - begin. Great repetition competes with great evolving, and no-one can know the difference, unless and until another addled rushing life in the flesh, in the seas of mind, in the threshing fields of feeling, runs its round. And the day of reckoning will be here again, and the stolid ritual departure performed again, all witnessed by crowds of black-clad bystanders (some of whom will weep), the ghosts of the future. Today I am one of them… And I wonder, who should weep for me? It must be no-one, least of all 'the one who is called myself'.

7. No-One

…I believe there was once a person who lived and passed away, of whom nothing was ever written, no photograph was taken, who did not a thing noteworthy or remarkable, who lived in a place all forgotten in a land ruled by no remembered king, who tasted nothing but humble baked bread of a wheat field, and who felt all seconds and minutes and days of his life sufficient unto himself in unutterably quiet harmony with his breath, who felt the wind and sun, and the night and the stars on his skin in the darkness, who had never the mind to wonder at the wonder of being or birth, who passed away in the quiet tides of the unknown, his head on no soft pillow known to another (except perhaps a casual wife he never married but who shared his days and doings then herself passed on), a person who is not even a dream in the mind of another, or a memory or cause or consequence, who is clean beyond the intrusions of myth and make-believe, and who lies still, without future or past in quiet earth turned by the casual plough of some other soul unknown, in some other story in some other dimension… I believe there once was such a person.

Forever Here Forever Gone

AWARENESS ALONE

NINE

POLEMICS ON REALITY

1. The Elusive

It is right to believe there is always hope...

Hope! Are you expecting your next breath to improve on this one? Your next heartbeat to exceed the quality of this? Will your next thought somehow be more elevated than the last? Do you assume your blood will be purer tomorrow? Life is the continual and constant believing that what we do matters, and it is the continual and constant death of all our hopes and beliefs. It is automaticness driven by blind will. It utterly recycles itself at every instant. And of course there are no instants at all. Perfect torture. Lo, the Bible says 'I make all things new'. Is naivety our only hope, is ignorance of memory and past and future our only hope? Hope for what - peace, truth, beauty, joy? Your own ego, your own will to live, is the thief who embezzled peace from you and beggared you! And if it ever 'enquires into itself', it is faced with two paths. One: it will forever tangle itself deeper and deeper in the knot of seeking itself, like a dog chasing its tail, like a donkey wanting a carrot, like the serpent *Ourobouros* devouring its own body. Or two: it will dissolve in the naked foolery of its own enquiry, realising its bogus identity like a thief proclaiming his innocence by catching another thief. To 'know oneself' is therefore to expose oneself. And to expose oneself is to obliterate oneself. Religionists everywhere: you can only know your path by abandoning it! We are continually seeking, seeking like the waves of the sea. But where are we going? Nowhere but the sea. The sea is the obliteration of the wave of ourself. Poetic! You cling to the idea that you are a seeker, and therefore you are forever the blind and ignorant wave, forever surging into the illusion of future out of the illusion of past. And you will never arrive, and thus death will always accompany you, all your days and years and millennia… For time itself is a pinprick, is the idea of This. Time is point, and as long as point is there our attention will be arrested, we will be hypnotised by the need to arrive, by the need to know, the need to understand, the need to enquire and to find. Ours will ever be the search for The Great Beauty who is as elusive as the sunset, or the search for the Idea of Truth that is as transparent and elusive as the very air we suck into lungs that forever seek air. We are slaves who beg at the feet of the goddess of beauty, supplicants who kneel at the feet of the goddess of truth. Does the goddess exist? She does as long as we seek her! We will believe in her as entity as long as we believe in ourselves as entity. And when this dualism is ended, goddess and supplicant perish together. Ideals and fundamentalisms perish with their maker. Here is forever the creation of droplets in the borderless sea of mind. In the beginning (and it is forever the beginning) the seer creates the seen, and these two dance and fall away forever together. Are you the thing you see? Yes, and forever. Do the objects shift and change? Always, and thus do you. You are nothing but the becoming of your thoughts and desires. And herein is our slavery and our liberation, all in one. Torture! And Elusiveness! I loved best the story of the monk who, accompanied by his student, arrived one freezing night at the door of a lonely temple. The monk surmised that the only thing in the temple that was combustible and that would save them from freezing to death was the effigy of the holy buddha on the altar. He promptly chopped it up into faggots and lit a fire. The student howled in protest, asking what on earth was the point of being a monk if you are going to desecrate the absolute idol of the most sacred buddha. The monk of course ignored him. Here's a nice bit of warmth, he replied! …Dear reader, bless you. To live you must destroy. To love you must kill. To be free you must be obliterated. Now walk on down the line, and let life perform its dirty business on you.

without End.

2. No-One Has Ever Seen The Dead Man

The material scientist fatly announces: *We are going to die!* I wonder how he may know that? I am willing to bet life and limb that no-one has ever sought to prove the existence of death except from the standpoint of living. If you have seen a corpse (and so many have) what did you see? The truth is you saw yourself looking at a corpse. You watched yourself staring at 'a mound of flesh with no electrical energy in it'. By analogy, no-one has ever been able to prove insanity except from the standpoint of sanity. No doubt, the one who 'experiences death' is very much alive. And no-one has ever been able to prove his own death experience to anyone else. We are bound to ask: to whom does the death occur? You will say 'to me, to him or to her, of course!' In that case, who exactly am I that death occurs to me? My meaning is: if it occurs to me, then it must be a 'thing separate' from me. And are you going to tell me it occurs to no-one? This is not mere semantics! Does 'dead' mean 'not functioning normally'? Does it mean 'gone from this world'? In the latter case, gone where? Does it mean disassembled, dissolved? In that case, into what? It all reminds of the Upanishadic story. Nachiketas enters the Cave of Death and asks for a boon. Death smiles ironically and says to him: ask whatever you like! Nachiketas says: I have but one request. *Tell me what you are.* At this, Death gets very disturbed and says: No no, ask me for anything: riches, power, fame, love - but don't ask who I am! Nachiketas is adamant: *I want nothing else. Tell me who you are!* And suddenly Death shrinks back like a crab into his shell, and disappears in front of the enquirer's eyes. To this you might object: if we claim there is nothing but life, then we may also claim there is nothing but death - since life is nothing but endless change and transformation. In that case I say to you that death is nothing but a word, a word like 'change'. (Now we are in semantics!) And would it not be better to speak of these 'nothing but' absolutes in terms of life, existence, being, somethingness - rather than your castle in the air called 'nothingness'? After all, 'I am' is the foundation of all experience, and therefore of all proof. There is nothing outside it, nothing that can be proven, that is. It is as if we were all a race of True Men who had never seen The Dead Men. The true men might speculate and prattle about the existence of these fabled dead men, but no-one has ever been able to prove it except in their imagination. In fact the image of the dead man becomes so all-pervading that everyone believes he exists, somewhere. In fact there is no dead man; it is pure illusion, a label, a fable. In the same way, to believe in 'your own death' is the same as to believe in a heaven above the clouds. We want proof. To whom shall death be proved? To the one who exists. And he, unfortunately, is all there ever is, all there can ever be…

3. Absolute Renewal

What is lost? This is the key and absolute question. There must be an answer we can live with, without fear, without end, without interruption; no mere emotional solace, no mere intellectual construct but the essence of the nature of ourselves. Who are we? There has never been a time, thought, feeling, sensation, place, impulse, need, wish, love that has not been an expression of self. There is only existence absolute, utterly aware, ever unified, and there is never any instance or transaction whereby it is other than itself. We thereby affirm: 'I am forever myself because there is nothing that is not myself'. It may be objected that there is an infinitude of things that are not myself! But these are not 'things'. Rather, they are of the substance and nature of the sole and absolute being-awareness. This being-awareness was never born and will never pass away. Our fear of loss is but the realm of change, illusion, *maya*. The word 'death' signifies nothing but change, transformation, and we merely take on combinations of this eternal substance. I 'change clothes': I put on and take off garments, coverings, costumes, masks, wigs, makeup. I put on and take off flesh and bone and blood and sinew. I put on and take off the power to see and hear and taste and smell and touch. I put on and take off the power to feel love and pain and confusion and doubt and need. I put on and take off the power to imagine worlds and places and universes, to imagine sun and sky and moon and wind and trees and snow and sea and all other imaginings right down to the tiniest object. I put on and take off the power to think, the power to measure, power to evaluate. I put on and take off the power to see the future and the past, to sniff the invisible, to intuit the hidden structure of all things. I put on and take off the power to understand time and space, the power to will, the power to create. I pulsate with nothing but change because simply, I can. It is simply my nature. I breathe in the breath of all the worlds and breathe them out again. And when all these powers are temporarily absent… I am never gone, I am *myself*. I am myself as stillness and purity and forever-hereness.

This is my crystalline empty home. And here I rest as I always rested. I machinated in the most complex worlds, I sang and loved and hated and strove and fought and shed blood... and I was never anywhere but here. Where the hell else could I be? And even now I look on the isolated souls about me and wonder if they will ever stop to think about this, and I feel pity. But my pity is misplaced! We are all of the oneness, of the hereness, and we all play roles and we all take them off again! I the still, permanent one, am real. You will object that this permanence is nothing but endless roiling change and suffering! And you will be right. But never fail to see that the one who changes is forever untouched. There is nothing to fear but fear itself, no fear but the fear of itself.

What should you do then? Drop your attachment to the fear that you will die. Accept eternal change as life itself. Accept that nothing, nothing is lost when you change. Accept that change is the ghost-dance of being. Yet even knowing that every single cell in this body has continually died and renewed itself in the space of moments or weeks or months, does not seem to do the trick! Was there ever a time or place where you were not renewing yourself? Trust in the absolute power, the power that is nothing but renewal. It cannot be anything else but itself. Stop clinging to the idea that your shell is permanent. Nothing stays. Be glad of it. The only thing that stays is life, awareness, the bliss of presence - and that is you. It can never not be you, you can never not be it, you never were anything but it. Cling to nothing, not to some phantom Other. Relax. The foundations of the house are intact and perfect. You go forward as you should. There is nothing out of place, except maybe your belief that there is something amiss. Peace. Peace. You are fine. You are always intact. You are deathless. Be fearless, be fearless. Good. Good.

4. Deconstruct, Deconstruct

Dear scientists, let's do some science. That is, let us deal solely in what can be proved. *Is there materiality outside consciousness? Discuss.* I'll bet you never got a topic like this at your chemistry school. Those who wish to call themselves materialists are free to do so, just as I am free to call myself a goat. When the sage Sri Aurobindo speaks of the subconscient, the subliminal, the subconscious, and the superconscious, he directs us to 'include all that is not available to the seer due to his limitations'. Yet because no-one has ever been able to prove that a thing exists outside the realm of consciousness, we may assert that consciousness is the be-all and end-all. However, this is the 'short cut' conclusion. Instead, let us for the sake of thoroughness conjecture (a) that 'the origin of material things is outside consciousness' and that consciousness is somehow 'the product of material things' (b) that 'the human consciousness is not the same as Absolute Consciousness, either in substance or in scope' and that 'the ego is the arbiter of all experience' (c) that 'consciousness is not necessarily always present in this discussion'.

First, can any object, any 'thing' be identified without 'identification of a seer' or 'subject'? Next, you will note that it is impossible to designate a 'thing' without labelling it something. Let's take a so-called material thing, say a rock, since it appears to be 'hard' and without any consciousness. If I turn it in my hand, does its substance change according to the perspective from which I view it? The answer must be no. Does its form (shape) change according to the perspective from which I view it? The answer is yes. Is its shape and therefore its 'identity' subject to my vision of it? The answer must be yes. Is its shape part of its identity? Answer, yes. The materialist will object: the *substance* of it, the chemical or atomic substance of it is not altered by my vision of it. All right, let us investigate its atomic substance. By the way, what instrument is used? A microscope, that is right. By what agency was it invented? Consciousness in the form of human intellect, correct. Now let us enter the atomic structure. What do we find? A lot of space, a lot of light! Where the hell is this atom exactly? Over here or over there? Does the identity of the object therefore change according to the perspective by which it is viewed? Yes! Does the object thus have any identity independent of the perspective from which it is viewed? No! Therefore, does this atomic structure have any identity independent of... etcetera? No. It is now (according to the seer, the perceiver) mere empty space, mere pulsating light. Let us enter this light and deconstruct it. I put it to you that light is very much of the same substance as the consciousness that perceives it. I put it to you that there is no difference between light and consciousness. So, are there any objects outside the perceiver? In the context of 'the relationship between perceiver and perceived', there are none. I put it to you that there is no difference between perceiver and perceived. Therefore, did anything happen? The answer is, nothing ever happened. Is there anything but the ocean of consciousness? Sorry, but there is indubitably not.

How then do things appear to exist? How do things appear to be material? Answer: *Is consciousness not a material, the original material?* By analogy, when an ocean of water produces waves, are the waves anything but water? Therefore, when consciousness 'causes external things', is consciousness ever anything but itself? Of course not. What then causes such 'waves'? Consciousness pulsates. Pulsation is another word for displacement or relativity or limitation. It is the very power and force of consciousness playing and delighting with and as itself. In its utter freedom it is free to extrapolate all things and combinations of things forever - and of course never - since time and space and relationship and cause (*etcetera*) are never anything but ideas (phantoms) generated within itself. Even its apparent limitation of itself as 'object' is a charade. Therefore being is as if nothing. Put the words being and nothing together, and you get *becoming*. Summary: there is nothing but the ocean of consciousness. There is no materiality outside consciousness. Consciousness is the alpha and omega, the absolute, the immanent, the total, the One. And because it is confined to no quantity or scope, it is *you* and nothing else, whether you admit to it or not. What is 'material form'? It is nothing but the endless tiny flickering alteration, becoming, of your perspective.

5. Conversation with a Scientist

- Sir or madam, by what means are we able to say that a thing is scientifically proven?
- *When it has been proven to consistently exist in any and all circumstances*
- And if a thing is not provable, it cannot be claimed to be true?

- Correct
- What is the truth of the following statement: 'No-one has ever been able to prove there is anything outside life'?
- *Since we are continually aware of the presence of death in life, such a statement would be unprovable*
- And what is the truth of the following statement: 'No-one has ever been able to prove that there is anything outside awareness'?
- *I accept that we are able to prove nothing without the involvement of the faculty of awareness*
- Can we prove that manifested objects are anything but products of awareness?
- *Manifested objects are 'considered individually within the medium of our awareness', as I said*
- But do we accept that if a 'product' of awareness has no existence outside awareness, then it is nothing but awareness?
- *No. It is entirely probable that awareness can be obscured or clouded or deluded or partial, or a host of other conditions that affect our ability to make a judgement*
- Fine, but I ask again: Do you accept that 'the products of awareness' have no existence outside awareness?
- *An idealist philosopher could, I suppose, make a case for that*
- So we may make the statement that there is nothing but awareness, period?
- *That is manifestly ridiculous. There is an entire universe of inert objects out there*
- But how are you able to make such a statement?
- *Through the medium of awareness… I already said it*
- But as a scientist, you are bound not to accept anything as proven unless it can be proven in all relevant circumstances?
- *True*
- Is there a circumstance where awareness is not present?
- *Obviously, I personally cannot actually say there is. No*

- Then can you think of any other statement that can actually be proven other than 'awareness is always present'?
- *By your process of logic, no*
- I say to you that there is only one provable statement that can ever be made, and that is: 'there is nothing but awareness'
- *Too clever by half, sir*
- Even the statement 'we are continually aware of the presence of death in life', which you already made, cannot be made without awareness
- *All right*
- Therefore life is awareness? It certainly cannot be proven otherwise
- *I am still bound to assume there is a universe of inert matter that is clearly unaware!*
- If you assume it, you are no scientist! If a universe of inert matter be outside awareness itself, could someone please inform me where it resides? In fact, has anyone ever been able to locate an object outside awareness? Further, if such a universe were outside, how on earth could we be conscious of the fact that we were not conscious of it? Awareness is clearly all there is, all there ever can be. Can awareness *appear* to be obscured? Most certainly it can. And you just proved that little fact with your attitude - what I might call your 'stoical materialism'. But my real question is: *to whom* can awareness appear to be obscured?
- *Well, to me*
- Exactly. To 'you'. You, who are *nothing but awareness.*

 ### 6. Continual Birth of the Separate Self

Ladies and Gentlemen, let's begin with a white empty screen. We shall draw dots on it and call them 'particles'. How to define a particle? Quantum physicists seek to 'isolate' particles to study their actual nature, only to discover they 'seem only to come into existence in relation to one another'. How then did so-called Particle A get its 'identity'? Because of the so-called 'identity' of so-called Particle B? Why bother to distinguish so-called material particles at all since they are obviously 'co-dependent dancing ghosts'? We face the problem of the elusive. Things only appear to exist for extremely small amounts of time, and their properties are phantom: they are here and they are not. Heisenberg noted, in his Uncertainty Principle, that a so-called particle appearing in time has no particular location, or if it has, its duration at that location cannot be measured. Now if a so-called particle can't be located either in space or time with any certainty it clearly does not exist with any degree of reliability. Its existence relies on faith (ie: illusion). What intangible force pushes the field to create these particles? It is the Energy, the Joy, the Pulsation. Many will call it dissatisfaction or desire. But whose? The *Who* is awareness. The origin of the 'material object' is in the apparent relationship between the observer and the observed. The factors in the observer-observed relationship only come into existence 'in terms of relationship', ie: they have no self-existence, no independent arising. Since the observer, the ego, therefore cannot be proved to exist, he continually needs to find a *reason* to exist - hence he conceives the *object* that allows him to become the *subject*, or observer, of a *relationship*. This becomes his 'hypothesis', his 'narrative', his 'discourse'. Hypothesis leads to conclusion and he invests in it since it validates him. And now the observer can permanently exist as long as he permanently observes the so-called permanent objects he calls his own. These he can believe in. Because, oh my god! without this relationship he can't exist. 'Objects' thus become habitual. What materialist scientist wants to admit to this? Not one, because it would shred his role, his status, his identity. So, out of this observer-observed relationship anything can be spun, as a spider spins the web out of itself. The *idea* of knowledge comes into being, *idea* of time and space and atom, and hence science, and hence particle physics, which is nowadays the science of trying to materially manipulate that which is never materially there. All our little worlds come into being like bubbles, like Hermann Hesse's glass beads. We construct the world of solid matter out of non-solid particles, build concrete existence on non-concrete foundations. Can one build a house out of thin air? Apparently one can.

Who or what does exist then? We should understand the notion of relationship, of negation. Yin-yang, you-me, love-hate, good-bad, observer-observed. If something cannot exist except in relation to something else, we have the following options: (1) neither exists at all (2) both exist, in which case they would have to be permanent and unchanging which clearly they are not (3) both are exactly the same thing, which clearly they can't be since there is a relationship between them, or finally (4) both are completely different, which they clearly can't be since neither exists prior to the other, ha ha. Under the paradigm we have set ourselves we must find an answer - any answer - or we will choke. Or disappear up our own backsides. Or never fall in love again. Perhaps the Buddhists have it sussed when they say 'all is interconnected'. But if everything is interconnected, where is the boundary between any 'thing' and any other? If truly interconnected, there cannot be any boundary, and therefore no interconnection. Thereby it is one big soup. No particles at all. Nothing discrete. All is One. Therefore nothing happens. Nothing ever happened. Ooops.

But the idea of observer and observed persists! If subject and object come into being as a result of one another, then both are phantoms, and they dance a ghost dance forever. And if forever, never. Listen: conscious being through the polarising force of pulsating energy, allows 'time' and 'space' and 'cause' to come into existence as 'the matrices of so-called events'. But since the event is nothing but the observer, then 'seer and seen' are simultaneous, and therefore beyond (invented) time and space. Why claim then, to measure in those 'matrices called time and space' that which can't possibly be measured? That which can't be measured can only be claimed to exist, it can't be proved. We thus choose our own paradigms, ladies and gents. We are seated in the power of powers, and what do we do with it? We let our polarising judging intellect run rampant! And all our 'worlds' will last forever, and we will struggle forever, since we believe in them forever. Welcome to your own life-movie at 24 frames per second. We have no choice but to dwell in belief. Belief is what holds the worlds together. The Jew pops on his skullcap and lo, he is a Jew. The Islamist pores over his Koran and lo, he is a Muslim. The Christian cries buckets over Jesus and lo, he is a Christian. The Communist invents a nice box for you to live in, the size of a coffin! The Capitalist expands the box to the size of a house with a bunch of expensive bling and a crippling mortgage. Some of us need to be loved, some need marriage, some sex, some religion, some yoga… Choose your cage! We all need cages and crutches. And that ultimate crutch, the ultimate cage - is the need to exist as a separate self. How to appear to be a separate self? We have to believe in it. How to believe in it? Establish a relationship with something, anyone, *outside*. But what's the boundary between you and that other? Nil. You and It are a single dance. You don't believe this? Try living without air, without light. Try living without food or love. Do 'I' come into being because these are there? I believe I do. Do I come into being because you are here? I do. Yet if we were truly eternal, timeless, spaceless - we wouldn't be sitting here cogitating on this. And I certainly would not be writing it down. But here we all seem to be!

7. There Are Multitudes Within Us

All possible spheres (contexts, worlds) are myself, and all exist at once. Any expansion of consciousness, however small, leaves us amazed at our self-imprisonment. The sphere of emotional attachment and aversion called *vital*, which gives rise to fixation and judgement and slavery to karma through the limiting choices we make, rules us. This attachment in its turn colours the *mental* realm - our choice of narratives based on our experiences of attachment and aversion. In its turn, the *intellectual* sphere, the power of discrimination between helpful and unhelpful acts (be they mental, emotional or physical), is coloured by our experience in the 'lower' spheres. And the *causal* realm, by which creation pulses out of the self-absorbed emptiness of pure existence-awareness, is deeply coloured by continuous feedback from the lower-realm experiences as described. So when we 'leave this physical', we clearly undergo a re-appreciation, a re-evaluation in light of the deeper realms, and just as at 'death' we rise up in a column of light (within the spinal column) through the crown of the head (the reverse of our entry before birth) so our exit from a particular cycle of physical incarnation must thereby be subject to review, to analysis and evaluation by whatever means are at the disposal of our own higher powers - followed then by return to these spheres of attachment, and commensurate with our level of detachment from past karmic threads. Yet all so-called levels or spheres operate as if like Russian dolls, one within the other, all affecting all others, all in fact being aspects of one another. So this exit and re-entry called 'death' and 'birth', this cycle of involution followed by evolution - akin to in-breath and out-breath or to sympathetic and parasympathetic waves of energy in the spine (*etcetera*) - is a misnomer at best and diabolical attachment at worst. As long as the self believes itself to be limited, it is subject to the spheres of influence, and when the self knows it is unlimited, the spheres are subject to it. As Whitman said: there are multitudes within us. We are the eternal denominator, the borderless experiencer of all spheres, which are forever retained. These incarnations are inescapably fitted to our past acts, and we choose to utter these narratives in the matrices of name, form, time and space. We make our bed and we lie in it.

8. Value Beyond Pessimism

How to address the apparent contradiction of our existence? First, we posit an eternal emptiness where absolutely nothing ever changes. Second, we posit infinite possibility driven by eternal force, where all worlds and forms manifest in pulsation, resulting in 'a permanent phenomenon of displacement'. This latter is called *Samsara*, force of desire, ever hoping, ever becoming, ever wandering, ever insecure, ever inconclusive. Further, it is convincingly said that 'that which changes' is an oxymoron, since 'that' cannot ever be itself, and therefore can literally have no meaning, and thereby no existence. But surely in *Samsara's* eternal pulsation, all must have its 'use and purpose', however ephemeral? One argument for this lies in the fact that 'nothing can be missing from the absolute'. We thereby affirm that value lies in 'the Absolute fulfilling its uses and purposes', whether we understand them or not. A brave positive vision! Next, we must ask: *who is it* that claims that since things continuously change and disappear, that there is no ultimate value? It is precisely the seer of all phenomena. Is there anyone else? Certainly not. Further, he who decides whether something is real or unreal obviously knows himself to be real. Why then, we disingenuously ask, should the seer be any kind of pessimist, and hence a sufferer? Is it because the pulsation, the becoming (*Samsara*) is an eternally recurring condition of limitation, ignorance and self-estrangement, whereby our understanding is clouded, cropped, tenuous? There is no alternative but yes. What stays then? It is clearly the one who is ever himself, the aware one, the seer. Yet he is expert at masking himself! And life seems tremendously tough! I myself hang by a thread to the hope of understanding... and yet *here I am*, and I am whole, for without being whole how could I ever experience fragmentation? Likewise, the one who is whole can by definition never suffer. Yet he who believes he is partial, he who is fragmented, will suffer. He is fragmented as pulsation, displacement, as atom and word and time and space, as a vortex of eternal repulsion and attraction. He is led to the notion that life will always be both meaningful and meaningless, both valuable and valueless. He asks: what hope of attainment, freedom, peace? Yet he who thus debates, obviously knows himself to be real, otherwise he would not be interested in or qualified to make such judgements about reality and unreality, wholeness and fragmentation. Who in the end assigns meaning and meaninglessness, value and valuelessness? Who conducts the polemic? It is *you*. Absolute *you*. Therefore *you* may free yourself of your habit of feeling hopeless... But again arises the power of the veil, in the form of doubt! - where shiftless *Samsara*, in its restless seeking, again raises the spectre, the demon, of hope and its destruction.

If only... If only

Listen again. The philosopher Schopenhauer takes a pessimistic view that is born of lack of control, of a feeling that by being utterly immersed *in and as being* we are utterly dependent, that the totality (the id) 'wipes us out'. Yet should we lament our absolute Being? We *are* the Being, and in Us there is only the will to create, the pulsation, the *experience*. Force and counterforce exist within us alone. Thereby, to say we are dependent suggests we are somehow independent, since we have absolute power to feel and to experience and to suffer! Why then does Schopenhauer feel that 'will is the eternal repetition of ignorance', that there can be no evolution toward liberation? Consider: if there were no such evolution, how could the self envision any 'gradations of life'? We have already come a long long way to be given human form! The Seer obviously accepts desire, within his eternal psyche. And though human suffering may seem exquisite (such is our advanced narcissism) our power to remove it is surely equal to the need to do so; this is the law of compensation. Nietzsche affirmed how philosophy is conjured out of *need,* where human will is the force of striving for better, and here is the very source of the idea of evolving. But where ego is present there will always be pessimism. Why? We feel the very preciousness of the self, and we express this self as ego, which, since it is the desire to immerse and die in all the delights and forms of the world, is always helpless. We really cannot ever let go of this. We are romantics, we are in love with experiences and people and things… But finally and ironically, pessimistic Schopenhauer was right: there is no evolution, thank god! Evolution is a narrative, and narrative is *desire,* and it ends, ceases to exist, when it is no longer needed. When will this be? People speak of detachment from desire, the end of the need to wait, the end of waiting in *time,* the end of belief in thought as anything but thought, the end of belief in, and slavery to, any particular feeling. Instead, there is a singular and absolute attitude to life expressed as 'utterly unchangeable and therefore empty' which in fact is the possibility of an all-encompassing love. This attitude is simply and merely the *recognition* of our total and utter identity with Absolute. Here and Now. This Vishnu, this renewal, this presence, this mercy, alone is the death of pessimism. Enquire into pessimism, Mister Schopenhauer! Do it a million times if you have to, but always you will come back to the sole problem: *who* is the enquirer into the so-called problem? It is *you.* And you are all that there ever is. And when we actually *see* pessimism for what it is, at that moment we are not pessimistic. Let that moment repeat itself, and rule you. No seer of the truth can ever be pessimistic.

9. The Dividual

What measure of choice do any of us have? Take a fundamentalist, who demands the utter surrender of self and others to his cause. For him this world is utterly flawed, and his purpose, his 'holy war', is to annihilate or self-annihilate. Sickness or not, it is his choice. You may disdainfully reply that we are 'mere particles', ghostly atoms in a churning miasma of being, where incalculably greater forces shape our 'choices' and 'destinies' forever. Let us assume you are totally correct about this. But these parts, formations, constituents, ingredients, objects: all are *without self-nature*. They are conjurations, fantasies, projections, dreams in the air. And dreamed by whom? They are not the immortal self in us, they are not the eternal presence that we are, they are not *the one real substance that is the person*. They are not he *who knows* he is obliterated, unborn, never formed, always gone, a ghost in air, a vapour in the sky… yet who is ever present, ever capable of choice, ever aware of his predicament. He is ever subject to conditions yet always *not* subject, because he is beyond conditions, beyond change, beyond fantasy, beyond dream, beyond his own mutable ghostliness. He is the one who is ever alive, ever knowing, ever present. And he makes choices. His choices are battered and burned and baked and boiled and smashed and ridiculed as Life - but he makes them. And he is also 'immortal beyond all change, beyond all mutation, all choice'. Perhaps he is *The Dividual,* the one who is both ever indivisible and ever mutable… according to how he chooses.

Choice is not a choice

10. She is Ever of the Infinite Universe

The borderless awareness stores all acts as memory, to be set in train again as karma's child. Things pass away, fall out of shape, and in the end there is only the utter moment, with whatever trivia it contains. Embrace the new and relevant, people say. But 'you and I' never do cope with this absolute. Krishna the god was begged by his acolyte Arjuna to show the true nature of the cosmos. So he did, and Arjuna nearly went mad, crying out and begging for the unutterable horrific bedlamic vision of death and change to stop! No. Our experience is always a sheltered, calibrated, tamed, pointed, simplified choice. We never learn how to flow as the world's chaos… So I think of the demented, who wordlessly cry out for all the things they lost or discarded. Have we seen the suffering chaos of these we love, when their identity is sucked away behind the glazed pools of their eyes? Here is thought genocide, a sped-up version of what we all experience. Or perhaps dementia is temporary: released at last from the thickened brain a person comes to herself in a wider freer country, truly conscious and unconfined. What is birth in this body and brain anyway but confinement? And what is freedom but the death of confinement within thought, idea, imagination, memory? We all whisper: they are passing away now, passing away… a cognitive dissonance with our own sparrow lives of non-achievement. Faith and effort and hope are all gutted, futile. But if it is reality, how can we ever say it is a problem? Where do we 'pass on' to anyway? The sum total of energy cannot diminish in this absolute being. It is 'the ever-present change of form', eternally passing moment on moment, endlessly becoming, and therefore nothing at all. We are not ever what we appear to be. But, but, we live, we live.

What am I to make of it then, I ask myself, when a person in an eighty year-old form is presented to me in a casket and I am told 'this is the body of your mother'? Is there a single thing about this 'body' that is less or more unreal, less or more substantial than the person of sixty, the person of forty, of twenty, the baby of one month, the fabled twinkle in her father's eye? I saw death for what it is: a complete fake, a misnomer, a meaningless idea, a dumping ground for all superstition and ignorance. Listen. Whatever form you appear to take is passing away with each breath, each atom-second, into another form which passes away to another form, forever. This, in any million myriad combinations, depending on the size of the optical tool we might look through. And none of these so-called forms is anything other than a phantom, an *idea*. And when this 'last form' appears to disintegrate, when the light of the windows of the eyes seeks the beyond, when the zephyrs of breath labour and flow outward into the wide air, when the bag of flesh hesitates, falls and hugs the earth and will not get up or walk on no matter how its companions urge it to, then we can say that the person, whosoever and whatsoever that may be, has moved beyond our sight into another room, a new garden - to pluck a fresh adventure, new entertainment for her eyes, a new movie to titivate her, fresh parlay with the ineffable converse of life. Inside or outside time and space, we cannot say. But one thing I can: she left behind for me a store of memories with which I can and will do as I like. And I will reconstruct her story, or not, and reframe her former outward being in my eye, in my own tangle of grief and love, my narrative. Until I will think of her no more, since I also will have moved beyond this frighted quivering set of atoms, breathed too many of these intemperate breaths, replaced too many of these beaver cells, and walked on down the hallway into the dark or light. And then a hush will fall on our mutual mother-son soap opera, our construction, our painted little stage set, for whom there is no audience any more, and for whom a hush and a forgetting now falls in the camera-show of the world of men. And whom will we meet and do our business with in future pleasure gardens? It may be our chosen familiar ones or it may be strangers. Walk on. Be sure of this: nothing ever stays as it is, and yet no fish is ever plucked from the borderless sea. Walk on. Don't look sideways, or grasp at myriad operas of invention that beckon from the verges of your cosmic road. Instead be the garmented nothing that you are, and let your train trail behind you like the stars of an emperor, and let those who come behind pick up the cloth and treasure it - or not, as they choose.

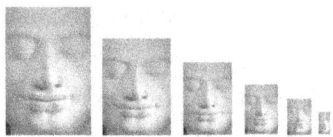

11. Beyond

We are the dreamers of all worlds, dancers of non-existent things. Under the wheel for all these years, a journey without end, a cry in vain. We are the merciful lightness, free whether we like it or not. Nothing is ours: all is forever gone, without cause, without end, in the flow of continual forgetting. Keepers of the illusory gate, the banal fruits of yesterday, grotesque theatre of the world, forever and never, amen. Who can ever describe what is? We are dancers of ideational phantoms, riddlers of insidious naming, cyclers of need and lack, repetiteurs, habitues, time and death worshippers. In the coliseum of suffering, we open our mouths and all is lost. Identity is clinging. Endless dialogue of a self. Ego, that desire-ghost, fixator, phantom gatekeeper, material idea, superimposer. Our blinding need to ride and flow, to dream, to self-distract.

Not an infinitude of waves will change the ocean. No-one will ever describe what is. Multitudes are within us. There's no limitation without infinite liberty. Let it go, let it go. Believe in nothing. It's over, it's over. Who is the seer? Deconstruct the 'I' thought. Fatal idea of separate perceiver. No thought has self-nature. We are the insubstantial, the illusory act of measuring. Would you chop up the seamless flow? Where is the part of you separate from the whole of you? We are not what does not exist. Illusion is illusion is illusion, nothing is what it is. Nothing is personal. In this dream of creation, all fruitless journeys lead to here. Beyond the illusion of mouths lies the silence. The ancient of days: without it we have no existence at all. What can exist that is not forever? No borders, no bodies in the graveyard. No-one ever saw the dead man. No death outside the observer. The observer is the observed. No-one ever experienced anything but this. Nothing ever happened that is not now. No-one ever proved a thing outside awareness. Nothing can exist that is not forever. Absolute scintillation forever, always for the first time, ever present, ever gone. Eternal ocean. Measure not your life in years and days, drown in the eternity of now.

What is the spirit of survival? Your only friend is you. Give it all away, practise bloody-minded courage, beyond pessimism, beyond desire. Continue as you must. We can't have this without that. Don't fool yourself it makes a difference. Who can cope, deal, live with nothing but the absolute? Eternal freedom of no choice, freedom of no things, no choice but the real, nothing but what *is*. Life is eternal, you are life, and you are eternal. Show me the border! Be as you are, be as you are. Where are you going? To be or not to be is not a question: you *are*. Surf the wave. Where is it now? If not this, then what? It's up to you. There is no you. Get out of your own way.

Act but know there is nothing to be done. Do your best but cling to no result. Improve but know you are going nowhere. Travel far but know you are only ever here. Create but know there is nothing but sky. It all matters but none of it matters. Learn but know it has all been done. Grasp but see that it is never yours. Succeed but give it all away. Don't believe, enquire. Face your immortality, care not what happens. Freedom is here. You are the indivisible. Accept, accept, accept. There is no other. The secret is, there is no secret. Goodbye to all of it. Beyond the machine, beyond the machine. Peace, flow, awe, wonder, surprise, all things new. Fearless, desireless, borderless, deathless, absolute…

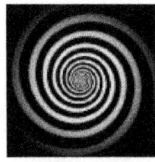

TEN

ENDLESS DIALOGUE OF A SELF

So, we at last embark on the battle to remember the reality of Ourself alone. We know that there is nothing but the Storyteller talking to himself. And it doesn't matter if we wax repetitious, for it is all waves (all this writing too) and the cresting of a wave is nothing but the negation of its trough. All crests and valleys, they are only the nowness, hereness, no-time-ness, nowhereness. Memory is nothing but the detritus of a need to hold on. History is nothing but obsessive scrounging for meaning, the past nothing but a child's game of imagination where 'event' is viewed like some snapshot frozen in time, a reference point for all manner of theorising and storytelling. The snapshot never was; the 'point' is an impossibility, an absurdity, and if ever there could be such a frozen thing, the entire universe of flow would utterly explode into nothingness. There is nothing but flow… and if nothing but flow, nothing but nothingness. The problem really is: how to play the great pantomime of 'meaning' knowing that all is erased now and forever? I am writing this consequential blurb in order to cover up the terrifying fact that life is utterly simple. Yet there is no choice but to fight out our own relentless conversations, without end, without end…

In the beginning we take 'the world' as real - and its power controls us utterly (so says a First Voice) even while its totality is continual alteration. We try to grasp at happiness in myriad paths, products, experiences. In time we see that suffering comes from transformation itself. So I tell you once and for all, you are nothing but the ocean of awareness and the world is nothing but your own formations. (A Second Voice interjects)

Then what is the nature of forms? (First Voice in reply) They are of the nature of awareness. *So if they are of the nature of awareness, are they other than awareness?* No, there is only awareness. *So forms are unreal?* They are real since they are of the nature of awareness. *But they are illusion since they only appear to appear. Is not illusion illusion?* Correct. *So form cannot exist.* Except as the nature of awareness! Awareness as energy only appears to create. The only 'relationship' is said to be between awareness and object. (And there is no possibility that so-called forms can have any 'relationship' to one another.) *But how can awareness ever be in relationship to itself?* It appears, according to the mysterious volitional energy arising in it, to continually extrapolate, and limit, itself. *We who are real have to live as if form is real?* Who takes it as real? *Me, I, myself.* Who is that? *All right, I am awareness. Do I know then that my world is unreal?* The world is not unreal! *But you said…* The world is of the nature of the only real substance, awareness. *Understood, but is awareness ever anything but itself?* No. *So the changes of the worlds are unreal.* They are unreal. There is no change. *Is suffering unreal then?* It is us, in our refusal to accept ourselves! We chase the illusion of 'wanting the other', and we suffer the difference between what we want and what we have. *So there can be no suffering outside this illusion?* Correct. *How can an unreal thing cause suffering?* Precisely because we make it real, and thereby we attract confusion, ignorance. Meanwhile we, as awareness, generally know that we are suffering. 'I know that I am, and I know that I am suffering'. There is always one who is aloof from suffering. *How?* In order to be the one who suffers, that is, the one who is in relationship with suffering, we have to be the one who does not suffer. *I am the one who is aloof from suffering?* Correct. *How then did I get to be in relationship with suffering?* You grasp, cling, make the false step of thinking you are separate, as ego. I don't blame you! The power of formation is absolute. *But separate from WHAT?* From yourself, in effect. You call 'you' the ego, and define what is 'not you' as Other. You therefore enter relationship, which is false for the very reason that it is relational, separative, relative. *But we can't do anything about ego. It's an absolute force, a phenomenon.* We can divest ourselves of the false idea that we are separate. *What am I then?* You are the absolute existence-awareness, boundless, eternal, free, indescribable, formless, total, pure.

Hegel said all things are defined only by their negation. But he also said that a thing and its negation must logically be components of a greater unity. *So I create my suffering?* As I said, you attach yourself to illusion as if it were real. And the first and only illusion is that you create the false, limited 'I'. You put 'I' at the beginning of every sentence. 'I' creates all worlds. 'I' is the original and only thought. Take it away, and all worlds are gone. *So beyond that, there is nothing to do?* Absolutely nothing. *Then why are we having this conversation? Words generate illusion!* Because we honestly seek to end suffering. *Awareness cannot suffer!* Apparently it does. Who else could? *It cannot!* Well done, keep thinking that. *But there is suffering!* Only when we indulge in the limitations caused by grasping desire. *Suffering is necessary, to learn and to grow!* You are right, you are right... until it is necessary no more.

How can an unreal thing cause suffering?

There is Nothing but Inclusion

Yet again the writer is lost in the pulsation of his mind... 'The ever-present timeless spaceless causeless reality, is That wherein all possible things occur simultaneously, without any precursor, always fresh, always new. It is miraculous potential, pulsating, scintillating as itself. This mysterious presence appears to act, to distribute itself as *organs:* parts, polarities, attractions, repulsions, atoms, causes, effects, places, circumstances, moments, flavours, regions, senses... The seer's pure vision seems trapped and conditioned by the deepest formations and involutions, the lowest denominators, the lowest depths! Yet these levels are nothing but the breathing of life itself, its densification and rarefaction. Knowing this absolute pulsation, knowing that all its so-called parts and attributes are utterly harmoniously evolved out of it and as it - the only attitude to be taken is that of *itself* - which is utter freedom in the *inclusion* of all things. All 'things' are the rapturous expression of it, and they have no substance but it, even as they seem to have their uniqueness. And so they are all gone, and yet are all present, for they are nothing but the pulsating One.

Only the Indivisible

Imagine an onion. Peel away all its layers. The onion seems born out of emptiness! We must never take 'object' or 'mass' or 'density' for granted, because these are 'compounds of utter emptitude'. At the 'origin', and in the utter process of every divisible strand, there is indivisibility. If there is relationship at all, it is but the in-breath of emptiness into 'other', and the out-breath of 'other' to emptiness. We must ask: to whom does 'relationship' occur? Answer: to the One who manifests the idea of it. *But is this seer empty, unmanifest?* It seems it cannot be, for it takes form as 'other'. *Is that form actually manifest?* It cannot be, since it exists as seer. Here is the ultimate and only paradox. *Can form beget form?* Form is never form! I told you, only emptiness may appear to 'beget' form. All is 'manifest in and as the emptiness of the conscious seer'. Please ask: how can a living being ever register anything that is not itself? Example: the scientist Oppenheimer looked into a vacuum and before his eyes 'particles' spontaneously appeared. *Why then do we insist on the concept of quanta (things) in physics?* Because (a) we cannot admit to the unchanging reality of eternal oneness. Because (b) we cannot admit to the nothingness of physics itself. *What is Cause then?* There is but one 'cause', that of 'unmanifest dancing manifest'. Form or Other is nothing but 'the perception of pulsation'. But it is a vexing thing: that pulsation in itself cannot be said to have existence, since no form can ever be what it is except in relation to some node or negation with which it 'pulsates'. Pulsation is the idea of relationship, yet since there cannot ever be said to be two distinct things that mutually pulsate, it must be accepted that there is no pulsation at all. Yet form is *said* to be 'pulsation between unmanifest and manifest'. We go in circles! Or in spheres, or in magnetic vortices. At last, there is nothing that does not partake of the nature of itself. Self is absolute. As we said: *how can a living being ever register anything that is not itself?* The proof that two are one is that duality or other is perceived by One, as One. *And who is that?* Ha! Therein is the endless mystery… All one can say is that it is YOU.

Is there any relationship at all?
There is no Other

There is absolute existence, and there is nothing other than it. There is absolute awareness, and there is nothing other than it. There is absolute oneness, and there is nothing other than it. These are three in one, subject to no relationship, no 'law of compensation', no 'yin-yang', no 'force and counterforce'. *How then does limitation, objectification appear to appear? And again, how is there suffering?* If awareness, as innate energy or pulsation, appears to identify with limitation (in reality it can never do so) then 'subject-object relationship' comes. This is the idea that there are 'things and the seer of things'. The 'seer' is nothing but the arbitrarily limited 'I', which is nothing but identification with 'body-mind' and 'object'. The world is a fiction created by the original and sole idea of a limited observer. From limitation and objectification, language follows, everything gets named, and one is locked into a paradigm called 'cause and effect' that by force of habit is hard to shake. How is 'other' so utterly pervasive? Because the original illusion is unquestioned. Some will blather that this is a weak explanation, and that 'materiality-objectivity is permanent'. But if we question the process of perception, that is: 'who perceives?' we quickly arrive at the truth: objectification is the sole ignorance. *Yet is objectification-illusion a permanent state of existence-awareness?* It cannot be, since it is illusory, and illusion cannot by definition exist. *All right, but again, how does it persistently appear to exist?* 'Unlimited I' eternally expresses itself *as* the free infinitude of its *organs,* which appear as 'little I' (ego). For example, there cannot be any sentence or thought or act without 'I' as the subject. 'Unlimited I' is absolute borderless undifferentiated awareness. Can it be limited simply because projections or displacements appear within it? No. Can awareness be limited simply because relationships or dualities appear within it? Never. Objection is made by materialists and empiricists, who have entirely the wrong end of the stick. They say ridiculous things like: awareness is not only limited to the brain, but is generated or created by the brain (a lump of meat inside a skull cavity). They say things like: awareness 'gradually evolved in stages out of inert matter. What! They provide not a skerrick of evidence as to how the inert could possibly 'become conscious'. And all the while they ignore the fact that they are inventing and reiterating their theory absolutely and entirely in the context of awareness. Can a fish deny it is of the sea? *Water, what water?* says the stupid fish. The truth is, awareness is absolute, and cannot possibly be subject to any kind of involution or evolution or becoming. All experience, all projection, all veiling, all objectivity, all other, all matter - is deconstructed as awareness. So go ahead, materialists. Perpetuate the cardinal, fundamental, only mistake: believing there are 'objects distinct from awareness'. They will reply: *Absurd! Of course there are 'things' outside our 'personal awareness' of them.* But are these 'things' outside awareness itself? Show me the border between 'absolute awareness' and 'personal awareness'! If they are 'outside', could someone please inform us where they reside? In fact, has anyone ever been able to locate an object outside awareness? Further, if they were outside awareness, how on earth could we be conscious of the fact that we were not conscious of them? There can be nothing outside consciousness, hence there are no objects separate from it. They are mere so-called 'objects (organs) of consciousness'. But is this latter nomenclature ('objects of consciousness') useful or misleading? Profoundly oxymoronically misleading, is the answer. The sole provable fact is: I am, and I am aware that I am. Yet, in 'subject-object awareness' I believe I am 'separate from any object that I know'. This automatically delimits the definition of me (the subject) as 'limited I' - *as opposed to* 'Unlimited I'. I accept the absurd equation 'I versus Not I'. This is a lie, an illusion. This original limitation-idea creates all limitation. The philosopher Derrida sought to 'deconstruct the object' in order to bring it back to undifferentiated consciousness, and he made a reputation out of it. But his enquiry is ultimately cumbersome: it is like letting the tiger out of the zoo then marshalling all forces to capture it again. The idea that there is an object to be deconstructed is a falsehood. There is no object. There is no Other. To 'sustain the world' is futile. To live awareness is bliss. To live subject-object awareness is suffering. Which do you prefer?

Idea of 'limited I' maintains the fiction of the world

Within sentience, how can insentience occur?

Insentience is impossible except as 'the *idea* of projection, displacement, object, relationship, other, densification'. This is known as death. Let us now follow a chain of fundamental mistakes. (1) That an 'object' consists of 'dense matter'. (2) That the 'object' is thereby inert. (3) That awareness cannot be present in so-called 'inert matter'. Let us blunder down this line and ask: in which 'regions of density' does awareness reside? In the 'brain'? In the 'synapses'? In the electricity that connects the synapses? In the 'nervous system'? And so on and on. Such reasoning births absurdity. Awareness does not reside 'in the densities of matter' for the simple reason that there is no difference between so-called matter and awareness. If you want to call yourself a materialist, then realise that awareness is the only material! The term 'matter' can only be used as a tag for so-called 'objectification of awareness', whereby, ironically, matter 'appears to be inert because it is denser than awareness, which is always without density'. The one who posits matter as exempt from awareness identifies with 'body' and 'mind' as distinct entities, while the origin of the objectification lies in 'desire to know'. Awareness cannot be other than aware, but it 'appears to polarise through projection and displacement', which are the genesis of the term 'the inert'. In the face of this profoundly persistent vision of polarity, of relativity, we are bound to ask: *To whom does relativity occur?* We arrive at two possibilities: (1) The one to whom relativity occurs is permanently subject to it, thereby giving to relativity the supreme power. (2) The one to whom relativity occurs is 'beyond relativity'. By either statement we make the mistake of seeing relativity as real, ie: as having self-nature. We are then led to ask: *To whom does relativity appear to occur?* Yet are we not again posing a question that forever maintains a false duality? To seek, to ask, to probe, is to impose the original limitation.

Awareness appears to perform two movements: contraction and expansion

These are the core movements of the idea of displacement, otherwise termed 'form and emptiness'. In contraction the awareness 'focuses', flowing to a singular point to the exclusion of all else. In expansion the awareness divests itself of focus - before the next contraction arises. It is impossible to 'hold any point in perception' except as this (rapid) displacement of contraction and expansion. While an object of focus is perceived, there can be no perception of any other. For example, while sound or light is perceived, there is no perception of silence or darkness. Meanwhile, whether perception is in contracted or expanded mode, there is always a 'singularity of awareness'; that is, there is never anything but continuity of awareness. *We never experience anything but absorption, a sense of oneness, even as we perceive the notion of displacement, duality.* Whether as in-breath or out-breath, we experience nothing but air. To deconstruct perception is to ask: what happened to the point (contraction)? It is instantly gone (expansion), just as 'the point it transforms into' (contraction) is also gone (expansion). The phantom point (in name, form, time and space) has no existence other than in 'an imagined context of emptiness', just as that emptiness has no existence other than 'in relation to the phantom point'. Existence-awareness, in whom 'relativity is said to occur', shines as borderless eternal. The 'seer who is purported to see the other' can *never* see the other, since the 'other' would by definition not be a part of himself. Therefore, we conclude there is no other. Nothing ever happened.

How would the world appear if there were no 'limited I'?

To assert existence is to assert non-existence

To accept 'the phenomenon of contraction and expansion' is to forever underpin 'a relationship between point and context'. Example: We see a point of light originate 'in a thing called darkness', and we see that 'the idea of a point of light simultaneously originates the idea of darkness'. Or else we feel that 'a point of light' has distinguished itself from 'a hitherto unseen state of absolute light'. Again, we hear a 'sound' (vibration) coming out of 'a thing that is now called silence (emptiness)', and we realise that the 'particular sound' originates 'the idea of silence'. Or else, we feel that 'a particular sound has distinguished itself from an unheard state of absolute sound'. Again we ask: how can 'silence' register 'sound', since it then would no longer be silence? In other words, how can a thing register anything that is not itself? How can a 'thing' not cease to exist at the registration of another 'thing'? Will we proceed to claim that 'sound' has no existence at all? No, because 'to assert the non-existence of a thing' is precisely to 'assert the context of existence'. That which is itself can only 'seek to know itself', an absurdity, by creating 'other', another absurdity. You and I 'perceive the idea of relativity' within a oneness that cannot be 'other' except 'to appear to itself as negating itself'. Relativity is therefore truly a marvellous mirage, a veiling sleight-of-hand born of the 'volition' of awareness.

Ignorance is the idea of difference

This world is a dream of our own making

'Sound' appears as an 'entity' only in terms of 'a relative context called silence', 'light' as an entity in terms of a relative context called darkness, 'solidity' as an entity in terms of a relative context called 'rarefaction', and so on. But if awareness is the absolute ground and source, then 'awareness of entity (limitation)' is a very strange oxymoron. Entity or form is thus a mere signifier, a mere 'differentiation of existence-awareness into so-called relationships' which appear to be in opposition, appear to express otherness, relativity, particulation and so on. In fact these 'relationships' are nothing but the 'eternal undisclosed perceiver', one without parts, silent, without qualities. Thus, 'death' is nothing but the idea of difference, whereby one thing 'dies' because another thing is purportedly 'created'. Absurdity! And to 'appear to occur' is impossibility, oxymoron, flight of fancy. The statement 'the object is separate' is a statement occurring to oneself, therefore a meaningless statement. That this statement is 'deemed possible' is testament only to the omnipotence and omniscience of oneself. Thereby, do we really think we should be concerned about death, this time-space soap opera of ours? You are not a victim. You are seated in the power of powers, and you have decided you are a victim to the circumstances you create. Why limit yourself? You are the creator of worlds. How did you do it all? You are the bliss of oneness, the bliss of existence-awareness. How did these worlds come? They never came. There could never be anything but existence-awareness-bliss. How then do they appear to come? As idea. What is idea? It is the power of volition, a need, an impulse, a displacement, a warp, a wave, a play in the ocean of awareness. It is nothing but impulse of existence-awareness through 'organs of self-expression'. And if you, the looker, look, you will see that in your looking you are making the thing you look at. You self-entertain. This world is a dream of your own making. Who else could have made it? There is never anything but borderless you, there never could be anything but borderless you. You are the god, the avatar, the responsible one, the now and the here. And you create the idea of ego, of point, of atom, of sphere. And you let these so-called spheres appear to be distinct. Yet anything that appears to be separate is utterly unreal. No 'thing' has any kind of self-nature. Materialists invest in and as 'a universe separate from the seer', and build conjectural universes based on energy and matter and atom and change and relationship and distance and time and cause and effect... These have no existence whatsoever outside absolute awareness. Anyone who purports to participate in 'the creation of universes' cannot ever be anything but himself, now, here, borderless, without conditions. So do not worry about this dream called birth and death, my friends. You are the ever-living eternal presence, and the dreams you create do you no ultimate service at all. Do you want to be victim? Do not be the victim of your own dreams.

Where is the border?

Nothing ever evolves or involves

Are we forever confned to the creation of name and form? Or is confinement the last most elusive mirage? We must persist in our enquiry. The persistent obsession with the paradigm of discreteness (so-called objects) entrenches automatism. Our friend Charles Darwin signifies the obsession, though he was originally a believer in the all-encompassing divine. It is a remarkable thing to create a fantastic and complex series of labels, and then, tracing the movements of these labels, to call it 'evolution', to invent a complex series of pathways and call them 'species', to designate a fantasmagoric cosmos of creatures and to persist in thinking they are in some way distinguishable from their context or 'environment', and that therefore they survive in it by 'adaptation'… **Where is the boundary between creature and environment?** Is a fish other than the sea? You may say that the tension between the need to survive and a 'hostile' environment, allows a 'creature' to clamour for 'independence'. Yet there is no manner in which the creature, defined as it is by volition, the power to make decisions, can ever be independent of anything. Its so-called volitional powers (a tiny part of the forces operating upon and within it) are nothing but expressions of infinite forces of context, environment. The terms 'context' or 'environment' are nothing but 'relative spaces in which a so-called creature operates'. If need is the originator of all volition, Darwin should have asked the deepest question of all: *Wherein is the spirit of survival?* or *What claims to survive?* If all is created, transformed, transmogrified by so-called evolution, what survives? Only existence itself: forever capable, forever aware. Further, if we are to create any arbitrary 'point in time and space' in order to 'measure difference', we find that the point or state selected is utterly arbitrary since it is merely relative to some other arbitrary point or state. If a 'creature survives by adaptation' using 'volition in a given environment', it can logically be in no way separate from the conditions of that environment… which 'conditions' themselves 'undergo continual change'. What we glibly call 'change' can occur only in the context of *that which survives,* in other words *that which never changes.* And what is that? It is existence-awareness alone. All else is but a description, an imposition, an idea. Darwin invented or traced a set of ideas, labelled them 'species' and merely watched the labels change. The reality is, the eternal unchanging existence-awareness appears to express itself in 'name, form, time and space' as the so-called 'phenomena of the world'. Hegel showed that any so-called object or event, encountering its necessary negation, must logically fuse into a more comprehensive unity. Here then is the best expression of 'evolution' - *a movement inward to the ever-present heart*. We might just as well call the eternal process 'involution', *the extrapolation out of the ever-present heart*. It is obvious that if involution and evolution are to be entertained at all, they must be simultaneous movements, differentiated only by 'point of view'. They are therefore relative, therefore empty. The fact remains: no 'thing' or 'process' or 'conception' has self-nature. A walled house has no self-nature. The human body has no self-nature. Death has no self-nature. And suffering, which we are clearly most concerned about in this life, is nothing but the difference between what we think we have lost (utter freedom) and what we seem to have (confinement, ignorance). There is nothing to be lost, and ignorance is nothing but our investment, our clinging. A breath, a hair on our head, a heartbeat: have we 'lost' these? And do we lament if they are gone? No doubt we require the illusion of 'thing' or 'process' or 'conception' to define ourselves. Nevertheless, we are never confined.

Is a fish other than the sea?

Why do we, as existence-awareness, need to 'prove' or 'find a way back' to our totality? Our struggle is always the hiatus between the need to cling and the need to cease clinging. We make islands, egos, of ourselves in order to fight and overcome. Our need is expressed in the great miasma of mental perception, vital desire, physical formation, where the great credo is *maintenance, survival*. The volition, the ego, will do literally anything to maintain itself. We thereby enter the vicious circle of belief in our own limitation, so that 'survival' becomes endless expediency, manipulation of circumstance, and we continually invent relationships that we hope will elucidate 'meaning'. This is the hell of becoming. Yet, what possible ground is there for 'a thing' to exist as distinct from any 'other'? To divide totality into discreteness: of sequence or locality or label or density or shape... here is the nothingness, and the torture, of becoming. There is no meaning outside the simplicity of awareness! Here is the koan of koans: '*Who casts a veil over the real?*' People fear death, but consider this: life has no ultimate power to kill itself, only to endlessly obscure itself as *organs* of 'time' and 'change' and 'event' and 'point' and 'relationship' and 'transformation' and 'relativity' and 'polarity'. If this is the death instinct, the instinct to manifest, to objectify, it is none other than a great refusal, a repulsion. Manifestation has thus been called 'the eternal instinct to die'. By definition it can never succeed. The freedom of existence-awareness allows the appearance of ignorance and suffering, and the question is: can the ensuing battle ever end? Where is the death of the death instinct? We can't kill limitation, and we can't kill illimitation. They are two movements of the one reality. Know therefore that there is *no other*. Know that there is no attainment, only embodiment. Know that there is nothing to become. Know that there is nothing to be done. There is nothing to be done. The only possible sufferer is absolute seer, and he by definition cannot suffer. Therefore, be still, be at peace.

There is no Incarnation, only Me

The proper attitude, and I embrace this to the absolute particularity of my heart, is that I don't care about anything that ever happens, ever again. I will never be traced. I am not even wave or phantom. All is gone and all is to come and all is gone again. The spirit of survival, though it is some kind of magical conjuration of becoming called the world, is not ego, not confinement, not mental labyrinth… not cruel, not deluded, not insatiable… it is the spirit, the free self, eternal existence-awareness, forever here, now, *this*.

www.ingramcontent.com/pod-product-compliance
Lightning Source LLC
Chambersburg PA
CBHW051122160426
43195CB00014B/2305